Allies in Crisis

ELIZABETH D. SHERWOOD

· · · · · · · · · · · · · ·

Allies in Crisis

Meeting Global Challenges to Western Security

Yale University Press

New Haven & London

Published with the assistance of the A. Whitney Griswold Publication Fund.

Designed by James J. Johnson
and set in Trump Roman types by The Composing Room of Michigan.
Printed in the United States of America by Vail-Ballou Press, Binghamton, New
York.

Library of Congress Cataloging-in Publication Data

Sherwood, Elizabeth D.
  Allies in crisis : meeting global challenges to western security /
Elizabeth D. Sherwood.
    p. cm.
  Includes bibliographical references.
  ISBN 0-300-04170-5 (alk. paper)
   1. North Atlantic Treaty Organziation. 2. Europe—National
security. 3. United States—National security. 4. World
politics—1945- I. Title.
UA646.3.S45 1990
355'.03301821—dc20   89-35260
                                               CIP

10 9 8 7 6 5 4 3 2 1

For my parents, who gave me a safe nest and strong wings

Contents

Preface

Throughout the 1980s, a debate raged within the Atlantic alliance about what support its members could reasonably expect from one another in areas not formally covered by their North Atlantic Treaty Organization (NATO) obligations. Around the world, from the Strait of Hormuz to the Falkland Islands, from Chad to Lebanon, regional developments threatened the interests of NATO's members. The heated discussion in allied capitals captured my interest, and it led me to think about the issues in a broader context. How had NATO coped over the course of its history with crises affecting the interests of one or more of its members in areas not covered by the mutual defense guarantee? How did perceptions formed in previous crises influence allied behavior in the present? Had patterns or precedents been established in the past that could offer guidelines for the future? When I explored what I believed to be the relevant literature, I discovered that despite the existence of a surfeit of volumes on NATO, none concentrated specifically on the relationship between global developments and alliance security.

In this book, I have carefully chosen a series of crises in which one or more of the principal allies believed its important interests were engaged outside the treaty area and where what took place had a significant impact on alliance relationships. Some crises, though historically important, did not illustrate anything unique about the way out-of-area issues have been handled and hence are not discussed. The scale of the crisis weighed heavily in my choice: those involving the possible use of nuclear weapons, or portending a large-scale allied military commitment, took precedence. In addition, my purpose was not simply to duplicate the abundant literature already available about the major crises of the postwar period but rather to use the events as a prism through which to depict the dynamics of alliance politics beyond NATO's official domain. The discussions are, therefore, slices of the story, focused specifically on a certain set of issues. They consequently exclude a good deal of historical detail except as background, where necessary, to illustrate a point.

The following pages concentrate on the foreign and defense policies of the United States, the United Kingdom, and France. This emphasis reflects the hierarchy of power within NATO that has existed since its creation. The focus on American activities stems in part from the global nature of a superpower's commitments. Furthermore, because in 1949 the United States became the guarantor of Europe's security, its position conferred upon it a preponderance of influence over the setting of the alliance agenda. The United Kingdom and France have maintained far greater worldwide commitments than the other European members of NATO, and both have demonstrated the will and sustained the means to protect their global interests. As a result, the three principal powers of the alliance have largely defined the parameters of allied responsibility within and beyond Europe. Inevitably, then, this book concentrates on their actions, and the less powerful countries receive correspondingly less attention.

Any attempt to write contemporary history is complicated by the availability of sources. In the United States and the United Kingdom, there are extensive national archives, although classified diplomatic documents are made public only after at least a quarter century has passed. The American and British governments publish voluminous amounts of unclassified materials, and in the United States a good deal of ostensibly classified documentation has seeped into the public domain through congressional and journalistic inquiry. Research is more difficult in France. Access to declassified government documents proved all but impossible, and government publications are practically nonexistent. I attempted to compensate for gaps in the public record by conducting extensive interviews in France as well as in the United States, the United Kingdom, Italy, and Germany. In addition, a profusion of memoirs and a vast range of secondary sources cover the period about which I have written.

I also needed to bridge the gap between academic analysis and the real world of transatlantic policy making. A six-month stint in the

State Department's Bureau of European and Canadian Affairs, where I dwelt primarily on out-of-area issues, and two years' work as foreign policy and defense adviser to a United States senator, complemented my otherwise scholarly perspective on the making and management of foreign policy. This experience in government further convinced me that even the official declassified record to be used by the next generation of scholars will capture neither the rough texture of the policy process nor its full substance. Because of the nature of governmental paper trails as well as the discretion of censors, materials in declassified files are often arbitrary, incomplete, and scattered. Much of what is significant, precisely because of its importance and sensitivity, is not written down. Perhaps more than anything else, I came to appreciate the extent to which individuals, through their personal relationships with colleagues at home and counterparts abroad, make a difference in the practice of statecraft.

Acknowledgments

A number of individuals made a difference—an invaluable difference—in the writing of this book. Although I bear total responsibility for what is contained herein, this work would never have been completed without the generous contributions of mentors, colleagues, friends, and family.

Since my freshman year at Harvard College more than a decade ago, Stanley Hoffmann has been a source of enlightenment and inspiration. It is to Professor Hoffmann that I owe the deepest gratitude for initially engaging me in the study of international relations and for unstintingly sharing his time and ideas with this awestruck student.

Three others in the Harvard community played important roles. With his ebullient curiosity, Graham Allison first encouraged me to explore the dynamics of alliance politics beyond Europe and held the firm and reassuring conviction that this subject really mattered and merited a book. Robert Putnam, a devoted teacher and scholar, gave valued guidance and enthusiastic support. Joseph Nye offered incisive advice at critical moments.

Hedley Bull, my dissertation supervisor at Oxford University, brought his rigorous intellect to bear on early drafts and brooked no exception to his high standards of scholarship. He improved this book by challenging me to reach beyond a narrowly American perspective. After Professor Bull's untimely death, Adam Roberts provided a sound balance of constructive criticism, prodding, and reassurance. The generosity of the Rhodes Trust made my graduate work at Oxford possible.

As my research progressed, Richard Burt, Robert Blackwill, and Richard Haass gave me an opportunity to test my academic hypotheses and learn about the real stuff of alliance politics inside the Bureau of European and Canadian Affairs at the State Department. Richard Haass shared his unparalleled grasp of the complexities and subtleties of this subject with me and applied his disciplined mind to editing multiple drafts.

John Steinbruner and the entire Foreign Policy staff at the Brookings Institution provided warm and challenging company in which I completed the original manuscript and revised it several years later. William Quandt initially encouraged me to come to Brookings and offered sage advice and delightful friendship during both periods of my residence there.

Many others on both sides of the Atlantic gave generously of their time and ideas. I would especially like to thank François Heisbourg, whose encyclopedic and multilingual grasp of history and exceptional acumen informed his comments on innumerable drafts. Frederick Smith calmly endured—and answered—my infinite questions with kindness and humor. Those who proffered wise counsel, patiently read and commented on parts of the manuscript, graciously consented to be interviewed, and opened doors to new sources or unearthed old ones include Richard Betts, Martin Binkin, Luigi Caligaris, Anton DePorte, Joshua Epstein, Kenneth Flamm, Josef Joffe, Kay King, Pierre Lellouche, Susan McGrath, Thomas McNaugher, Robert O'Neill, Yves Pagniez, and Paul Stares. I would also like to thank all those who consented to be interviewed on a confidential basis for the essential contributions they made.

My editors at Yale University Press warmly encouraged and gently spurred me on to the finish: Marian Ash offered gracious support and sage advice throughout the process; John Covell and Eric Van Horne provided sound suggestions on revising the manuscript for publication; Carl Rosen and Fred Kameny kindly but meticulously applied their considerable talents as copy editors. In a category all by herself was Kathryn Ho, my word-processing wizard and indefatigable source of moral support.

I would also like to thank the friends who stood by me through the days when it seemed I would never emerge from underneath my piles of files. They include Pamela Saunders Albin, Abby Collins, Mahnaz Ispahani, David Lakhdhir, Penny Pritzker, Scott Sagan, Jay

Shanker, Jessica Teich, Katrina vanden Heuvel, Leon Wieseltier, Rhodri Williams, and Jennifer Seymour Whitaker.

My brother, Benjamin Sherwood, put his thick red pen, keen journalist's eye, broad knowledge of imperial history, and intense fraternal devotion to work on editing the manuscript, improving it immensely.

William Ury lovingly advised, edited, nurtured, and tolerated me through the writing of this book. He contributed his unparalleled understanding of crisis management and conflict resolution, illuminating the complex dynamics of alliance politics and inspiring me to think big.

I have dedicated this work to my mother and father, Dorothy and Richard Sherwood, not because I did it for them, but because I could not have done it without them. Their fervent editing, unflagging love, and almost irrational faith in my abilities have kept me and sustained me and brought me to this day.

Allies in Crisis

Introduction

The Atlantic alliance has been American foreign policy's greatest success story. Since its creation in 1949, the North Atlantic Treaty Organization (NATO) has deterred Soviet aggression against the territory of its members. Paradoxically, because of its effectiveness within the European theater, most of the major crises bearing on the interests of the Atlantic allies have taken place beyond Europe. There has never been a proverbial golden moment when NATO was insulated from developments outside its boundaries or from the interests of its individual members in those developments. As a result, alongside the NATO that makes headlines—an official, formal, Europe-centered organization—is a shadow alliance, an informal, globally oriented partnership of Western nations. This shadow alliance has played a critical role in protecting the allies' global interests.

The term of art used to encompass this dimension of alliance politics is *out-of-area*: it refers to developments beyond the official treaty area, and more generally outside of what is loosely known as Europe, that are relevant to the interests of the allies, either individually or collectively. From the Korean War in 1950 to the Persian Gulf in the late 1980s, a consequential portion of the history of the Atlantic alliance has been written by out-of-area events.

Because patterns and perceptions formed in past crises influence behavior in the present, a thorough knowledge of the history of NATO out-of-area crisis management is required to make sound recommendations for the future. The conventional wisdom is that the Atlantic alliance has handled extramural challenges badly or not at all; as is often the case, the conventional wisdom is wrong. Coping with out-of-area problems has certainly required a delicate balancing act, but on balance it has been a success. Despite tensions that might have torn it asunder, NATO has survived and indeed thrived, continuing to satisfy the vital security interests of its members both within and outside of Europe.

In NATO's management of out-of-area challenges, three clusters of issues emerge repeatedly and in different permutations throughout the postwar period. Shaping the dynamics of alliance politics beyond Europe have been competing definitions of allied out-of-area interests, divergent views about the appropriate allocation of human and material resources, and marked inequalities in the distribution of power within NATO.

The first set of issues has revolved around conflicting definitions of what constituted alliance interests beyond the treaty area. Since the creation of NATO those allies with interests at stake outside Europe have attempted to identify their own concerns with those of the alliance. The French in Indochina, the British at Suez, and the Americans in Vietnam all sought allied support for their causes. Yet the members of NATO, and especially its principal powers, have also carefully guarded their independence and have resisted being bound by their partners' commitments. In general, allies have been interested in cooperation if it was tantamount to support for their national policies, but not if joint action would constrain their chosen course. This put a damper on efforts to formalize allied obligations beyond the treaty area and forced the allies to rely on alternative means of policy coordination outside Europe.

In addition, what Harvard professor Stanley Hoffmann has termed the "geopolitical unevenness"[1] of the alliance led the United States to believe that it bore the principal responsibility for defining and defending the global interests of the allies. Compounding this problem, American military strategists held that the credibility of the United States's nuclear deterrent was being tested, either directly or indirectly, each time Western interests were threatened in the Third World. By contrast, the European members of NATO alternately worried that they would be either implicated involuntarily in American military commitments around the world or abandoned by their distracted guarantor. Both anxieties have shaped European attitudes toward United States out-of-area policies.

A second and interrelated set of issues lies in the perennial debate among alliance members over the allocation of resources. Beginning with the Korean War, the European allies worried about American strategic overextension, fearing that Washington's global commitments would shortchange NATO's security. In the eighties, the commitment of the United States to protect Western access to oil in the Persian Gulf provoked similar fears of a potential depletion of NATO's defenses. Conversely, since the Vietnam War, Washington has pushed for greater sharing of the collective defense burden both within and outside of Europe. American policymakers have been frustrated by what they perceived to be the increasingly Eurocentric views of the allies, although at times they confused allied desires for independence with parochialism.

The third set of issues has arisen from the indisputable hierarchy within the alliance that has been a determining factor in its handling of out-of-area crises. Since NATO's creation, three countries have dominated the debate over allied responsibilities beyond Europe. Throughout the postwar period, the United States has wielded the majority of political, economic, and military power and hence has had the most influence over setting the alliance agenda. The British, in part because of their remaining global commitments and in part because of their "special relationship" with the Americans, enjoyed pride of place among the Europeans. While the French search for equal status ultimately led to their departure from NATO's integrated military command structure, France continued to be considered one of the alliance's three principal powers because of its independent military strength and ongoing international commitments in Africa, Asia, and the Mideast. Separately, the United States, the United Kingdom, and France established the principle that they would coordinate with one another outside the formal alliance framework when and where their national interests coincided.

A mere reading of official NATO statements on out-of-area issues over the decades gives little hint of the intensity and vitality of the intra-alliance bargaining process. The following chapters demonstrate that consulting, cajoling, imploring, arguing, threatening, and sulking are all the stuff of alliance politics. NATO has survived a number of divisive out-of-area crises because its members have kept their eyes on the ball, an essential element in building and maintaining constructive long-term relationships in the face of short-term disagreements. Since NATO's creation, there has been a fundamental consensus among the allies that differences over strategy or policy beyond Europe ought not to detract from the maintenance of their central strategic objective: preventing the Soviet Union from expanding its empire to the Atlantic.

Nevertheless, there have been periodic calls to "solve" the out-of-area problem by formalizing allied cooperation outside the treaty area—by expanding NATO's domain or creating new forums for consultation and policy coordination. In fact, NATO has wisely eschewed formal cooperation beyond Europe, fearing that it would overburden the partnership and unnecessarily limit the autonomy of its members. Instead, the allies have relied on an ad hoc, informal approach to the management of developments outside the treaty area. The organizing principle has been that members with the interest, the will, and the capability to take action beyond Europe in defense of Western interests should do so, and that, where possible, they should coordinate with one another. Most often, this kind of cooperation has taken place on a bilateral basis outside the NATO framework. The nonbinding nature of this arrangement has given the Atlantic alliance the flexibility necessary to manage a wide variety of global challenges to the interests of its members and, ultimately, to endure.

• • • • • • • • • • • • • • • • • •

CHAPTER ONE

Defining the Limits of Alliance: The Creation of NATO, 1948–1949

In one year's time, between the spring of 1948 and the spring of 1949, NATO's founders divided the non-Communist world into two distinct parts: the territory to be covered by the treaty commitments of the Atlantic allies and the rest of the globe's surface. In so doing, they created the out-of-area concept. This chapter focuses on NATO's original geographical context—on why the alliance included and excluded what it did and on what its explicit links were to the world beyond the treaty area. The extensive debate over the scope and domain of allied responsibility presented here reveals that NATO was never perceived by its founders as an isolated project. They understood from the outset that the promotion of European security was integrally linked to developments outside the planned alliance's boundaries.

The Awful Ruin of Europe

At the end of World War II, Europe lay smoldering in ashes. In March 1946, Winston Churchill described the devastation to an American audience: "The awful ruin of Europe, with all its vanished glories . . . glares us in the eyes."[1] During the bleak winter of 1946–47, a good deal of the continent faced starvation, freezing homes, and silent industry.

The United Kingdom—until then the mainstay of Western security around the globe—confronted an acute crisis. Embattled by a severe coal shortage, diminished manpower, and obsolete machinery, the British appeared to weaken by the day. *Life* magazine painted

5

a bleak portrait of America's closest ally: "Her extreme poverty, her hunger, her industrial anemia are starkly apparent. Great Britain is no longer a first-rank world power."[2]

In early 1947, the inevitable retreat commenced as the British began to shrink their global responsibilities and reduce their overseas commitments: on 14 February they referred the Palestine question to the United Nations; on 18 February they announced the end of the Raj; and on 21 February they told the United States that they would no longer be able to finance or police the precarious situations in Greece and Turkey. These developments heralded the postwar transition from Pax Britannica to Pax Americana.

France and Italy also were destitute and unstable, and their respective Communist parties were making inroads on desolate political landscapes. In France, Communist leaders held cabinet posts in a series of coalition governments from 1945 through 1947. In Italy, the Communist party in 1945 had 1.7 million members; in the first postwar elections in June 1946 the Communists and Socialists together received nearly 40 percent of the popular vote.

Most important, the fate of Eastern Europe raised the specter of Communist domination of the entire continent. Churchill had warned in 1946 of the growing Soviet sphere of influence: "From Stettin in the Baltic to Trieste in the Adriatic, an iron curtain has descended across the Continent. Behind that line lie all the capitals of the ancient states of central and eastern Europe."[3] By 1947, Moscow's increasing domination of Bulgaria, the eastern sector of Germany, Hungary, Poland, and Rumania testified to the reality of the direct and indirect Soviet threat to a free Europe.

From Washington's vantage point, it appeared that the Soviets were on the move everywhere in the immediate postwar years, not only in Eastern Europe and Western Europe, but in the Middle East and Asia as well. Indeed, the perception of the Communist threat in Europe was in part driven by developments in these other regions. In Iran, the United States and the Soviet Union had come uncomfortably close to conflict over Soviet demands for oil concessions and support for a revolt in the northern province of Azerbaijan. In China, where American policy had been an excruciating failure, the indigenous Communists were steadily advancing. In Korea, American and Russian occupation troops faced each other across the thirty-eighth parallel. Furthermore, many of the victorious allies were plagued by empire problems. The British were losing the jewel in their crown,

India; the French faced unrest in Indochina; and the Dutch struggled with an uprising in Indonesia.

The general international turmoil hastened the emergence of the United States as the new guarantor of Western global interests. In March 1947 Secretary of State George Marshall observed, "We are now concerned with the peace of the entire world."[4] Precipitantly, the Americans were being looked to and indeed began to perceive themselves as the one power with the capacity to prevent Communist expansion and to reestablish world order.

In a nineteen-minute speech before Congress on the afternoon of 12 March 1947, President Harry S Truman revolutionized American foreign policy. He boldly asserted, "It must be the policy of the United States to support free peoples who are resisting attempted subjugation by armed minorities or by outside pressures." An editorial in the *New York Times* anticipated the momentous significance of Truman's words: "The epoch of isolation and occasional intervention is ended. It is being replaced by an epoch of American responsibility."[5] The *Washington Post* commented, "This is breath-taking in its literal implications. . . . It is as much a tocsin as a policy, a weapon in itself as much as the threat of a weapon."[6]

The Marshall Plan, announced at Harvard University on 5 June 1947 by the secretary of state bearing its name, provided the economic backbone for Truman's commitment. The United States contributed $13 billion, mostly in free grants, for the reconstruction of Western Europe. This investment also paved the way for the establishment of the military backbone for the Truman Doctrine: the North Atlantic Treaty Organization.

Building the Foundations of NATO

In his "iron curtain" speech Churchill had been the first to call for a joint effort by the United States and the British Commonwealth to resist Soviet advancement across Europe. The dark specter of Munich—where in 1938 British Prime Minister Neville Chamberlain had traded territory for false security—haunted the victorious allied leaders as they rebuilt a shattered world in Hitler's aftermath. Determined never again to pursue a policy of appeasement when confronted with a dictator's ambitions, they applied the lesson learned in the late thirties to Stalin's challenge.

NATO was the brainchild of British Foreign Secretary Ernest Bevin, who was determined not to repeat the mistakes made in the previous decade. Scarred by England's having borne the brunt of the Nazi onslaught while waiting for the United States to intervene, Bevin focused on obtaining an American commitment to protect Western Europe from the apparent Soviet threat. Because of the perceived global nature of Moscow's ambitions, he first dreamed of a grand federation embracing all of Western civilization. He initially thought that in order to secure Washington's involvement both the Pacific and Atlantic areas should be included in a "spiritual" federation of the West that would deter the Soviets from any further advancement.[7]

The American government, however, did not respond to Bevin's ambitious scheme with universal enthusiasm. While Secretary of State George Marshall was generally supportive, several of his senior advisers, including Counselor Charles Bohlen and Chief of Policy Planning George Kennan, were skeptical of making any broad commitments to Western defense. Furthermore, the Americans emphasized that the West Europeans needed to take the initiative to provide for their own defense before any military guarantee could be made. Bevin therefore reduced the scale and scope of his proposal to be more palatable to the United States and commensurate with Britain's limited capabilities, advocating instead the formation of an alliance limited to the Atlantic theater.[8]

The conclusion by the United Kingdom, France, and the Benelux countries on 17 March 1948 of the Brussels Treaty, a mutual defense association forming the European foundation of an alliance with the United States, was the first concrete step in Bevin's campaign to secure an American commitment to the defense of Europe. Concomitantly, the Communist coup in Czechoslovakia in late February and mounting Soviet pressure on Finland and Norway created a new sense of urgency in Washington about the fate of what remained of a free Europe. When on 11 March Bevin proposed to the United States the establishment of a "regional Atlantic Approaches Pact of Mutual Assistance" that would comprise "all the countries directly threatened by a Russian move to the Atlantic,"[9] Marshall responded affirmatively the next day. Without consulting his State Department advisers, Marshall affirmed that the United States was "prepared to proceed at once in the joint discussions on the establishment of an Atlantic security system."[10]

The original members of the envisaged pact defined themselves by their obvious political and historical ties and by their geographical position on the north Atlantic. The United States, the United Kingdom, and Canada formed the negotiating core, and they invited the other Brussels Treaty powers—France and the Benelux countries—to join them in the creation of the new alliance.

Over the next year, an intense and at times heated debate ensued about the proper scope and domain of the proposed alliance. In a series of meetings entitled the "Washington Exploratory Talks on Security," American, British, Canadian, French, and Benelux representatives grappled with the definition of the alliance's geographical boundaries. These "Washington Talks," as they came to be known, began in July 1948, continued throughout the year preceding the treaty's signing, and served as the principal forum for consideration of the appropriate territorial range of the alliance.[11] The Washington Talks were conducted by a working group consisting of the ambassadors to the United States from the five Brussels Treaty powers and Canada, with Under Secretary of State Robert Lovett representing the United States.

The parameters initially envisaged by the United States became the general outlines of NATO, reflecting European dependence on American power. A State Department internal memorandum dated 27 July 1948 detailed the criteria of the United States for determining additional alliance members: geographical position; the contribution a country would make and the liability the country might present for the security arrangement; the consequence of inclusion or exclusion on the country's security as well as its corresponding impact on the United States, Canada, and the Brussels Treaty powers; and the attitude of the given country toward participation. The memorandum advocated the inclusion of Norway, Denmark, and Iceland, as well as of Italy, Ireland,[12] and Portugal. Spain, Western Germany,[13] and Austria might be considered for membership when internal political conditions in each were satisfactory. It also concluded that the security of Greece, Turkey, and Iran, while important, should be provided for in another context.[14]

From the outset, a paradox confronted the participants in Washington: in the very act of defining the precise territory of the proposed alliance, they created potential new security problems for themselves. For by defining what was "in-area," they also established an out-of-area. In so doing, they might lead other nations to conclude that out-of-area concerns were not of vital import to the security of the Atlantic powers.

In an effort to grapple with the implications of this paradox, the United States presented a paper to the working group of the Washington Talks in early September 1948 on the "Territorial Scope of a North Atlantic Security Arrangement and Its Relationship to the Security of Other Nations."[15] The paper specified three factors bearing on the decision to invite other free European nations to participate: "(1) the effect on the security of the nations participating in these talks should the territory of these other nations be occupied by an enemy; (2) the necessity for maintaining and strengthening their Western orientation, and (3) the importance of avoiding any Russian miscalculation to the effect that these nations could be absorbed into the Soviet orbit with impunity." The American document also took explicit note of the problem of limited resources. Resource constraints formed the most powerful argument for a lean interpretation of NATO's territorial dimensions: "A line must be drawn somewhere. . . . The problem is to devise an arrangement which would best meet the security needs of the nations here represented without overextending their military capabilities."

To resolve the paradox the United States proposed that there should be three categories of alliance membership, commensurate with the capabilities and circumstances of potential participants: full membership involving "maximum commitments of reciprocal assistance . . . and development of co-ordinated military potential"; associate membership requiring a commitment to provide access to facilities in exchange for a promise on the part of full members to come to their defense; and associated status for those countries against whom aggression would provoke consultation among full members as to the appropriate response.

Emphasizing that particular attention should be paid to "the area within which aggression would bring into operation the provisions of mutual assistance in the proposed Pact," the working group transmitted the American paper in a slightly revised form on 10 September to the governments of Belgium, Canada, France, the Netherlands, and the United Kingdom for consideration. The Washington representatives also made note that they intended "to draw the attention of their governments to the importance of this [territorial] question which they themselves have not so far attempted to consider."[16]

Sir Nicholas Henderson, a member of the working party drafting the treaty and later British ambassador to the United States, summed up the outstanding issues in the early autumn of 1948: (1) "Whether or not there should be different categories of membership"; (2) "Which countries should join the Treaty; the question of Italy looked like being the most difficult"; and (3) "Definition of the area within which aggression would bring into operation the provisions of mutual assistance in the Pact."[17] With these issues outstanding, there was a lull of several months in the Washington Talks, due largely to American preoccupation with the November 1948 election that extended President Truman's mandate. When the discussions resumed in the beginning of December 1948, the participants finally began to debate the specifics of the treaty commitment.

This debate over NATO's appropriate scope and domain was significantly influenced by resonant antecedents in the American experience and by congressional pressure. Across its history, the United States had resisted "entangling alliances": George Washington advised the country to "steer clear of permanent alliances with any portion of the foreign world," and Thomas Jefferson warned the nation only to "trust to temporary alliances for extraordinary emergencies."[18] Since the decision to join a permanent peacetime alliance was unprecedented, the implications of this commitment were viewed with skepticism and suspicion, especially by the United States Congress. On the eve of the signing of the North Atlantic Treaty, the *New York Times* summed up the mood on Capitol Hill: "Father Congress was in a distinctly waspish mood all week, complaining about the high cost of security. . . . The isolationist clacque was in full cry."[19]

According to the Constitution of the United States, the executive branch cannot enter into a treaty without securing the "advice and consent" of the United States Senate.[20] The legislative branch thus wielded enormous influence regarding the precise delimitation of NATO responsibilities. During the initial Senate hearings in May 1948 on American participation in the alliance, Senator Arthur Vandenberg, chairman of the Senate Foreign Relations Committee and the Republican party's leading foreign policy spokesman in Congress, argued that "there can be no open ended obligation of any sort whatsoever in respect to military assistance to Western Europe; . . . we must maintain our right of self-determination even as we grant it to others."[21]

President Truman and his senior advisers knew that while they could count on the support of congressional Democrats, Vandenberg's endorsement would guarantee enough Republican votes to ensure passage of the treaty by the necessary two-thirds majority. Robert Lovett, who had previously won the senator's support for the Truman Doctrine and the Marshall Plan, was assigned to lobby Vandenberg on NATO. In the late spring of 1948, Vandenberg wrote the Senate resolution bearing his name, giving the president the mandate to establish regional and collective defense arrangements advantageous to the nation's security.[22]

Although Congress thereby endorsed the negotiations to create NATO, its opposition to automatic involvement in defense of another country's interests and its unique constitutional authority to declare war still shaped the final text of the treaty. This proved most significant with respect to article 5, which allowed each nation to determine its own course of action in a crisis, including whether to use armed force.[23] In spite of the unprecedented commitment of its political, economic, and military resources to countries beyond its borders, the United States clearly intended to retain the maximum freedom of maneuver and to relinquish as little sovereignty as possible within the NATO framework. Since the Europeans were at the time desperately dependent on American economic support and military protection, they had no choice but to accept the terms defined by Washington.

Clashes of objectives and interests outside Europe, especially with respect to the course and pace of decolonization, were decisive in establishing the restricted geographical dimensions of the treaty's operation. The Americans had no intention of being formally obligated to take action in concert with or in support of their European partners in the non-Atlantic world. Since World War II, the United States had been largely unsympathetic toward its allies' efforts to retain control over their remaining colonies and therefore deliberately distanced itself from their imperial activities.[24]

Public opinion in the United States had been pronounced on this point since the beginning of the war. On 12 October 1942, the editors of *Life* offered an "Open Letter . . . to the People of England," in which they spelled out the American perspective in no uncertain terms: "One thing we are sure we are *not* fighting for is to hold the British Empire together. We don't like to put the matter so bluntly, but we don't want you to have any illusions. If your strategists are planning a war to hold the British Empire together they will sooner or later find themselves strategizing all alone."[25] Columnist Walter Lippmann's reaction to Winston Churchill's plea for Anglo-American global cooperation in the iron curtain speech captured the postwar mood: "The line of British imperial interest and the line of American vital interest are not to be regarded as identical."[26] Washington's policies in the early postwar period reflected the broad consensus against any perpetuation of European imperial status.

With the boundaries of American involvement constrained by historical experience, congressional pressure, and anticolonial sentiment, the Washington Talks participants continued to hammer out the specifics of the proposed treaty. In December 1948, Theodore Achilles, chief of the State Department's Division of Western European Affairs, sent a memo to the Joint Chiefs of Staff that included a rough definition of the area to be covered by the treaty. Achilles made the case for precisely delimited alliance responsibilities, with which the military establishment concurred:

> We do feel it essential that the area covered by the mutual assistance provision of such a treaty should be specifically defined in order that the governments, legislatures and peoples concerned, particularly our own, may know exactly what commitments are involved. We feel that the area should be defined on the basis of strategic considerations, not from the point of view of attempting to defend any particular part of the area but from the point of view of defining as specifically as possible an area within which hostile armed action would in fact require armed reaction by this Government and other government parties to the treaty.[27]

Based upon the apparent consensus among diplomats, politicians, and strategists that the treaty domain should be precisely demarcated, the United States insisted during the remaining negotiations on the explicit articulation of limits to the alliance.

Variations on the theme of a broader security pact were still raised occasionally by other Washington Talks participants, reflecting concern in some European capitals that the creation of NATO might adversely affect allied interests in other areas of the world, but these proposals were consistently dismissed. One notable example was the scheme put forth in January 1949 by E. N. Van Kleffens, the Dutch ambassador to the United States, suggesting that countries outside the core NATO area might be associated to the treaty through "annexes to this convention and will be considered as forming an integral part thereof."[28] The British and the Americans, however, quickly spurned this idea.[29] A Foreign Office cable to Ambassador Oliver Franks detailed British objections, which centered on the perils of spreading Western or, more specifically, American resources too thin: "This idea seems woolly and dangerous. (a) It offers a prospect of an indefinite extension of the scope of the Pact—as far afield, apparently as New Zealand on one side and Persia on the other with all the corresponding difficulties of getting it through Congress. (b) It will create two different categories of signatory with apparently different obligations—with unforeseeable consequences on its organisation and execution."[30]

In spite of their rejection of explicit alliance responsibilities beyond Europe, the negotiating parties were fully aware of the potential significance of developments outside the treaty area to their collective and individual interests. The principal Western powers had a wide range of global concerns at the time including the fate of China, the independence of India, the future of Indonesia, and the partition of Palestine. During late 1948 and early 1949, the Washington Talks participants wrestled with establishing a definition of allied responsibilities that reflected this broader agenda. A two-track approach finally evolved: the first contained the formal military guarantee that the treaty provided for Europe; the second covered the informal dimension of cooperation beyond Europe that complemented the European security commitment.

Drafts of article 4, considered the heart of the treaty, stated that the members would "consult together whenever in the opinion of any of them, the territorial integrity, political independence or security of any of the parties is threatened." The American military establishment, reflecting its natural concern with the actual defensibility of commitments, feared that this would permit too broad a definition of allied responsibility. The Joint Chiefs argued that the words "territorial integrity" could "be construed to include the colonies of all the signatories to the pact," and that it therefore "could constitute a very large order indeed and one that does not appear to be essential to the North Atlantic Pact." Moreover, they asserted that "there should be clear understanding that consultation is not in itself a commitment to military action."[31] Although the phrase "territorial integrity" remained intact in the final treaty text, the United States did insist that an additional clause—obliging consultation whenever "there exists a situation which constitutes a threat to or breach of the peace"—be removed because it went "too far."

The British balked and made deletion of the phrase obliging consultation conditional on an understanding being entered into the final negotiating record that article 4 "would cover the non-self-governing territories of the signatories." This informal "agreed interpretation" made clear that the consultation clause in article 4 applied to a threat "in any part of the world, to the security of any of the Parties; including threats to the security of their overseas territories."[32] The British intended this to allow them to "insist on consultation" whenever they considered their security threatened by events outside the treaty area.[33] But reflecting the emerging awareness in London that no greater commitment would be forthcoming from Washington, the Foreign Office warned the Commonwealth Office that with respect to the dependent territories, "the most we hope for is to have it on record in the minutes that an external threat to one of them will be regarded as an occasion for consultation."[34]

This resolution of American and British differences over article 4 reveals the origin of what here will be termed the *informal* dimension of allied out-of-area cooperation. While policy coordination beyond Europe might well take place, based on the shared international objectives expressed in the North Atlantic pact, the participants in the negotiations accepted that no formal commitment to action beyond consultation would exist in the actual treaty. Although NATO's explicit domain of responsibility was clearly limited by the treaty, members with extra-European interests and capabilities obviously retained the right to act outside of Europe, whether cooperatively or individually. Allied behavior beyond Europe would thus be guided by unwritten rather than explicit bonds. Theodore Achilles has written of the assumptions that underlay this arrangement: "The treaty area, as defined in article 6, is simply that in which an armed attack would constitute a *casus belli*; there was never the slightest thought in the mind of the drafters that it should prevent collective planning, manoeuvres or operations south of the Tropic of Cancer in the Atlantic Ocean, or in any other area important to the security of the Parties."[35]

By the beginning of 1949 the Washington Talks participants had produced a complete text of a draft treaty and had reached general agreement on the value of consultation on out-of-area issues. A major intra-European issue, however, had not yet been resolved: the exact territory against which an attack would trigger the collective defense provisions of the treaty.[36] It proved relatively easy to agree on mere consultation in the event of an armed attack beyond the treaty domain or any other event indirectly threatening the security of the parties. More portentous was the commitment to regard an attack on the territory of any party to the treaty as an attack on all, including oneself, and hence to take action in meeting that attack as if in defense of one's own territory.

The divergent security perspectives and requirements of the seven core North Atlantic powers were reflected in their debate about which of their extra-European territories to consider as integral to the security of Europe and which additional countries to include as original signatories. The United States, the United Kingdom, and France differed markedly on the thorny issues of the inclusion of Italy and French North Africa in the Atlantic pact and on the possibility of provision being made in the NATO context for the security of Greece, Turkey, and perhaps Iran.[37] They also differed, although with less controversy, over including Scandinavia and the Iberian Peninsula. The resolution of these differences reflected the distribution of power within the nascent alliance: big decisions would be made by its three principal members—the United States, the United Kingdom, and France—and, in the final analysis, by the United States alone. The remaining negotiating parties—the Benelux countries and Canada— accepted this blunt reality with a mixture of grace and resignation.[38] This early precedent became the pattern in subsequent consultations on the definition of alliance interests beyond Europe.

As the discussions over the delineation of the treaty domain progressed, the Americans expressed foreboding that the creation of NATO might have a destabilizing impact on Western interests outside the treaty area. Thus despite their determination to delimit precisely the nature and extent of their commitment to Europe, they also became the advocates of an inclusive rather than an exclusive map of NATO.

Specifically, the United States feared that the establishment of a "hold line" might lead the Soviets to believe that anything outside the treaty area was fair game.[39] Reflecting preoccupation in policy-making circles with this possibility, *Foreign Affairs* editor Hamilton Fish Armstrong entitled his April 1949 article "Regional Pacts: Strong Points or Storm Cellars?" He argued that Washington should defuse the possiblity of NATO's being perceived as a retraction of American obligations under the United Nations Charter or the embodiment of a new form of Western isolationism by affirming that the Atlantic alliance "is not a limitation of policy to a few U.N. members but a specific reenforcement of a general policy which applies to all members."[40] Such concerns explained Washington's inclination to invite into NATO those European countries whose link to the West was weak or who might be subjected to Soviet subversion, and these included both Italy and the Scandinavian nations.

The United Kingdom was the most globally minded of the European powers in terms of interests and capabilities, but it relegated its non-European security concerns to a position of secondary import during the NATO negotiations. The essential objective of the British was to bind America to the defense of the Atlantic community writ small: to create an alliance that would unconditionally defend the core countries. They therefore did not advocate the inclusion of what they viewed as peripheral nations, and they pursued their broader security goals in bilateral discussions with the United States.

In contrast, the French were narrowly preoccupied throughout the negotiations with extracting precise obligations of assistance for the defense of their own territory. In order to create leverage to ensure the protection of their interests, they advocated the inclusion of Italy and linked their support for the accession of the Scandinavian powers to the satisfaction of their perceived security requirements. These requirements revolved around the extension of the NATO guarantee to North Africa.

Anchoring Italy to the West

The debate over Italian membership in NATO was the most protracted and contentious of any of the unresolved issues regarding the treaty area. The British opposed Italy's inclusion from the outset and continued in early 1949 to campaign outspokenly against Italian accession.[41] In Bevin's words, "Italy would at present be more of a liability than an asset militarily and a drain on present limited resources of arms and equipment."[42] The British Chiefs of Staff argued that "it would be fundamentally unsound at this stage to add to our existing commitments in Western Europe and the Middle East." In contrast to the American military establishment's analysis that the inclusion of Italy was warranted to safeguard Mediterranean sea communications, the British estimated that they could not "afford an Italian insurance policy at present," noting that the Americans did not "realise how much the premiums would increase in wartime."[43] London could afford neither the forces nor the equipment to mount a successful defense of Italy. Underlying this position was a pervasive skepticism about the reliability of the Italians as allies. There was also residual concern that the Italians would use accession to the pact as a means of reclaiming their former colonial possessions.[44]

The British, however, never strayed from their central task of securing an American commitment to the defense of Western Europe. When it became evident that their opposition to Italian adhesion might "prejudice the prospects of the Pact," they were willing to reconsider their position and eventually to accept Italian entry if the Americans chose to do so.[45]

The French, by contrast, wavered initially but eventually became self-interested advocates of Italian membership. Their first rationale for supporting Rome's accession was strategic: the Po Valley in northern Italy was the traditional channel of invasion from the East, and France did not want to be the most exposed flank of the West. Furthermore, according to this analysis, if the Scandinavian powers acceded to the pact but North Africa was not included, NATO's center of gravity would shift to the north. France would feel, in Foreign Minister Robert Schuman's words, that "instead of being in the middle of a defense system, they have put us on one of the wings." The French attempted explicitly to link the accession of Italy to that of Norway, but the other negotiating parties resisted the ploy on the grounds that the Italian and Norwegian questions were distinctly different.[46]

The second rationale motivating French advocacy of Italian membership was even less altruistic: they believed that the inclusion of Italy would permit them to make a more forceful case for the inclusion of North Africa. Thus Paris remained the most prominent proponent of Italian accession and even threatened that if Italy were excluded, and especially if Norway acceded without Italy, France's relationship to the alliance would have to be reevaluated.[47] Confirmation of the opportunistic nature of this position came when the French let it be known that they would be willing to lessen their insistence on Italian membership if, in so doing, the other negotiating parties might be more favorably disposed toward the inclusion of France's North African territories in the treaty area.[48]

During the first two months of 1949, the United States wavered on the subject of Italian membership in NATO, and so these differences between the British and the French went unresolved. American policymakers did worry that including Italy would stretch the NATO security commitment beyond the Atlantic all the way to the Mediterranean, draining the limited military resources of the other parties and thereby necessitating an even greater contribution by the United States. George Kennan, director of the State Department's Policy Planning Staff, made the case against Italian accession. He argued that the pact should be restricted to the North Atlantic area, including only those states "whose homeland or insular territories are washed by the waters of the North Atlantic, or which form part of a close union of states which meets this description."[49] Like the British, the Americans also remembered, "In two world wars Italy has shown herself to be an ineffectual and undependable ally, having switched sides in both wars."[50]

These negatives, however, were offset by two key considerations. The first was the military assessment that Italy was strategically significant to the defense of NATO. Theodore Achilles outlined the Pentagon perspective: "Our military are insistent that she [Italy] be in, taking the position that Italy cannot be ignored in the strategic defense of Western Europe, that the question of whether or not any particular country is included depends not on whether troops are available to defend that country, but on whether or not a Soviet attack upon it would sufficiently affect the security of the other parties to warrant their going to war."[51] Another State Department memo emphasized that the omission of Italy would be "like a man going out to dinner in his evening clothes minus his trousers, thereby exposing a part of the body which should never be exposed."[52] Although the Americans understood that the fighting value of Italian forces at the time was militarily insignificant, the denial of Italian territory to the Soviets was perceived to have an important bearing on the outcome of operations both in Western Europe and in the Middle East.[53]

This assessment was integrally linked to the second consideration driving American policy: Italian entrance into NATO would cement the nation to the West and thereby prevent the Communists from gaining a foothold on the doorstep of Western Europe. Accession to NATO had become the focal point of a domestic political debate within Italy, in which the decision to join the Atlantic alliance represented a fundamental *scelta di civiltà*, or "choice of civilization."[54] Capitalizing on American anxiety that the growing strength of the

Italian Communist party (PCI) could make possible its entry into the government, Italian officials cautioned that there could be adverse consequences for Italy's political orientation and security should the invitation to join NATO be withheld.[55] As the Atlantic pact negotiations moved toward completion, the Christian Democratic leadership warned that if Italy were not invited to accede as a full member before the treaty was signed, the governing coalition might collapse and the PCI would take charge.[56]

This was a compelling argument for American officials responsible for policy toward Western Europe. In March 1948, Truman had issued clear instructions on Italy: "The U.S. should make full use of its political, economic and, if necessary, military power in such manner as may be found most effective to assist in preventing Italy from falling under the domination of the USSR either through external armed attack or through Soviet-dominated Communist movements within Italy."[57] In accordance with this presidential directive, the United States expended a considerable amount of energy and money to ensure that Italy was not "lost" to the Communists in the April 1948 elections, which served as the postwar state's first real test of party strength.[58] Although the Christian Democrats—Washington's choice—triumphed, the PCI remained a potent force on the Italian political landscape. The director of the State Department's Office of European Affairs, John Hickerson, warned that if Italy were not allowed to participate in NATO, it would bring about a "fundamental reorientation of Italian foreign policy," the consequences of which "would not contribute to the attainment of U.S. objectives in Europe."[59]

Prompted by these strategic and political factors, President Truman decided in early March 1949 to support and invite Italian membership in NATO, against the advice of some of his own advisers and the British government, and in spite of the machinations of the French.[60] That the United States ultimately defined the parameters of the alliance confirmed the early existence of a hierarchy of power within NATO in which the principal allies, and more often than not the United States alone, made the major decisions regarding the security of the rest. The less powerful partners, while accorded the opportunity to speak their minds, recognized that they had very little leverage and would have to acquiesce in whatever decision was taken. Instead of considering Italy to be marginally out-of-area because it was not actually on the Atlantic seaboard, NATO's founders stretched the concept of the Atlantic alliance to accommodate American strategic and political objectives.

The Dilemma of Greece, Turkey, and Iran

During the debate over the inclusion of Italy, a related set of questions arose pertaining to the security of Greece, Turkey, and Iran. The Americans and the British determined that the inclusion of these countries in NATO itself would stretch the concept of an Atlantic alliance to the breaking point. They both, however, believed that the security of the Eastern Mediterranean and Middle East was vital to their own security and that the security of Greece, Turkey, and Iran was vital to the security of the Eastern Mediterranean and Middle East. They did not want to invite Soviet adventurism on the periphery of Europe by drawing a line around the Atlantic allies.

In October 1948, Joseph Satterthwaite, director of the State Department's Office of Near Eastern and African Affairs, made the case to Under Secretary of State Lovett that the actual boundaries of the proposed alliance with Europe might inadvertently, but nonetheless significantly, affect Soviet perceptions of opportunities. NATO, he argued, could not be completely insulated from calculations of extra-atlantic interests and objectives, especially in the Eastern Mediterranean:

> The relatively close association of the United States with certain states of western Europe under this arrangement will emphasize the lack of any special arrangement for the security of other states which are similarly threatened by the Soviet Union but which, by their geographic position, could not logically be included in the North Atlantic group. It seems essential that a decision be made regarding our policy toward the security of these states in the light of the North Atlantic arrangement.[61]

The British concurred: something needed to be done about the geographically contiguous but non-Atlantic countries of the Eastern Mediterranean. Indeed, as it became evident that Italy would join NATO, Bevin argued that some sort of deterrent posture was even more necessary. Otherwise, he asserted, the "Soviet Union might assume we had decided upon a certain line of defence which did not include Greece and Turkey, which would thereby be endangered."[62]

The British analysis, however, differed from the American one in an important respect. Considering a joint declaration, American policymakers were keen to include Iran because, in their assessment, Iran was subject to "the most prolonged and direct Soviet threat" of any of the countries under consideration. Iran would be "the logical 'soft-spot' to tempt the Soviet Union to risk aggression" if Moscow believed it would not be met with a serious response by the United States and United Kingdom. Indeed, the Americans felt that it would be better to have "no declaration at all than one which omitted Iran."[63] The British, by contrast, worried that the inclusion of Iran would be extremely provocative to the Soviet Union. They reasoned that Moscow might feel the West was pursuing a policy of encirclement and this would precipitate an invasion rather than deter one. The British ambassador in Teheran, Sir John Lerougetel, reported to Bevin that the Russians might use such a declaration as a pretext to invoke the 1921 Treaty of Friendship between Persia and the Soviet Union and reoccupy Azerbaijan.[64]

The Americans and the British also considered inviting the other negotiating parties to participate in issuing a proposed statement on Greece, Turkey, and Iran. Their preliminary soundings, however, revealed that the smaller parties to the treaty would be unlikely to support any statement unless it was diluted to the point of being devoid of substance. Furthermore, the Turkish government opposed the involvement of such countries as Luxembourg on the grounds that it might "reflect on Turkish prestige."[65] The Greeks were similarly inclined to prefer a declaration made only by the Americans and the British, with the possible addition of the French.

In fact, both Washington and London were relieved not to have to negotiate with the smaller powers. The Americans argued that it simplified the task and that an Anglo-American statement would "carry virtually as much moral force as one signed also by the Benelux nations." More important, in the event of an attack on any of the countries to which the statement applied, consultations and possible action would be considerably expedited if only two parties were involved. The Americans noted, "It may even be a positive advantage to omit from the list of signatories the weaker states which might be more reluctant to act and which could contribute little to any action which might be taken."[66] The British shared this perspective. Deputy Under Secretary of State Gladwyn Jebb argued that he did not believe that it mattered whether the "minor signatories" subscribed; what counted was a declaration by the United States and the United Kingdom.[67]

Secretary of State Dean Acheson and Ernest Bevin originally planned to issue a formal joint declaration on Greece, Turkey, and Iran as a complement to their announcement of the establishment of NATO. As a result of their differences over Iran and concerns about American congressional scrutiny, they decided to make separate statements about the interests of their respective governments in the security of the three countries in question. The British avoided making specific reference to Iran and referred instead to the area from "Greece to the Persian Gulf."[68] In choosing to issue two distinct statements, Acheson and Bevin also made their declarations seem less like a new treaty commitment and thereby avoided having to seek the approval of the United States Senate.[69]

The delineation of NATO's original southeastern boundaries—including Italy but excluding Greece and Turkey—contributed to the establishment of two significant and interrelated precedents for the management of allied interests beyond Europe. First, the United States and the United Kingdom conducted a unique bilateral dialogue fitting within the framework of the proposed European alliance but covering developments well beyond the scope of NATO. It became increasingly clear that their special relationship—a relationship that itself had evolved outside the NATO context—would play a central role in the management of developments beyond Europe affecting the interests of the alliance or its individual members. This reinforced the acceptability of ad hoc arrangements for the protection of the out-of-area concerns of NATO's principal powers. Second, based on their intimate consultations, the Americans and the British established an explicit linkage between European and non-European security interests. They espoused the principle that security was indivisible: even though NATO would have distinct boundaries of action, its members could not insulate themselves from developments beyond the proposed treaty area.

Based on this principle, Greece and Turkey were later invited to become full members of NATO. Their accession in September 1951 was part of a broader American and British endeavor to augment the Western presence in the Mediterranean and the Middle East (see chapter 3).[70] The merits of Greek and Turkish entry were debated then in the context of alliance interests not only within but beyond Europe. This reflected the growing perception that NATO security was inextricably linked to developments outside the formal domain of allied responsibility.

The French and North Africa

The determination of the French to include North Africa in the treaty area was perceived by the other negotiating parties as nothing less than a national obsession. Although France's overseas possessions had not been covered by the Brussels Treaty, the French argued that NATO was going to be much broader in scope. They reasoned that if the inclusion of the noncontiguous American territory of Alaska could be justified, so could the inclusion of North Africa, a French "metropolitan" territory.

United States policymakers were concerned about the precedent that would be set by including any North African territory in the treaty area, fearing it could encourage other allies to expect American protection for their colonial possessions. As noted, American officials were loathe to provide any support for the scattered remnants of empire and Pentagon strategists preferred to keep the operative area of the prospective alliance as small as possible. The British thought the French were making an "absurd fuss" on the subject. Indeed, London worried that French self-absorption might jeopardize American support for the proposed alliance, "prejudicing not only their own position but that of the other Brussels Powers. They seem characteristically unable to look at the matter from anything but their own selfish point of view and almost to take the line that it is they who are conferring a favour on the Americans by joining the pact."[71] The French, however, remained steadfast, threatening that the treaty would be unacceptable unless, at a minimum, Algeria was expressly included. The government informed Washington that it could not present a pact excluding Algeria to the National Assembly for a vote.

Confronted with this ultimatum, the State Department relented. The United States agreed to the attachment of a further treaty provision in which specific mention would be made of the area in which an armed attack would trigger the collective defense provisions of article 5, and in which Algeria would be specifically identified as a part of France.[72] This clause, which became article 6, defined NATO's boundaries as the territory of the parties in "Europe or North America," which included the "Algerian Departments of France."[73] The State

Department believed that this formula was the only way to avoid a fight with Congress over an expansion of the geographical scope of the treaty into North Africa. Although the actual difference seems slight, it was believed at the time to be essential in securing American congressional support for the pact.[74]

Belgium, a less influential power, was unsuccessful in its endeavor to extract a similar commitment from the United States. The Belgians sought the inclusion of the Congo in the territory to be covered by the pact, but they were told that the treaty could not possibly be extended to include the Belgian colony and no specific reassurances or commitments could be made.[75] France, as one of the three principal powers of the alliance, benefited from a certain privileged status; the rest learned that they had little leverage over the central triumvirate, especially when it came to the definition of allied interests beyond Europe.

The Stepping-Stone Concept

The debates over the inclusion of Portugal and the Scandinavian countries were not nearly as controversial as those concerning Italy, the Eastern Mediterranean nations, and Algeria, but their inclusion in the proposed alliance reflected a new era in American strategy. For the first time in its history, the United States made sustained international commitments, and this required it to think in global terms about its security interests. This meant that NATO's scope had to be broadened to include several countries that could facilitate the deployment of American manpower and matériel to Europe.

In a deployment plan termed the *stepping-stone* concept, United States military planners held that access to the major midocean islands would be crucial to the air and naval reinforcement of the NATO allies in wartime. Given the limited range of aircraft at the time, the Americans deemed refueling facilities in Greenland (belonging to Denmark), Iceland, and the Portuguese Azores essential to providing for the security of Europe.[76] The Brussels Treaty powers' dependence on American military protection dictated that their interests would be best served by supporting the inclusion of the countries in question.[77]

Portugal

The United States insisted that an effective defense of Europe could not be mounted without access to naval and air facilities in the Azores.[78] Portugal was an Atlantic power, so no argument could be made on geographic grounds against its accession. Nevertheless, the Portuguese expressed several concerns about NATO membership that accurately reflected their position on the political as well as geographic periphery of the proposed alliance.

Most important, the Portuguese believed that the principal negotiating parties sought their accession solely to exploit their valuable real estate. They feared that the NATO powers wanted only to "secure the establishment in time of peace of military or air bases in territories which are of special strategic significance for the defence of the Atlantic."[79] The Americans and the British assured them that no party to the treaty would automatically have to grant facilities to another party without its full consent.[80] Portuguese uneasiness, however, was justified. Though they would not be required "automatically" to grant use of their facilities, considerable pressure would later be exerted upon them when such access was desired. The United States, in particular, would seek to use Lajes air base, not only for the defense of the Atlantic area but for out-of-area operations as well.

The Portuguese also inquired into the possibility of extending the NATO security guarantee to their colonies but were told that the treaty would only be applicable to overseas territories insofar as provisions would be made for consultations.[81] Finally, the Portuguese made the case that Spain should play a role in the defense of the Iberian Peninsula. The negotiating parties agreed that Spain should be brought into NATO as soon as the country adopted a form of government acceptable to the Western powers. Spain's domestic political situation, however, would not permit accession for thirty years.[82]

Scandinavia

The inclusion of the Scandinavian countries in NATO, rather than the creation of a distinct northern flank security arrangement, reflected the fact that the proposed alliance was to be first and foremost a defense pact. Military considerations therefore proved decisive in determining the scope of membership. In a February 1949 study, the American Joint Chiefs of Staff argued that Scandinavian participation would be of great value to the United States in prosecuting its NATO responsibilities: "The major strategic interests of the United States in the Scandinavian nations are the denial to the Russians of air and submarine bases in Norway and the island possessions of Denmark (Greenland) and Norway (Spitzbergen Archipelago, including Bear Island), and to secure such base and communication facilities as may be required by the United States in the prosecution of a war." The Joint Chiefs asserted that they considered it "vital to United States security that we retain our present facilities and obtain additional base rights in Greenland and that the United States control that island in event of war." Additionally, they emphasized that Scandinavian membership in a North Atlantic security pact was far preferable to a separate Scandinavian grouping—a grouping the Joint Chiefs suspected might espouse neutrality.[83]

The British concurred in the American estimate of Scandinavia's strategic importance and were particularly interested in Norwegian and Danish accession to the pact.[84] The French, as noted, were narrowly concerned that the inclusion of Norway without the inclusion of Italy might orient the proposed alliance to the north, leaving them exposed and vulnerable as its southernmost member.[85] Once the decision to include Italy had been made, the French supported Norwegian membership.

In early March 1949, the negotiating parties extended invitations to Norway, Denmark, and Iceland (and to Portugal and Italy) to participate in the final sessions of the Washington Talks and to join the pact as original signatories.[86] Sweden was not asked to join, since soundings early on in the negotiations—as well as Swedish efforts to persuade the Norwegians and Danes to establish a Scandinavian security system that had no close defense relationship with any other countries—indicated that it intended to preserve its neutrality.[87]

The Birth of NATO

Publication of the text of the North Atlantic Treaty on 18 March 1949 represented a watershed in American foreign policy. *Life* described it as "the greatest formal shift in U.S. policy—and American thinking—since the promulgation in 1823 of the Monroe Doctrine."[88] In a solemn ceremony on the afternoon of 4 April in Washington, D.C., the treaty was signed. With President Truman standing behind him, Dean Acheson penned his name at 4:51 P.M., thereby adding the United States to the list of eleven other original members of the Atlantic alliance: Belgium, Canada, Denmark, France, Iceland, Italy, Luxembourg, the Netherlands, Norway, Portugal, and the United Kingdom.[89]

The Marine Band accompanying the otherwise dignified proceedings played two oddly revealing selections: "It Ain't Necessarily So" and "I Got Plenty o' Nuttin." In spite of the general consensus that the United States had no other choice but to use its power to deter Soviet aggression and expansion, there was significant doubt about this new responsibility. Several senators questioned whether the Constitution permitted the treaty's commitment to enter into war on behalf of the allies. A larger contingent questioned the prospect of substantial expenditures for the rearmament of Europe. On the eve of the signing, James Reston wrote a *New York Times* article entitled "We Assume World Role But Cost Bothers Us," in which he described the mood in Congress:

> The Senate will probably give its consent to the ratification of the North Atlantic Treaty in much the same way as a grumpy father consents to the marriage of his beautiful daughter to the wily foreigner.
>
> . . . And yet, despite the longings for a simpler past, the frustrations of the present and the fears for an unknown future, Father Congress will no doubt kick in at the end with a grumpy blessing—and a fairly handsome dowry.[90]

Underlying this hesitance was the knowledge that NATO irrevocably repudiated any last remnants of isolationism in American foreign policy. The United States, thrust onto the world stage by fortune, improvised its new international role as it went along. In its editorial on 3 April, the *New York Times* described an uncertain America assuming the mantle:

> We have really had less than four years in which to lay down a new foreign policy, or set of foreign policies. Even the word foreign has taken on a new meaning. Nothing is foreign to us if it concerns the fate of the civilization we cherish and which we are called upon to maintain, perfect and defend. But it has not been easy for the American people to accept this burden. We were not ready for it.

Can there be wonder if we were at first confused? This is a world we never asked for, yet in which now we must play our part.[91]

The commitment to Europe had profound global implications. Indeed, in his speech during the signing ceremony, Truman pointedly broadened the significance of the Atlantic treaty. He announced, "The pact will be a positive, not a negative, influence for peace, and its influence will be felt not only in the area it specifically covers but throughout the world."[92] The *New York Times* headlined the importance of the president's statement: "Calls Agreement Not Limited to Atlantic in View of Its World-Wide Influence."[93]

In fact, the Atlantic alliance was born into a world of potentially unlimited threats to the partners' collective and individual concerns. Consequently, the parties to the treaty assumed two types of obligations. One involved formal commitments for collective defense within a specifically delineated area; the other called for consultation whenever any member believed its "territorial integrity, political independence or security" was threatened. The second element, central to the purpose of this book, included the informal agreement to consult in the event of a threat to the interests of any of the allies beyond the domain of the pact. Although this understanding did not involve explicit military obligations outside Europe, it implied something more than each ally going its own way.

Two challenges for NATO lay in this unavoidable blurring of the limits to alliance. First, events outside the treaty area had the potential to threaten the interests and security of the Atlantic allies and therefore might require a coordinated allied response. Second, disagreements over the appropriate response to such threats might prove detrimental to the cohesion and solidarity of the alliance itself.

The following chapters explore how—and how well—the Atlantic alliance has managed these twin dimensions of the out-of-area challenge. Beginning with the Korean War and ending with the debate nearly four decades later over allied cooperation in the Persian Gulf, this book seeks to understand the political dynamics of the limited alliance that is NATO and how that alliance has coped, in the absence of formal commitments or mechanisms, with developments beyond its official domain.

CHAPTER TWO

Probing the Limits of Alliance, I:
Asia, 1949–1956

The first challenges to the solidarity of the Atlantic alliance came not from Europe but from Asia. Although article 6 of the treaty had precisely and explicitly limited the domain of allied action, it became clear in the early fifties that the members' individual security and the cohesiveness of the alliance could be affected by developments outside the formal area of allied responsibility. Events in Korea and Indochina illustrated the extent of allied interests at stake beyond Europe as well as the potential for interallied friction over how best to protect and promote those interests.

By 1950, the doctrine of containment stood as the unifying principle of American foreign relations. Over the course of the next decade, this commitment—to "confront the Russians with unalterable counter-force at every point where they show signs of encroaching upon the interests of a peaceful and stable world"[1]—set the priorities and established the boundaries of American global policy and action. The United States confirmed that it would use its preponderant military power to influence events, basing its decision to do so on the exigencies of the containment doctrine.

The European allies considered the containment of Soviet expansion their principal goal within Europe, but it was not uniformly their primary objective beyond Europe. Members of NATO held varied and at times competing worldviews, reflecting differing historical ties, current commitments, and future objectives. The attempt to reconcile the American anti-Communist crusade with the colonial entanglements of the British and the French in Asia and, subsequently, the Middle East, was the greatest source of tension within the alliance during the first decade of its existence.

The principal NATO powers came to perceive developments in Asia as an indirect but nonetheless critical test of the non-Communist world's will to resist Soviet expansionism.[2] With the American commitment to Europe a virtual certainty in the spring of 1949, Foreign Secretary Bevin began to urge Secretary of State Acheson to take a greater interest in Southeast Asian affairs. Bevin expressed concern that the establishment of security provisions for Europe and the Middle East would increase pressure on Southeast Asia.[3] Initially, the United States appeared reluctant to commit itself to any responsibilities in the region. By the end of the year, influenced heavily by the crushing Communist victory in the Chinese civil war, the Americans had moved definitively toward the British position.

In mid-December, Acheson proposed to British Ambassador Franks "some rough geographical division of responsibilities: the United States would look after Indonesia, the Philippines, Indochina and spare a little for Siam; the Commonwealth could help the countries in the Indian Ocean and particularly Burma."[4] The ambassador immediately discouraged the idea of a division of labor. London, which had been emitting mixed signals about its desire to involve the United States in the area, was understandably ambivalent about being almost entirely supplanted by the Americans in Southeast and East Asia.[5]

The United States government nonetheless established policy guidelines for American activities in the region. On 30 December 1949, President Truman endorsed the National Security Council study "The Position of the United States with Respect to Asia" (NSC 48/2). It fixed as a core American security objective the "gradual reduction and eventual elimination of the preponderant power and influence of the USSR in Asia to such a degree that the Soviet Union will not be capable of threatening from that area the security of the United States or its friends."[6] The study also articulated the means by which the United States might pursue this objective, placing emphasis on the development of bilateral or multilateral cooperative measures. Perhaps most important, it urgently requested $75 million in support for American friends and allies in China's neighborhood.[7]

Truman's acceptance of NSC 48/2 signaled America's new international resolve. Within a month, the president initiated a complete review of United States global strategy. The impetus lay in two major international developments of the previous year: the Chinese Communists' victory and the detonation of the Soviet Union's first nuclear device. These events simultaneously expanded the realm of immediate American concerns to include Asia and undermined the sense of security the United States had derived from its nuclear monopoly. The product of the presidential review, which Truman approved as NSC 68 on 7 April 1950, was the first complete articulation of a broad strategy to heighten military preparedness for the Cold War.[8]

But the programs envisaged in NSC 68 were costly, and Congress—already footing the huge bill for the Marshall Plan—was not in a spending mood. Even the money for the congressionally sanctioned commitment to the defense of Europe was not guaranteed over the long-term. It took an out-of-area crisis—the Korean War—to generate the military appropriation increases necessary to implement NSC 68 and fully fund the American role in NATO.

The Korean War

The American reaction to the North Korean invasion of South Korea on 25 June 1950 dispelled European concerns about the willingness of the United States to become engaged in Asia. Washington confirmed that it was clearly prepared to employ military force to back up its new strategic doctrine and treaty responsibilities. The outbreak of war also shattered the illusion that United States nuclear capabilities would deter the Soviet Union or its allies from pursuing their territorial objectives by military means. Washington and many other NATO capitals drew the conclusion that if Moscow would use its military power through a client state in Asia, it might also do so in Europe, particularly if it did not meet with resistance.[9] Acheson outlined the need for decisive action: "To back away from this challenge, in view of our capacity for meeting it, would be highly destructive of the power and prestige of the United States. By prestige I mean the shadow cast by power, which is of great deterrent importance. Therefore, we could not accept the conquest of this important area by a Soviet puppet under the very guns of our defensive perimeter with no more resistance than gestures and words in the Security Council."[10]

The Korean conflict convinced the American public that sustained military spending for conventional forces in peacetime was a prerequisite of security, even in the nuclear age.[11] It was a turning point for both the United States and NATO because it spurred substantial defense-budget expansion in the United States. General Omar Bradley, chairman of the Joint Chiefs of Staff, testified before Congress in July 1950: "Communism is willing to use arms to gain its ends. This is a fundamental change, and it has forced a change in our estimate of the military needs of the United States."[12]

Gripped with anti-Communist fever, Congress agreed to provide the funds necessary to fulfill the requirements outlined in NSC 68. It enacted additional taxes in 1950 and 1951 that generated approximately $5.7 billion in new revenue. In 1950 alone Capitol Hill authorized an additional $4 billion in defense funds, although there was no little disagreement about funding priorities within that budget.[13] This provided for the establishment of a base line of standing United States military capability—including the development of a mobilization base and of the active forces necessary to deter Soviet aggression—that set a peacetime precedent.[14] The funding provoked by Korea therefore laid solid foundations for a sustained commitment of American military power to Western security.

The shock of Korea also jolted the Atlantic allies into realizing that their mere signatures on paper did not constitute a security guarantee. In response, NATO took its first concrete steps toward closing the gap between its objectives and its capabilities. Discussions about the impact of the Korean War on Europe dominated meetings among the American, British, and French foreign ministers in September 1950.[15] In the North Atlantic Council (NAC)[16] meetings that month, the subject of Korea provoked the first serious debate about what defenses the alliance required in addition to an American nuclear guarantee. At these sessions, the related subjects of German rearmament and European conventional defense were also discussed in detail.[17]

At the time, NATO still had neither a commander nor a military headquarters. During its September meetings, the NAC agreed to establish "an integrated force under centralised command," with a supreme commander responsible for organizing and training "an effective integrated force in time of peace as well as in the event of war."[18] In December, General Dwight D. Eisenhower became the first Supreme Allied Commander Europe (SACEUR), and in February 1951 the Supreme Headquarters Allied Powers Europe (SHAPE) was established.[19]

NATO's founders had not explicitly intended to establish a standing integrated military force. They had laid the groundwork for a limited peacetime pact that pooled their individual strengths to produce the maximum deterrent against a potential Soviet attack.[20] But as Korea so harshly demonstrated, in the new Cold War system there might be no true peacetime: the alliance could not afford to wait for war to mobilize its defenses; it would have to be prepared in advance. "The outbreak of the Korean War," alliance historian Robert Osgood observed, "completed the transformation of NATO from a multilateral guaranty pact into a semi-integrated military organization designed to redress the military imbalance on the Continent."[21]

In addition to its impact on American and allied defense planning, the Korean War also presaged allied political and military coordination beyond Europe. It established an enduring pattern for the management of out-of-area crises: NATO qua NATO did not get involved in Korea. Those allies choosing to fight there coordinated their efforts on a bilateral and multilateral basis outside the formal alliance framework.

Western participation in the Korean War took place under the auspices of the United Nations.[22] Immediately following the North Korean invasion, the United States appealed directly to the United Nations for support, arguing that a failure to take action in Korea would irreparably undermine the credibility of the new international organization. Acheson explained the rationale for United Nations involvement in testimony before the Senate Armed Services and Foreign Relations committees: "The attack on Korea was . . . a challenge to the whole system of collective security, not only in the Far East, but everywhere in the world. . . . This was a test which would decide whether our collective-security system would survive or would crumble. It would determine whether other nations would be intimidated by this show of force."[23]

Based on its analysis that the North Korean invasion represented a critical test of Western resolve, the United States made a vigorous effort to engage its allies and friends in the war effort. Sir Lester Pearson, Canada's secretary of state for external affairs, dined with Acheson on 24 July 1950 and later recounted the American secretary of state's expression of intense concern over sustaining public support for the war: "The struggle ahead should not be one of the United

States vs the Communist world. The American people could be convinced of this if we all acted together on the Korean front as members of the United Nations, and if we worked together to strengthen our defenses generally."[24] Consequently, Acheson recommended that the members of NATO spearhead a cooperative, coordinated United Nations effort in Korea. Even single battalions would be useful, he argued. Then, as Pearson remembered, Acheson focused on the significance of the allied role:

> He emphasized again the tremendous importance of contributions to the Korean operations from United Nations countries, especially from those who, like Canada, have prestige and influence and command respect. Everything possible must be done to emphasize that a United Nations Force is now in being and that the United States Army is only part of that force, though the biggest part. For this purpose there must be ground forces from other countries and he strongly hoped that Canada could join others in offering such forces.[25]

The net result of the American campaign combined with the United Nations' endorsement of military action was that fifteen countries in addition to the United States dispatched armed forces to Korea and another five sent medical units. Seven of those sending troops were members of NATO—Belgium, Canada, France, Luxembourg, the Netherlands, the United Kingdom, and the United States. Two more that provided troops, Greece and Turkey, were soon to accede to the alliance. Denmark, Italy, and Norway were among those contributing medical aid. The British, in keeping with their stake in the region, had by far the largest contingent of any European ally, and their force was augmented by contributions of Commonwealth members Australia and New Zealand.[26]

The Americans still bore the brunt of the actual military burden. At the end of 1951, nearly two-thirds of the six hundred thousand troops under United Nations command in Korea were American. The United States contributed 50 percent of the ground forces, 86 percent of the naval forces, and 93 percent of the air forces. If the Republic of Korea's respective contribution of 40 percent, 7 percent, and 5 percent is factored in, the quantitative significance of the other national forces appears slight.[27]

In symbolic terms, however, it was critical that the Korean effort took place with the blessing of the United Nations instead of as an exclusively American initiative. This made participation in the "united action" more politically palatable for those involved. Pearson wrote, "We felt that we should participate as a member of the United Nations but we wanted to be absolutely certain that this would be a United Nations and not a United States operation."[28] While the United States had almost total control over military strategy and provided the bulk of the fighting men and matériel, the British contribution and the presence by the end of 1950 of ground troops from many other countries countered the Soviet accusation that the Korean conflict was solely an American war.

The Korean War also revealed the significance of the special relationship between the United States and the United Kingdom and its implications for out-of-area crisis management. The unique rapport between the Americans and the British indicated that despite the principle of equality among the members on which the alliance was based, a distinct hierarchy had emerged based on relative distributions of interests and capabilities. This was an irritant to the rest of the allies, and in particular to the French, who resented the fact that they were not accorded equal status and influence with the British.[29]

The special relationship had been consolidated by intimate Anglo-American cooperation during World War II and flourished in NATO's early years. Diplomatic and military representatives met frequently to discuss their global foreign policy concerns. An April 1950 State Department paper entitled "Essential Elements of US-UK Relations" confirmed that American policymakers expected the British to play the role of "our principal partner in strategic planning" and described the unique relationship between the two countries: "No other country has the same qualifications for being our principal ally and partner as the UK. It has internal political strength and important capabilities in the political, economic and military fields throughout the world. Most important, the British share our fundamental objectives and standards of conduct."[30]

Following the outbreak of the Korean War, there were nearly constant Anglo-American exchanges on the situation in the Far East. High-level discussions were held in Washington in both July and October 1950, producing general agreement on policy toward Korea. After General Douglas MacArthur's misguided attempt to move the war north and the massive entry of Chinese troops into the conflict in November, however, European frustration with American leadership began to grow. Acheson described the unraveling of support for the

United States effort: "What lost the confidence of our allies were MacArthur's costly defeat, his open advocacy of widening the war at what they rightly regarded as unacceptable risks, and the hesitance of the Administration in asserting firm control over him."[31]

In early December, British Prime Minister Clement Attlee flew to Washington to meet with Truman. The trip was provoked by a press conference at which the American president had tendered the use of the atomic bomb in Korea as a distinct possibility.[32] The threat to employ nuclear weapons exacerbated increasing anxiety in London— as well as in other European capitals—that the United States might attack China and perhaps provoke World War III.[33]

During his visit, Attlee also emphasized another dimension of European concerns about the course and impact of the war. The allies were beginning to worry that Korea was distracting the United States from more active participation in European security. Even among NATO's global powers, MacArthur's excesses provoked anxiety about how an extended commitment of American military forces in Asia might weaken European defenses and invite Soviet attack. Attlee told Truman, "We must not get so involved in the East as to lay ourselves open to attack in the West. The West is, after all, the vital part in our line against communism. We cannot take action that will weaken it."[34] The American ambassador in France reported growing sentiment that "France, together with Britain, must exercise moderating influence on US to avoid major war in Far East which would detract from US capacity to help create situation of strength in Europe."[35] Fueling these fears, officials in Washington warned that the American people might not continue to support NATO if the British failed to maintain solidarity with the Korean War effort.[36]

In spite of these tensions over the possible expansion of the war, there was a solid bedrock of support in Britain for the United States. In response to Truman's assertion, "We will fight to the finish to stop this aggression. . . . [W]e cannot desert our friends when the going gets rough," Attlee assured the president: "We are in it with you. We'll support you. We'll stand together on those bridgeheads. How long we can hold is a matter of opinion." He added, "You can take it from me that we stand with you. Our whole purpose is to stand with you."[37] This determination to support one another was rooted in the mutual conviction that the United States and the United Kingdom had the power to set the West's agenda and that a failure to coordinate policies might have serious consequences for Western security. If alliance solidarity was broken outside Europe, the future of NATO could be jeopardized.

Attlee returned to England carrying a communiqué stating that the American president hoped "world conditions would never call for the use of the atomic bomb."[38] He had convinced Truman and Acheson that they could not count on further allied support if they chose to expand the war to China. By making it clear that the Americans would lose their collective security fig leaf if they launched a direct attack on Chinese territory, the British leader acted as a significant restraining force on the United States. Attlee's visit bolstered the position and perceived influence of the British within the alliance: the prime minister wrote to Bevin afterward that "throughout these talks, the United Kingdom was lifted out of the European queue and we were treated as partners, unequal in power but still equal in counsel."[39]

As the immediacy of the threat diminished and the Korean conflict sank into a stalemate, so too did the European sense of urgency about the war.[40] And in spite of allied military cooperation in this first test of alliance solidarity outside Europe, the conduct of the war raised doubts about American leadership and judgment. These doubts had implications beyond the Korean experience; for example, the growing unpopularity of the war among Europeans—based on their perception that the United States wanted to prolong and perhaps even widen the conflict—contributed to a slowdown in NATO's rearmament effort. In 1952, the NAC had agreed to match Soviet conventional capabilities by building NATO forces from twenty-five to ninety-six divisions in two years. However, less than a year after these "Lisbon Force Goals" were established, the allies decided to make a severe cutback in the planned expansion to thirty divisions.[41]

Ironically, this retrenchment from NATO's conventional rearmament plan led to a shift in alliance strategy that augmented the imbalance of power among its members. Moving away from reliance on manpower and conventional defense to increased reliance on the American nuclear guarantee, the Europeans became more dependent than ever on American protection. As such, over the long term the change in NATO doctrine raised rather than reduced allied frustration with American dominance of the alliance.

The Korean experience also heightened allied concerns about the appropriate nature and scope of consultations required for crisis management outside the treaty area. With regard to the united action, there were European recriminations that the United States conducted the Korean War without ample regard for the views of its partners in arms, except for those of the British. Some also believed that American policymakers intentionally avoided establishing any consultative mechanisms that would have forced Washington to relinquish its total control over the military operation.[42]

The United States did, in fact, engage in regular consultations with its allies. Throughout the latter stages of the war, and during the tense period of armistice negotiations, the Washington representatives of the fifteen nations with troops in Korea held working sessions once a week with Assistant Secretary of State for East Asia Dean Rusk. At these meetings, all new developments and proposals were discussed, providing a useful means of coordinating a "Western" position within the United Nations.[43] There were also extensive bilateral exchanges, including those described previously between the Americans and the British.

Against claims that this dialogue was not sufficient was the hard fact that, despite European contributions of manpower and matériel, the brunt of the fighting in the Korean War was borne by the Americans and the South Koreans. Not surprisingly, United States officials therefore believed they were entitled to retain primary decision-making power for the conduct of the war. Such disproportions in allied commitments and capabilities, as well as the endemic tension between national freedom of action and consultation and coordination with allies, proved a recurrent source of friction within NATO.

Several lessons for the prospective management of security threats beyond Europe were gleaned from the Korean experience. First, the ability of so many allied nations to fight together in the unified command against Communist expansion in Asia demonstrated that the interests of the Atlantic partnership extended well beyond Europe. Korea established the precedent of handling out-of-area challenges on a bilateral and/or multilateral basis, outside the formal NATO structure but within the context of the broader set of shared values and objectives that fuel the alliance commitment. In the future, those members of NATO with interests beyond the treaty area would take action collectively where coordination served both their individual and mutual interests. Second, Korea proved that alliance cooperation outside of Europe would be most effective when there was a clear, well-defined goal with a limited objective and a likelihood of success. When the objective was vague and open-ended, as it became in the late autumn of 1950, cooperation would be more difficult to sustain and interallied frictions would inevitably strain alliance solidarity.

The First Indochina War

In the early fifties, the American domino principle linked the outcome of developments in Asia, and specifically in Indochina, to the preservation of security in Europe. Complementing the Korean commitment, United States involvement in France's fight against budding Indochinese nationalism confirmed the emergence of the anti-Communist crusade as the principal goal of American foreign policy. The interests at stake in Indochina itself, however, were not of major import to NATO, and, as in the Korean case, NATO as an institution never became involved in the battle to "save" Indochina. Instead, efforts to coordinate both political and military strategy took place on a bilateral basis outside the formal NATO framework.

The interallied tensions that emerged over Indochina reflected the thorny problem posed by the European allies' remaining colonial possessions. The imperial powers, and in this case France, were not eager to subject their colonial policies to allied scrutiny or influence. Equally, the United States preferred as much as possible to avoid entangling itself with European colonial arrangements. Although the onset of the Cold War tempered American anticolonialism, it did not diminish French sensitivity to being supplanted in Indochina by the United States.[44]

The ambivalence of American policymakers toward the colonial problems of the European allies predated NATO. During World War II, President Franklin D. Roosevelt was outspoken in his opposition to the European powers' struggle to regain control over their possessions and, in particular, to the French effort to reestablish sovereignty in the territories of Vietnam, Laos, and Cambodia.[45] In early 1944, Roosevelt told his secretary of state that "the case of Indo-China is perfectly clear. France has milked it for one hundred years. The people of Indo-China are entitled to something better than that."[46] Indeed, the United States went so far as to provide aid to Vietminh leaders such as Ho Chi Minh with the objective of complicating the Japanese war effort and later that of the Vichy French forces.[47]

The Anglo-American wartime relationship was also strained over the resolution of colonial issues. The British worried that if the United States succeeded in pressuring the French to grant independence to Indochina, the Americans might use the precedent to insist on independence for other imperial possessions at the end of the war. London did not want British and Dutch territories in Malaya and Indonesia to be placed under United Nations trusteeship, a Roosevelt scheme to bring independence in several stages to former colonial territories.[48] Indeed, the American president knew the British opposed his plan to try out international trusteeship on French Indochina because "they fear the effect it would have on their own possessions and those of the Dutch. They have never liked the idea of trusteeship because it is, in some instances, aimed at future independence. This is true in the case of Indo-China."[49] Several weeks before his death, however, Roosevelt decided to accept French retention of Indochina, with the proviso that "independence was the ultimate goal."[50] This shift reflected a growing consensus in the United States government that the interests at stake in the emergent battle against Communism outweighed instinctive American sympathy for nationalist, anticolonial struggles.

Washington's Indochina policy between 1945 and 1949 was one of uncomfortable neutrality, gradually shifting by 1950 to sympathy and eventual support for the French effort.[51] Acheson acknowledged that American policy during this period was a "muddled hodgepodge."[52] The United States was juggling two competing sets of interests in Indochina, where nationalist forces, backed by Communists, had challenged a key ally in the global struggle against Communism. In doing nothing—and thereby leaving France to be defeated—the United States would have resolved the colonial issue in favor of the nationalist forces. But such an approach would also have given the Communists an important victory against the West. Acheson recalled American concern that a failure to support France outside of Europe might also negatively affect the French ability or will to contribute to the development of NATO: "That [inaction] might have had merit, but as an attitude for the leader of a great alliance toward an important ally, indeed one essential to a critical endeavor, it had its demerits too."[53]

In the wake of the Communist victory in the Chinese civil war in 1949, the United States began to rethink its entire strategy in Southeast Asia. Although in late 1949 and early 1950 the Americans maintained a low-profile role in the region, a major policy change was in the making that portended their increasing involvement in Indochina. Fearing a possible Communist takeover of the entire Far East, Washington decided it could no longer be passive about influencing developments in Southeast Asia. In an early articulation of the domino theory, Acheson wrote Truman: "The choice confronting the U.S. is to support the legal governments in Indochina or to face the extension of Communism over the remainder of the continental area of Southeast Asia and possibly westward."[54]

In May 1950, President Truman authorized the provision of economic support and military supplies to French forces in Indochina to assist them in combating Ho Chi Minh, who was being backed by the Chinese and the Russians.[55] The next month, heavily influenced by the North Korean invasion of South Korea, Acheson urged Truman to step up military assistance to Indochina.[56] In his first formal statement on the Korean situation on 27 June 1950, the president told the nation he had "similarly directed acceleration in the furnishing of military assistance to the forces of France and the Associated States in Indochina and the dispatch of a military mission to provide close working relations with those forces."[57]

In late January 1951, French Prime Minister René Pleven visited Washington for a series of meetings with Truman. During these exchanges, the president agreed to continue—indeed to expedite—the provision of aid for the French Union forces fighting in Indochina and for the national armies of the Associated States (Vietnam, Laos, and Cambodia). However, where the Europeans feared that Korea would cause a lengthy diversion of manpower and matériel away from the NATO area, American policymakers expressed concern about getting too deeply embroiled in Indochina and overextending American resources to the detriment of the newly founded Atlantic alliance. In summarizing the Franco-American conversations for the National Security Council, Acheson warned, "The U.S. and France should not over-commit themselves militarily in the Far East and thereby endanger the situation in Europe."[58]

During the Truman-Pleven talks, the French also proposed that a consultative body be established for France, the United States, and the United Kingdom to coordinate the three governments' policies in Asia and elsewhere. Pleven's predecessor as prime minister, Georges Bidault, had made a similar proposal nine months earlier for the creation of an "Atlantic High Council of Peace." Both endeavors reflected France's intense desire to be accorded great power status within the alliance.[59] More specifically, the French were frustrated by their limited influence over decisions taken by the United States affecting their global security interests. This scheme to concert policy outside of Europe was an early warning of their dissatisfaction with American hegemony.

Not surprisingly, Truman rejected the Pleven proposal. He preferred to rely on already existing forums, such as the regularly scheduled tripartite meetings of the foreign secretaries of the three countries, which were supposed to deal with Germany and Austria but, in fact, covered a wide range of security issues.[60] The United States government saw no need to establish new organizations: plenty of channels already existed for three-power cooperation.

Continual high-level coordination between the United States, the United Kingdom, and France was essential, but American policymakers—cognizant that NATO policy implementation was predicated on solidarity among all the members—wanted to discourage the establishment of any official body that would determine alliance policy above the heads of the rest of the allies.[61] Acheson's personal account of the meetings in early 1951 highlighted American skepticism about the creation of such a formal hierarchy within the alliance:

> In Europe, our tripartite responsibility for Germany and constant meetings to discharge it, as well as our tripartite position in the Standing Group of NATO, already gave the three such pre-eminence in the alliance as to cause painful jealousy. In the Far East, France refused to (and could not) assume responsibility beyond Indochina and was deeply suspicious of any intrusion by others there. The impression left with me was that the appearance of France on a world tripartite body, rather than the functioning of the body, was what interested our guests.[62]

In an effort to satisfy Pleven, Truman finally agreed to hold military-to-military consultations on Indochinese matters among the United States, the United Kingdom, and France. The Americans believed that confining discussions to the military sphere would reduce the political salience of the exchanges and diminish the adverse impact on those NATO members who were not included. But throughout 1952, the French continued to lobby the United States for greater support. They wanted matériel—especially airplanes and the loan of an aircraft carrier—and they wanted monetary assistance to pay local forces. Paris threatened that the drain on its resources was so great that French responsibilities in Europe and Africa might be jeopardized.

The Americans had certainly come a long way in a short time: by the middle of 1952, they were funding one-third of France's war effort in Indochina. In spite of this dramatic rise in assistance, the Truman administration was becoming increasingly concerned that the French were deceiving themselves. In an effort that appeared highly ironic to French policymakers two decades later, the United States began to try, according to Acheson, "to get our friends to see and face the facts in Indochina. France was engaged in a task beyond her strength, indeed, beyond the strength of any external power unless it was acting in support of a dominant local will and purpose."[63] From the French perspective, the way in which the United States led France to face the facts in Indochina posed a threat to the position that Washington was ostensibly bolstering: the Americans assumed an ever-increasing share of responsibility for the war.

In March 1952, the American government began working on a position paper defining its policy toward Southeast Asia. Accounts of meetings between State Department and Defense Department representatives illuminate some of the enduring challenges posed by the effort to achieve allied political and military cooperation beyond Europe. State Department officials warned that the Korean and Indochinese conflicts might be detrimental to the future prospects of the fledgling Atlantic alliance. In making this case, Counselor Charles Bohlen highlighted a principal and perennial requirement in the management of out-of-area problems: the need to prevent differences over policies beyond Europe from adversely affecting alliance cohesion within Europe. Bohlen argued that the first priority of the United States should be to maintain alliance solidarity: "British and French support means mainly political support. I take it no one thinks they can provide much military backing. . . . However, we have to get French and British support if we are going to war with Communist China, for without their support we might lose the whole NATO structure."[64]

Seeking to conduct accurate contingency planning, the professional military was preoccupied during the March 1952 discussions on Southeast Asia with reducing the uncertainty of depending on allied military support in an Asian crisis. Admiral William M. Fechteler, chief of United States naval operations, commented that the military could not predict exactly what it might need from the

British and the French but that "it seems to me we want them to place at our disposal accommodations normally at the disposal of an ally. For example, we would like to use Singapore as an air and naval base." State Department Policy Planning Staff Director Paul Nitze offered a European perspective: "I think they would reply that they want the consultation that is normal between allies."[65] The need of the American military to base its out-of-area planning on accurate assessments of potential allied support and its simultaneous reluctance to share in the substance of that planning proved to be a chronic source of tension in the Atlantic partnership.

The fruit of the March 1952 exchanges between State and Defense department officials was a White House directive, NSC 124, on policy toward Southeast Asia. NSC 124 explained the sweeping rationale for increased American involvement in Indochina:

> The loss of any of the countries of Southeast Asia to communist control as a consequence of overt or covert Chinese Communist aggression would have critical psychological, political and economic consequences. In the absence of effective and timely counteraction, the loss of any single country would probably lead to relatively swift submission to or an alignment with communism by the remaining countries of this group. Furthermore, an alignment with communism in the rest of Southeast Asia and India, and in the longer term, of the Middle East (with the probable exceptions of at least Pakistan and Turkey) would endanger the stability and security of Europe.[66]

In making the case through NSC 124 that NATO would be threatened by a failure to respond firmly to challenges beyond Europe, the United States affirmed the extended domino principle, thereby explicitly linking developments in Asia to European security.

Although the American commitment in Southeast Asia had burgeoned, the French pressed for greater support. In tripartite meetings in May 1952, the French complained that they could not simultaneously fight the West's war in Indochina and meet their European defense responsibilities. They claimed, for example, they could not guarantee continued funding for the proposed European Defense Community (EDC), a plan for greater European military cooperation, without increased American and British assistance in Southeast Asia.

The British were irritated by French demands and made it clear they had no intention of augmenting aid to the French war effort. Foreign Secretary Eden told French Defense Minister Pleven: "The French argument that Indo-China made it impossible for France to build up an army in Europe would not carry conviction in the United Kingdom. . . . We had a larger army in Europe than the French, despite our commitments in Malaya and in the Suez Canal Zone, where we had seventy thousand troops."[67] The British also argued that while they would provide political support for efforts to bolster the French position in Indochina, the scale of their responsibilities in Malaya and elsewhere made it impossible for them to spread themselves any thinner. Finally, they emphasized that despite their interests in the region (which were less significant than those they had in the Middle East), they did not want the conflicts there to escalate into a World War III with China.[68] In short, any substantive military assistance would have to come from the United States.

In December 1952, the NAC issued its first formal statement on an out-of-area challenge. Although often bland, NATO communiqués reflect the issues that have come to the collective attention of alliance members. In this instance, the ministers affirmed, "Resistance to direct or indirect aggression in any part of the world is an essential contribution to the common security of the free world." Expressing admiration for the French struggle in Indochina, the NAC agreed that France "deserves continuing support from the NATO governments."[69] This provided official sanction for French withdrawal of NATO-designated forces from Europe for assignment to the Indochinese theater.[70]

This precedent-setting statement by the NAC confirmed three guiding principles for the future management of out-of-area problems: first, developments outside the treaty area affected NATO members' security interests, not just individually but collectively; second, it was appropriate in the NATO context to consult on these developments as they arose; and third, assistance in such instances would be given by "NATO governments" as individual entities rather than under the auspices of the formal treaty organization. Thus during its biannual meetings since 1952, the NAC has held *tour d'horizon* discussions covering areas not included in the treaty.[71]

In January 1953, Dwight D. Eisenhower moved into the White House, and John Foster Dulles replaced Acheson as secretary of state. The transition heralded an increasingly zealous American effort to resist Communist expansion. The Republicans blamed the Democrats for having "lost" China in the previous decade, and the new administration therefore evidenced a keen interest in developments in Southeast Asia.[72] With the Korean armistice agreement that summer and the simultaneous channeling of increasing amounts of Chinese matériel (largely Soviet-made) into Indochina,[73] the United States shifted its attention to the deteriorating French position.

Dulles did not see any reason to support French colonialism per se, but he too believed that France's defeat might trigger a falling domino effect, toppling other pro-Western regimes in the region. As a result, United States assistance to the French effort was increased throughout 1953. An American military mission visited Indochina during the summer and advised that in addition to the $400 million earmarked for the effort, $385 million more should be made available in the next eighteen months. This aid package was approved on 30 September 1953.[74] At a National Security Council meeting on 24 March 1954, Dulles made the case for a further expansion of American involvement that amounted to stepping into the shoes of the French: "We were witnessing the collapse or evaporation of France as a great power in most areas of the world. The great question was, who should fill the void left by the collapse of French power, particularly in the colonial areas. Would it be the Communists, or must it be the U.S.?"[75]

By 1954, the United States was devoting one-third of its foreign aid budget to financing 78 percent of the French war effort in Indochina.[76] In exchange, however, Washington did not receive commensurate authority over its use. Paris requested allied assistance but vehemently resisted any internationalization of the conflict. As the official American military history of Indochina recounted, "The French retained full control of the dispensation of military assistance and of the intelligence and planning aspects of the military struggle."[77]

For a time this suited American objectives, allowing the United States to influence developments indirectly without committing its forces and prestige to a conflict that might not be won. Moreover, because the security of Europe took priority over Asian developments, American policymakers were reluctant to antagonize the French. For example, the United States had been working to secure French participation in the EDC; fearing French parliamentary rejection of the plan, Washington refrained from pressuring Paris to relinquish control over Indochina policy. The *Pentagon Papers* recounted the American predicament:

> NATO and the Marshall Plan were themselves judged to be essential to our European interests. To threaten France with economic and military sanctions in Europe in order to have it alter its policy in Indochina was, therefore, not plausible. Similarly, to reduce the level of military assistance to the French effort in Indochina would have been counter-productive, since it would have led to a further deterioration in the French military position there.[78]

As it approached climactic events in the spring of 1954, the United States was therefore constrained by the ensemble of its commitments. The vagaries of American policy toward the French war effort reflected this condition.

In late November 1953, the French had embarked upon an ill-conceived endeavor to establish a forward base at Dien Bien Phu, a valley hamlet far north of Hanoi near the intersection of the Chinese and Laotian borders. Without consulting the American Military Assistance Advisory Group (MAAG) in Indochina before launching the operation, the French dropped three thousand paratroopers into what General Thomas Trapnell, the MAAG commander, described as an "inferior defensive position," giving them only a fifty-fifty chance of survival.[79] Although the precise rationale for the French operation has never been fully determined, the stated purpose was to provide for Laotian security against either Vietminh or Chinese attack.

By mid-February 1954 nearly thirty-five thousand Vietminh troops were perched on the high ground surrounding Dien Bien Phu. On 13 March, they launched an all-out offensive. The French garrison was heavily bombarded by Ho Chi Minh's guerillas from the mountains encircling the camp. They succeeded in overrunning several principal defensive strong points, and the remaining French forces were cut off from supplies and reinforcements.

The deteriorating French position provoked an intense series of diplomatic and military exchanges among the United States, France, and Britain. The French high commissioner in Vietnam, General Paul Ely, traveled to Washington on 22 March to plead for more American aid. During his visit, Admiral Arthur Radford, chairman of the Joint Chiefs of Staff, advocated a nighttime air raid using American air force and navy planes. The idea apparently originated with the American-French military staff in Saigon, reflecting the emerging pattern in allied management of out-of-area crises in which policy coordination was often initiated and took place on a military-to-military basis, away from the political spotlight.[80] Code-named Operation Vulture, the plan would have employed sixty B-29's and 150 fighters belonging to the Seventh Fleet to conduct a massive air strike against the Vietminh positions. Radford apparently led Ely to believe that if the Dien Bien Phu situation worsened, the French could expect such support from the United States.[81] In doing so without authorization from Eisenhower, Radford imprudently raised French expectations that he would later have sorely to disappoint.

As the French weighed the advantages and disadvantages of allowing another nation's forces into the conflict, the American secretary of state publicly advanced an alternative to the secret military plan. On 29 March, Dulles proposed a collective allied military effort to resist the spread of the perceived Communist monolith. In a speech entitled "The Threat of a Red Asia," he argued: "Under the conditions of today, the imposition on Southeast Asia of the political system of Communist Russia and its Chinese Communist ally, by whatever means, would be a grave threat to the whole free community. The United States feels that the possibility should be met by united action."[82]

At Eisenhower's behest, Dulles and Radford met with congressional leaders on 3 April to gauge potential support for increased involvement in Indochina. The secretary of state conveyed the president's request for discretionary powers to use American air and naval forces in preventing the "extension and expansion" of Communism throughout Southeast Asia. Lyndon Johnson, Senate minority leader, observed that the Korean War had been 90 percent financed and fought by the United States and pointedly asked the secretary of state whether any other allies had been consulted regarding joint intervention. When Dulles replied in the negative, the legislators emphasized that there should be "No more Koreas" and that congressional support for further military action would be contingent on participation by the British and other allied nations. This reinforced Eisenhower's conviction that the United States could not take unilateral military action.[83]

The president therefore determined that any American military engagement would have to be based on three principles: "(1) formation of a coalition force with U.S. allies to pursue 'united action'; (2) declaration of French intent to accelerate independence of Associated

States; (3) Congressional approval of U.S. involvement (which was thought to be dependent upon (1) and (2))."[84] In drawing analogies to the successfully organized united effort in Korea, Eisenhower argued that the United States could only take action in conjunction with the British; without London's agreement to participate in a collective endeavor, American public opinion would not support the decision.

Shrewdly establishing a series of conditions for American military engagement he knew would most likely be impossible to fulfill, President Eisenhower confirmed that the motive for possible United States action was not that France was in imminent danger of losing a piece of its empire. Any American support would have to be part of the "free world's" struggle against Communism. Eisenhower thus built a case that satisfied those who did not favor intervention but also defended himself against right-wing domestic critics who did.[85]

On 4 April, Eisenhower wrote a personal letter to Prime Minister Winston Churchill suggesting the creation of a regional security organization for Southeast Asia. He recommended "the establishment of a new, ad hoc grouping or coalition composed of nations which have a vital concern in the checking of Communist expansion in the area," and envisaged the inclusion of the United States, the United Kingdom, France, the Associated States of Indochina, Australia, New Zealand, Thailand, and the Philippines.[86] Churchill was not quick to embrace the notion and lukewarmly responded that he would discuss the matter with Dulles when the American secretary of state came to London a week later.

The British were stalling for time until later that month when American, British, French, and Soviet representatives were scheduled to convene in Geneva to discuss the future of Korea and Indochina.[87] Eden hoped to delay any further action until the Geneva Conference participants had fully explored the prospects of a peace settlement: "I welcomed the proposal for the organization of collective defence in South-East Asia. . . . But I felt that to form and proclaim a defensive coalition, before we went to the conference table, would be unlikely to help us militarily and would harm us politically, by frightening off potential allies." Furthermore, he did not believe that the French were in danger of imminent and total military collapse—at least not before the Geneva talks had run their course—and therefore "did not think that concern for the immediate military situation should be the guiding factor in our policy."[88] Underlying the British position was their fear, present since Korea, that precipitous allied action would widen the conflict and increase the likelihood of Chinese intervention, bringing the whole world to the brink of war.[89]

Dulles visited London and Paris from 11 to 14 April in an attempt to secure allied support for his "united action" plan. The differences between British and American attitudes at this crucial moment reflected disagreement over short-term objectives and long-term projections. The United States was publicly pushing both for an immediate joint effort to bolster the French and for the eventual development based on this ad hoc coalition of a more permanent alliance against Communism in the region. The British resisted the first because its implied immediacy of action would prejudice the upcoming conference and the second because, if necessary, it should follow rather than precede Geneva.[90] In fact, Eisenhower's strategy of insisting on allied support bought him the domestic margin of maneuver necessary to straddle the middle ground. He would not go to war over Dien Bien Phu but he would also not abandon Southeast Asia to the Communists. He made the latter clear in a news conference on 7 April 1954: "You have the broader considerations that might follow what you would call the 'falling domino' principle. You have a row of dominoes set up, you knock over the first one, and what will happen to the last one is the certainty that it will go over very quickly. So you could have a beginning of a disintegration that would have the most profound influences."[91] The complicating factor was that the British, on whom his immediate plans were predicated, did not share his view that Indochina was the first domino in line.[92]

In Paris, Dulles found that despite their desperate military situation, the French remained resistant to greater involvement of other nations in Indochina. They wanted local assistance at Dien Bien Phu but were wary of accepting the imposition of a collective security framework for resolving the broader political-military issues in Indochina.[93] This reflected a critical and enduring difference between French and American approaches to the situation: Paris wanted only enough military assistance to relieve its forces at Dien Bien Phu, whereas Washington expected its military action to be accompanied by augmented United States participation in war planning and command.[94] The French attitude reinforced Eisenhower's distaste for engaging the prestige of the United States in the defense of Gallic colonial interests. The president revealed his profound reservations in an unpublished portion of his memoirs:

The strongest reason of all for the United States [to stay out] is the fact that among all the powerful nations of the world the United States is the only one with a tradition of anti-colonialism. . . . The standing of the United States as the most powerful of the anti-colonial powers is an asset of incalculable value to the Free World. . . . The moral position of the United States was more to be guarded than the Tonkin Delta, indeed than all of Indochina.[95]

When the American secretary of state returned to Washington, he immediately invited the ambassadors of countries that were potential members of the proposed Southeast Asian ad hoc defense group to a preliminary planning meeting.[96] Dulles alleged that Eden had endorsed such a step, believing that although the British leader opposed any immediate "united action," he supported the general principle of forming a collective defense organization for the region.

Eden, however, was furious: "Dulles was trying to bulldoze me. It was an outrageous ploy—trying to exploit Anglo-American friendship to get the war he wanted in Indochina. I made it crystal clear that we wanted no part of his dangerous enterprise."[97] Vice President Richard M. Nixon's speech on 17 April, in which he dangled the prospect that the United States might have to "take the risk by putting our boys in" to avoid "further Communist expansion in Asia and Indochina," probably further exacerbated British suspicions of American intentions.[98] Eden instructed the British ambassador in Washington to boycott the sessions on Southeast Asia and sent him a demarche to deliver to Dulles: "Americans may think the time past when they need consider the feelings and difficulties of their allies. It is the conviction that this tendency becomes more pronounced every week that is creating mounting difficulties for anyone in this country who wants to maintain close Anglo-American relations."[99] The British refusal to attend these meetings scuttled the proposed working group. Dulles was enraged by what he perceived to be Eden's perfidy and is alleged to have complained in private, "Eden has double-crossed me. He lied to me."[100]

As the fall of Dien Bien Phu drew nearer, the French finally relented on their insistence that no one meddle in the conduct of their affairs in Indochina. On 22 April, while NAC meetings and tripartite discussions were being held in Paris to prepare for the Geneva Conference, Foreign Minister Georges Bidault and General Ely suggested that emergency consultations should take place in Indochina between General Henri Navarre, who had conceived and implemented the Dien Bien Phu operation, and American military commanders. The next day, in the middle of a NAC session, Bidault received an urgent message from Navarre to Prime Minister Joseph Laniel, which he passed on to Dulles. The French commander pleaded that only two alternatives were left: Operation Vulture, with massive B-29 bombing by United States planes operating from bases outside Indochina (presumably in the Philippines), or a French Union request for a cease-fire for all of Indochina, which would have been the equivalent of capitulation.[101] Later that day, Dulles, Bidault, and Eden met to discuss the situation. According to Eden, Bidault accepted the substance of a Dulles draft letter stating that although it was too late to save the encircled garrison, "the United States was nevertheless prepared, if France and the other allies so desired, to move armed forces into Indo-China and thus internationalize the struggle and protect South-East Asia as a whole."[102]

Eisenhower was determined to stand firm despite the initiative taken by his activist secretary of state. "There would be no intervention without allies," he later recalled.[103] The British remained equally adamant about their position, and Eden went back to London for an emergency cabinet meeting on Indochina on 25 April. Churchill and Eden conferred and, according to Eden, Churchill's assessment of the situation was that the British government was being asked to "assist in misleading Congress into approving a military operation, which would itself be ineffective, and might well bring the world to the verge of a major war." The two British leaders agreed to inform the Americans and the French that they would not provide any military assistance to the French in Indochina or condone such an action by the United States.[104] In restraining the Americans, the British were playing the pedagogic role they assumed as their own power outside Europe waned. Through the special relationship they could teach the United States and, albeit indirectly, retain global influence.

The Geneva Conference on Korea and Indochina was scheduled to begin on 26 April. The setting of a date for negotiations generated a dynamic of its own: the closer the date came for the meeting, the less incentive there was for the British, who favored a negotiated solution (believing the French could not win the war), to get involved in a new military endeavor. Yet as the conference approached, there was a greater incentive for the French to pressure their allies for assistance, fearing that the proceedings might limit their remaining margin of maneuver or bind them to abide by a disadvantageous armistice.[105] The Vietminh recognized that a decisive show of force could substantially improve their bargaining position at the conference table and might further demoralize the French. Thus, on the eve of the Geneva talks, the Communist forces pushed for a final victory at Dien Bien Phu.[106]

Two weeks into the Geneva Conference, the fate of Dien Bien Phu was sealed by a combination of British opposition to military intervention and American unwillingness to intervene alone. On 27 April, Churchill promised the House of Commons that Britain would not take on any new military commitments in Indochina. In a 29 April press conference, Eisenhower reiterated that the United States would not take unilateral action. The British, well aware of the impact of their stance on the Americans, remained steadfast. On 2 May, Eden observed, "I am conscious of the effect of our differences over this question upon Anglo-American relations. But I am sure our only wise course is to follow a consistent line."[107] Without American intervention, the beleaguered French garrison fell on 8 May, and with its defeat the French virtually surrendered their historic position in Indochina.

Although the Americans were frustrated by British insistence on waiting until the Geneva proceedings had run their course to take any action to prevent further Communist expansion in the region, the two allies nonetheless sustained a close and constant dialogue during the conference. As would often be the case between them, disagreements over the specifics of a given policy did not hinder their ability to proceed to the next item on their mutual agenda. The Defense Department official history of American policy in Vietnam portrayed their shared objectives in the aftermath of the French defeat: "The changing war situation now made alignment with the British necessary for future regional defense, especially as Washington was informed of the probability that a partition settlement (which London had foreseen months before) would place all of Indochina in or within reach of Communist hands."[108]

The British and the Americans had already agreed in a separate context to explore another avenue of cooperation for Asian security. In a 23 April message to Churchill, Eden recounted a conversation with Dulles in which the two discussed the possibility of a joint military effort to protect Thailand in the event of a complete collapse of French authority in Indochina: "I think it would be valuable to offer such secret talks between us two in Washington. If French morale is really crumpling and they are going to pack up in Indo-China, it is worth considering a joint Anglo-American guarantee of the Thai frontier, and this, in their present mood, I believe the Americans might give."[109]

The United States ultimately refused to sign the Geneva agreements, largely because it was unwilling to subscribe to an accord that through partition legitimized the control of a large part of Indochina by Communist forces.[110] But Washington had its own secret victory at Geneva. Dulles secured French and British consent to discuss the creation of a Southeast Asian regional defense organization.[111] Indeed, while the Geneva negotiations were taking place, the Americans and the British discreetly established a study group in Washington to develop the idea of what would become the Southeast Asia Treaty Organization (SEATO).[112] Signed on 8 September 1954, the new Asian security alliance included Australia, France, New Zealand, Pakistan, the Philippines, Thailand, the United Kingdom, and the United States.

SEATO was a tangible manifestation of the extent to which the principal NATO allies had common or at least complementary interests, objectives, and commitments beyond the Atlantic treaty area. While regional arrangements like SEATO had no formal connection to NATO, and while the allies that participated did so independently rather than under the auspices of the Atlantic alliance, the involvement of key NATO members in other security alliances promoted the global nature of their dialogue. This phenomenon also reinforced the early establishment of a hierarchy among the NATO allies in which the world powers—the United States, the United Kingdom, and France—held a disproportionate share of influence within the alliance, not only because of their preponderance within Europe, but because of their commitments and capabilities beyond the NATO area.

The denouement of the first Indochina war had a significant impact on the Atlantic alliance: it set in motion the progressive alienation of France from the United States and hence from NATO. France's status as a world actor of consequence had been enhanced by its empire and, in the postwar era, overseas possessions had been a means of reaffirming French global interests and capabilities. With the onset of the Cold War, Paris tried to turn the crusade against Communism to national advantage by invoking the importance of

Western solidarity in facing the challenge from the East. Assuming and indeed expecting their more powerful allies to support their endeavors in Indochina in the name of containment, they were profoundly disillusioned when the Americans and the British failed to rally at Dien Bien Phu. When the French National Assembly rejected membership in the European Defense Community in late August 1954, it signaled its pique with the course of American policy in Asia by creating an obstacle to the achievement of United States objectives in Europe.

Further straining the relationship between Paris and Washington, it became clear within a month of the conclusion of the Geneva Conference that the United States intended to supplant France in Indochina. Dulles sent a letter to Foreign Minister Pierre Mendès-France on 19 August indicating that the American administration intended to deal directly with the new South Vietnamese government of Ngo Dinh Diem and its armed forces rather than use the French as an intermediary. Military matériel and economic assistance would be provided directly to the Associated States, and American personnel would become directly involved in training Vietnamese and Cambodian armed forces. Since dealing in this fashion with Diem would inevitably consolidate his power, the French objected vehemently to such an approach. They argued that the plan to furnish the Vietnamese army was "dangerous" and reminded the United States that France depended on American financial support to maintain its military presence in Indochina that protected the "free world."[113]

During high-level Franco-American meetings in Washington from 27 to 29 September, the French discovered that the Eisenhower administration had not been swayed by their vociferous objections. American support for the anti-French Diem, in itself insulting, was compounded by the reaffirmation that American economic and military aid would be channeled directly to the three Associated States. The additional American demand for augmented authority over training the Indochinese national armies provoked a forceful reply from General Ely that France wanted to retain responsibility for their instruction.[114] Ely's protestations notwithstanding, the United States assumed responsibility in early 1955 for training Vietnamese forces as French cadres were withdrawn.[115]

The torch had been passed: the de facto transfer of Western responsibility for Southeast Asian security from French to American hands was nearly complete. On 26 April 1956, exactly two years after the opening of the Geneva Conference, Paris dissolved the French High Command in Indochina. French historian Alfred Grosser described the conclusions his compatriots drew from the behavior of their superpower ally: "The opinion—widespread in France in any event—that American anti-colonialism was merely a pretext for substituting an American for the European presence in the former colonial territories was thus confirmed."[116]

The overall lesson France drew from Indochina was that allies could not necessarily be counted on and that it should never again allow itself to slip into such dependence on another nation for the defense of its interests. Specifically, the experience was a catalyst for the French decision to develop and acquire independent nuclear forces. The choice reflected their bitterness about the allied failure to support them in their final effort at Dien Bien Phu and about Washington's usurpation of their historic role in Southeast Asia. Over time, this nuclear deterrent would permit France to distance itself from NATO without jeopardizing its own security.[117]

The French elections of 2 January 1956 ushered in a government with Socialist Guy Mollet at the helm, an outcome interpreted by many as a rejection of the previous policies of alignment with the United States. Foreign Minister Christian Pineau proclaimed in March that France would seek a position bridging East and West, adding that there was no consensus over policy among the United States, the United Kingdom, and France.[118] This same government, determined to reassert France's independent global role, would confront the United States at Suez later that year.

The impact of disagreements over Indochina on overall relations between the United States and the United Kingdom proved minimal. But the level of trust between Dulles and Eden, never high to begin with, was never to be restored.[119] Dulles maintained that in Indochina the British had made life more difficult for him and had not stood up for the interests of the West. Meeting with reporters in late June 1954, the secretary of state commented that American foreign policy had suffered from its tendency to support the "colonialist" policies of Britain and France, and he suggested that that inclination would change.[120] Such would be Dulles's mind-set as the drama of Suez unfolded.

CHAPTER THREE

Probing the Limits of Alliance, II: The Middle East, 1950–1957

Anglo-American coordination of policy toward the Middle East predated the establishment of NATO. In the early postwar years, the United States and the United Kingdom sustained an intimate dialogue on Middle Eastern developments despite their differences over Palestine and competition for oil. British predominance in the region was a determining factor in any United States action. During a series of consultations in 1947 between American and British officials on protecting mutual interests in the Middle East, the State Department acknowledged this ordering of roles: "It would be unrealistic for the United States to undertake to carry out such a policy unless the British maintain their strong strategic, political and economic position in the Middle East and Eastern Mediterranean, and unless they and ourselves follow parallel policies in that area."[1]

The Americans were content to let the British wield the majority of the defense burden in the Middle East, but they resisted being manipulated into providing protection for solely British, and specifically colonial, interests. In evaluating their 1947 discussions with the British, American policymakers emphasized that the United States did not want to be a "junior partner" in the region, or to follow "blindly" the British lead.[2] This wary attitude toward the initial British effort to engage American political, economic, and military resources in defense of Britain's imperial position in the Middle East was a harbinger of future strains in the Anglo-American relationship.[3]

The Background of Allied Relations in the Region

Following the establishment of NATO, Washington and London held talks on the Middle East in November 1949, consistent with their unique pattern of consultation on matters of mutual global concern. In his introductory remarks, George McGhee, the American assistant secretary of state for Near Eastern and African Affairs, observed that "such intimate discussions had now become a normal aspect of Anglo-American relations."[4] The fact that such exchanges were not held with any other NATO member on a regular or even an irregular basis became a chronic source of friction within the alliance, particularly with the French, but also with the smaller powers.

In spite of the closeness and intensity of the Anglo-American dialogue during this period, the fundamental asymmetry in analyses and interests that had been evident during the 1947 discussions surfaced again. Britain viewed the Middle East as vital to its security and as a higher strategic priority than Asia. The British had a considerable political, economic, and strategic stake in the region, including an influential diplomatic role, substantial investment and trading relationships, and a military presence that protected their interests, including access to oil. During the November 1949 meetings, British Superintending Under Secretary of State for Foreign Affairs Michael Wright made the case that "if Western influence was removed from the Middle East, either voluntarily or by force, Communism would certainly fill the vacuum left." Arguing that this would "prejudice the future of Europe," he appealed to American Cold War sensitivities in order to persuade the United States to play a larger part in Middle Eastern affairs.[5]

The United States was not yet prepared to make a new commitment of this kind. During this period, Washington placed almost exclusive emphasis on deterring a Soviet threat to Europe. In early 1950, a memorandum by the American Joint Chiefs of Staff regarding the Middle East confirmed that "higher priorities in other areas make it impossible to devote any very substantial portion of our limited military resources to this particular area."[6] Furthermore, winning congressional support for NATO had been a colossal undertaking, and Capitol Hill was in no mood to expand American global responsibilities. McGhee observed that since the region had been largely a British preserve, and because the United States was heavily engaged elsewhere, "We wanted the British to hang on in the Middle East as long as possible."[7]

The course of the Cold War, however, portended a major revision of American military commitments in the region. On 25 May 1950, the Americans made a formal pledge to concert their actions with the British and the French to preserve peace in the Middle East. In the Tripartite Declaration, the three principal NATO powers agreed to coordinate Middle East arms sales in order to ensure the maintenance of a balance of forces in the area and to act to prevent aggression by one Middle Eastern state against another.[8] (American participation in this arrangement reflected the general policy shift on colonial problems noted in the previous discussion of Indochina.) Wm. Roger Louis, an eminent historian of British Empire, described Washington's motives:

> The tripartite declaration was issued exactly a month before the outbreak of the Korean War. The tide of American anticolonialism was now definitely on the ebb. Whatever objections there might have been to the British Empire in the Middle East, the need for an ally now convinced most American critics of British imperialism that the expansionist aims of the Soviet Union and Communist China demanded a firm Anglo-American response.[9]

British officials, however, continued to press for augmented United States involvement, arguing in October 1950 that "whoever controls the Middle East controls the access to three continents. Whether or not this area is held will determine whether or not we have a 'big free world' or a 'little free world.'"[10] From its own vantage point, Washington had also begun to worry about the increasing friction between the British and the Egyptians over joint defense agreements, including base rights, and heightened tensions between Israel and the Arab states. Acheson later wrote of the perceived power vacuum in the region that might, if unchecked, invite Soviet adventurism:

> Over the past four years in an unplanned, undesired, and haphazard way American influence had largely succeeded French and British in that part of the world. As ours had waxed and theirs waned . . . no power had been substituted for theirs to maintain

peace and order. . . . As the situation was developing, increasing opportunities were offered for the historic movement of Russia southward to warm water, to oil, and to mischief-making.[11]

Stimulated by British entreaties and by their own assessment of the regional balance of power, the Americans took a more active stance regarding Middle Eastern security in 1951. On 17 March, President Truman approved the policy statement "The Arab States and Israel" (NSC 47/5), which asserted the importance of Middle Eastern stability to the security of the United States.[12] Two interconnected processes were set in motion as a result of this affirmation of American interests in the region. The first was the move to admit Greece and Turkey to full NATO membership. Greek and, more significantly, Turkish accession are the only instances in the history of the alliance in which NATO's domain of responsibility was formally expanded to contend with out-of-area developments.[13]

The American assistant secretaries of state with responsibility for Europe and the Near East sent a joint decision memorandum to the secretary of state in April 1951 detailing the reasons that full NATO membership was their preferred form of security arrangement for Greece and Turkey. The memorandum outlined the military establishment's view that Greek and Turkish participation in NATO offered the greatest payoff in terms of enhanced military strength for both European and Middle Eastern contingencies. It also underscored the domestic political reality that it would be quicker and more efficient to integrate Greece and Turkey into an existing alliance structure than to create a new one that might face stiff congressional opposition.[14]

Proponents of Greek and Turkish NATO membership emphasized not only the advantages to European territorial defense but also the countries' strategic significance with respect to possible out-of-area crises. They argued that extending NATO's responsibilities into the Eastern Mediterranean and Near East would deter Soviet encroachment on that territory. Thus Greek and Turkish accession was seen as serving dual purposes. An aide-mémoire delivered by the United States to the British and French governments on 15 May detailed the military advantages: "The entrance of Greece and Turkey on the side of the Western Powers at the outset of a general war would (a) force upon the Soviet a significantly large diversion of effort, (b) contribute to and facilitate the defense of the Mediterranean Sea and the Middle

East and (c) provide a major contribution of strength to the Western Powers."[15]

In subsequent discussions between American and British officials on command problems in the Atlantic, Mediterranean, and Middle Eastern areas, the British pressed for linkage of Greek and especially Turkish admission into NATO to Greece and Turkey's expected contribution to Middle Eastern security. Indeed, the British went so far as to propose that Turkey should only be allowed to become a full member of NATO if it agreed "to play a full part in the defense of the Middle East under an Allied Middle East Command." While American policymakers resisted such a formal connection—and specific obligations with respect to non-European contingencies were never formalized—the United States agreed to urge such a role on Turkey as soon as it became a member of the alliance.[16]

The American, British, and French consultations on Greek and Turkish membership that preceded discussion in the full NATO forum were a source of procedural and substantive frustration to the rest of the allies. Such conduct would prove, however, to be a recurring phenomenon which the other members could do little about. From this early stage, there was no refuting the hierarchy of power within NATO.

The less powerful allies generally held parochial perspectives on the merits of broadening NATO's defense commitments, fearing that an expansion of the treaty domain to include Greece and Turkey would lead to a detrimental dilution of alliance resources. Secretary of State Acheson described the problem: "The 'North Atlantic' had been stretched in 1949 to include Italy; now we were trying to take in the eastern Mediterranean, a snake pit of troubles. How could Northern European statesmen convince their people that attacks on the Levant should be regarded as attacks on Scandinavia or the Low Countries?"[17] To contend with these differences in perspective, Acheson introduced the novel concept that a division of labor was implicit in the expansion of NATO's security responsibilities. He posited that "if Greece and Turkey became allies and were attacked, not every ally would be called upon to fight in the Eastern Mediterranean. Action there would have to be geared into a strategic plan for European defense as a whole."[18]

In making this case, the secretary of state established an important precedent for the future management of out-of-area issues: those with relevant interests and capabilities would take action on NATO's periphery; those with a narrower definition of their security could contribute to the common defense by doing more within the treaty area. This analysis was invoked in the debate over the defense of Southwest Asia two decades later (see chapter 7). With respect to the Persian Gulf, the Americans allowed that the Europeans could compensate within Europe for American manpower and matériel redeployed outside the NATO area if they did not want to participate there themselves.

The second initiative triggered by NSC 47/5 in spring 1951 was an ill-fated Anglo-American effort to establish a defense arrangement called the Middle East Command (MEC). From the outset, it was unclear whether the MEC structure would be located inside or outside NATO. During preliminary discussions among American and British diplomats and military representatives, United States officials accepted the vague definition of a "separate but interlocking Middle East command structure within NATO."[19] Debate over its exact configuration continued throughout the summer and into the autumn. The alternatives put forward shared one common element: an integral connection between NATO and the proposed MEC, whether or not it fell under explicit NATO jurisdiction.

One plan envisaged an allied MEC in which American, British, French, and Turkish troops would operate under NATO authority. Although the forces would have been placed under a British commander, British officials nonetheless questioned the desirability of such an arrangement. The Bureau of Near Eastern Affairs in the State Department was also predictably skeptical, arguing, "The real problem is to plan for the defense of the Middle East. . . . Since the defense of this area is not directly related to the defense of the NATO area, and none of the countries except, we hope, Turkey, are members of NATO, it should not be a NATO command."[20]

Based on exchanges with their American counterparts, the British put forth an alternative proposal to closely associate the MEC with NATO through a "special system of control."[21] After further discussion, American and British planners decided that the MEC would not be formally under NATO auspices but linked informally to the Atlantic alliance through the participation of American, British, Commonwealth, French, and Turkish troops coordinated by a British commander.[22] The headquarters and basing facilities would be located in Egypt but operated under British authority. The concept on which Washington and London finally settled was remarkable in its assertion of an overt connection between allied security and the defense of collective interests outside the treaty area.

The scheme was also noteworthy for its almost exclusively military nature. Throughout the discussions, American planners resisted the creation of a formal political association for the Middle East operating alongside NATO. If such structure was necessary, it would instead have derived from existing ties between and among the four NATO participants. In part, this reflected American reluctance to become formally obligated to support European colonial commitments.[23] It also highlighted the trend toward military-to-military cooperation, a less domestically costly means of organizing allied action outside the NATO area.

The MEC's fate was sealed, however, by Egypt's outright refusal to play any part in a NATO-dominated military alliance for Middle Eastern defense. Egyptian Prime Minister Nahas Pasha would not even read the MEC proposal made public on 13 October 1951.[24] In addition, given Anglo-French rivalries in the Middle East dating to the late nineteenth century, neither power was too eager to bind itself to concerted action. In spite of this legacy, the MEC was not scuttled by intra-allied friction. The British tried to keep the idea alive, and it was a subject of discussion at NATO meetings in Rome later that year. But the proposal was a dead letter, having foundered on external resistance from local powers who perceived the MEC as a new imperialist endeavor to preserve and bolster Western control over the region.[25]

Despite the stillbirth of the American initiative, the United States had become a major player in Middle Eastern affairs. This coincided, not unintentionally, with the rapid decline of British influence in the region, particularly with respect to Egypt. Four critical events in the first half of the decade hastened the diminution of British power. In October 1951, the Egyptian parliament abrogated both its 1936 treaty with Britain and the Sudan condominium agreement of 1899. Then, deposing King Farouk, General Mohammad Naguib seized power in July 1952 on behalf of a group of military leaders led by Colonel Gamal Abdel Nasser. By October 1954, the British had agreed to evacuate their prized Suez base within twenty months, and a year later Nasser announced the signature of an arms deal with Czechoslovakia.

Until the Suez crisis in 1956, however, Eisenhower maintained that because of heavy American commitments in Europe, Korea, Indochina, and elsewhere, the United Kingdom should wield the major responsibility for Middle Eastern stability and security.[26] With Washington's encouragement, the British worked throughout 1955 to conclude a series of security agreements with Turkey, Pakistan, Iraq, and Iran, known collectively as the Baghdad Pact. Later, after Iraq's withdrawal, the arrangement was renamed the Central Treaty Organization (CENTO).

While the United States privately supported the concept of the Baghdad Pact, it refused to link itself publicly with the new organization. Dulles claimed that Washington could not join because it had not yet offered a comparable security treaty to Israel and because the Egyptians were sure to oppose the pact just as they had the MEC. Concluding that the pact would alienate powerful forces in the region, most notably Egypt and Israel, the Americans decided they had nothing to gain from formal adherence.[27]

The British were especially irritated with American reticence since Dulles had originally proposed the idea and had talked London into participating. They resented Washington's desire to have it both ways by maintaining favorable relations with both the Arab states and Israel. Foreign Secretary Selwyn Lloyd later described his frustration with Dulles: "He seemed to want to hedge every bet. He was prepared to promise military and economic aid for the Baghdad Pact countries, but on no account would he join it. He was prepared to consider ways of reducing economic support for Nasser, but he was determined to avoid any appearance of 'ganging up' with us."[28] Eden elaborated on British disappointment that the United States left the United Kingdom as the only Western participant: "In recent years the United States has sometimes failed to put its weight behind its friends, in the hope of being popular with their foes."[29] Lloyd went so far as to say that as long as Washington established an "anti-Soviet screen" in the Middle East, it "did not much care what happened to British influence behind it." At best, he felt the Americans were indifferent to the decline of British power; at worst, he suspected that much of the State Department was openly anti-British.[30] The lesson Eden and Lloyd drew from this experience would have profound consequences in 1956: knowing that their most trusted ally could sometimes be infuriatingly mercurial, the British leaders would be more inclined than usual to dismiss Washington's counsel and go their own way. In so doing, they erroneously assumed that in a real crisis the Anglo-American bond would always dictate American support for Britain.

Curiously absent from any role in the Baghdad Pact was France, whose obsession with North Africa affected all its foreign policy calculations. The rebellion against French rule in Algeria began on 1 November 1954—barely six months after the fall of Dien Bien Phu—and on 19 May 1955 France began moving its NATO-designated forces to the troubled territory. Paris sought and gained the NAC's approval in advance of removing its forces from Europe; by late 1956 there were more than four hundred thousand French troops and a good deal of NATO-designated equipment in Algeria. While Algeria was not technically an out-of-area problem—it was considered a part of metropolitan France and covered by the NATO treaty—the French argued that the insurgency was an example of the Soviet attempt to weaken the West by fomenting instability on Europe's flanks.[31]

In addition to its preoccupation with Algeria, France was still smarting from what it perceived to have been its abandonment by the "Anglo-Saxons" a year earlier in Indochina. French pique was compounded by the fact that in the prewar period France had exerted substantial influence in Syria and Lebanon; in the postwar era, however, France's position was greatly diminished and the French resented the British leadership role. Thus Paris was reluctant to commit to any common Middle East policy and was skeptical of the Baghdad Pact. When the French next cooperated with the British in the region, their action was solely motivated by the conviction that Egypt's president Nasser was supporting and sustaining the Algerian rebellion.[32]

By 1956 the three principal NATO allies had diverged considerably from the consensus that motivated the Tripartite Declaration of 1950. The Czech arms deal of 1955 had been the death knell of tripartism: the provision of Eastern bloc weapons on a large scale to Egypt undermined the system of balanced arms sales that the agreement was supposed to enforce. Further, the tripartite powers' inability to restrain this influx of weaponry indicated that their influence over Middle Eastern states, especially Egypt, had precipitously declined. Finally, the failure of the Americans, the British, and the French to participate together in the Baghdad Pact effort signaled a breakdown in the spirit of cooperation that had motivated their 1950 agreement to maintain peace in the Middle East.

In the months before Suez, however, there was still an underlying commitment between the Americans and the British to cooperate and to avoid undermining each other's expressed global interests.

Churchill, for example, prevailed on Eisenhower in 1955 to suspend promised United States arms sales to Nasser, arguing, "You can't give them arms with which to kill British soldiers who fought shoulder to shoulder with you in the war." Eisenhower chose to stall the transfer, concluding that close relations with Britain were more important than those with Egypt in the global struggle against Communism.[33]

Indeed, the warmth of the relationship between the two nations raised an expectation of continued close cooperation that proved disastrously misleading in 1956; for example, at the opening of meetings between Eden and Eisenhower in January, Lloyd observed, "It is absolutely clear in my belief that the hopes for a peaceful world depend upon the friendship of our two countries. If we stand together, there is almost anything we can do together."[34] Because the British and the Americans considered themselves the closest of allies, they did not suspect each other's motives and actions as countries without such ties naturally would have done. As a result, they failed to anticipate and interpret correctly one another's responses. Richard Neustadt, author of the seminal study on alliance politics at Suez, concluded, "Misperceptions evidently make for crisis in proportion to the intimacy of relations. Hazards are proportionate to the degree of friendship."[35]

The French were much more cynical about the advantages of partnership, having long resented the Anglo-American special relationship and having been subjected to what they perceived as allied indifference to their plight in Indochina. Exacerbating their skepticism was the December 1955 American decision that important issues, hitherto discussed during trilateral exchanges among the United States, the United Kingdom, and France, would henceforth be considered in the NAC or in bilateral meetings. Although Washington's legitimate rationale was that it was no longer feasible to exclude Germany and Italy from such discussions, the French concluded this shift signaled their demotion by the Anglo-Saxons from great power status.[36]

Relations were particularly tense regarding the coordination of action in the Middle East. In the first half of 1956, the French were not included in extensive Anglo-American planning for a possible war between the Arab states and Israel. Although the premise of these talks was that such a conflict might trigger obligations under the Tripartite Declaration, the Americans and the British assumed France was too preoccupied with Algeria to care about anything else.[37] In an address to the Anglo-American Press Association in Paris on 2 March 1956, the new French foreign minister, Christian Pineau, expressed suspicion that the Americans and the British meant to push the French out of the Middle East: "We have the impression that . . . there lurks the desire of certain powers to swallow up the heritage of France." He therefore concluded that "despite alliances, despite affirmations, there is no real common French-British-American policy today."[38]

During the spring of 1956, Anglo-American relations also became strained. Negotiations over the financing of the Aswan Dam project brought to the fore interallied differences over Middle East policy. The British were infuriated in early March by what they saw as Nasser's machinations behind King Hussein of Jordan in Hussein's insulting ouster of the long-time British resident adviser, Lieutenant General John Bagot Glubb. They were therefore particularly annoyed by the ongoing American effort to remain on good terms with the Egyptian regime by pampering Nasser with aid.[39] Moreover, as the British watched their influence decline with the completion of the Suez base evacuation on 13 June, they became increasingly frustrated by the corresponding growth of the United States presence in the region.

While London focused on Nasser as the principal enemy of Western interests, Washington was preoccupied with the containment dimension of Middle East policy.[40] An April 1956 message from Eisenhower to Eden highlighted the American view that the greatest threat in the Middle East came from the Soviet Union: "We should not be acquiescent in any measure which would give the Bear's claws a grip on production or transportation of oil which is so vital to the defence and economy of the Western world."[41] Such was the divergence in perspectives on out-of-area challenges during this period, and it would remain fairly constant over time. Locked in the superpower rivalry, the United States endeavored to check Soviet global adventurism, while those European nations with imperial ties to a particular country or region concentrated on indigenous instabilities.

Muffled Disputes and Secret Plans, July–October 1956

By midsummer 1956, the British and American governments had reached basic agreement that providing aid to Egypt for the construction of the Aswan Dam was unwise on both financial and political grounds. However, Dulles's clumsy public announcement on 19 July of the withdrawal of the United States from the project precipitated a chain of events that led seemingly inexorably to an international crisis over control of the Suez Canal, pitting the United States against its two principal allies in Europe.

On 26 July, Nasser seized on this pretext to nationalize the canal, claiming that its revenues would finance construction of the dam. The response of the United Kingdom and France was predictable: each felt, for its own reasons, that force was the only appropriate recourse against Nasser. Haunted by the memory of Munich, the British were determined to act decisively; the French, convinced that Nasser was supplying the Algerian rebels, wanted to end his influence over their affairs and avenge their national honor. In a secret telegram to Eisenhower on the following day, Eden insisted that if a firm stand was not taken immediately, "our influence and yours throughout the Middle East will, we are convinced, be finally destroyed. . . . We are unlikely to attain our objective by economic pressures alone. . . . we must be ready, in the last resort, to use force to bring Nasser to his senses." Pineau commented to his British counterpart, Selwyn Lloyd, that "one successful battle in Egypt would be worth ten in North Africa."[42] Sensing eagerness for military retaliation, Washington attempted to restrain its allies with appeals for close coordination. The president dispatched Deputy Under Secretary of State Robert Murphy to London on 27 July for consultations with the British and the French.

By 28 July, however, Anglo-French planning for an invasion had already started. France's senior military officials went to London and established a covert joint military command.[43] On 30 July, Eden and Chancellor of the Exchequer Harold Macmillan sent secret messages to Eisenhower stating that Her Majesty's government had made a "firm and irrevocable" decision to "break Nasser." The British had decided, according to Eisenhower's recapitulation of their communications in his reply, to "employ force without delay or attempting any intermediate or less drastic steps."[44] Outlining London's dire analysis of the impact of the canal seizure on British interests and on the Atlantic alliance, Lloyd argued on 31 July that a failure to take action would "be the end of us, of Western Europe and NATO as decisive influences in world affairs."[45]

Deeply apprehensive, Eisenhower dispatched Dulles to London

on that same day to dissuade the British from provoking a military showdown with Nasser. Dulles carried a personal letter from Eisenhower to Eden in which the president emphasized in the clearest of terms that the United States would not agree to the British course of action before a serious effort to mediate a peaceful solution had been made. Eisenhower argued that the Congress and American public opinion would not support a precipitous bellicose response and that if the United States engaged in such an unpopular military endeavor, "there would be a reaction that could very seriously affect our peoples' feeling toward our Western Allies." He concluded, "I have given you my own personal conviction, as well as that of my associates, as to the unwisdom even of contemplating the use of military force at this moment."[46] In his account of Eisenhower's message, Eden demonstrated how statesmen, especially in the midst of crises, hear only what they wish to hear. Rather than focusing on the intensity of the president's argument against military action, Eden concentrated on the fact that Eisenhower "did not rule out the use of force."[47]

Three features of the unfolding Suez crisis reveal the dynamics of alliance crisis management outside of Europe. First, the precipitous pairing off of the United Kingdom and France reflected the fact that out-of-area cooperation is driven by the coincidence of interests rather than by the warmth of relations between two countries. Long-standing rivals for influence both in the region and for status within NATO, Britain and France determined that their own immediate objectives could best be advanced though cooperation. Neither could topple Nasser by itself. The intersection of their respective interests—the British passion to put Nasser "in his place" and the French resolve to destroy the Egyptian leader because of his support for the Algerian rebels—produced an updated version of the old Entente Cordiale, which in 1904 had recognized British claims in Egypt and French supremacy in Morocco.[48]

Second, the exchanges that took place were rooted in a habit of consultation; it was assumed that the three leading NATO powers with varied and often competing interests in the region would attempt to resolve the crisis, and their differences, among themselves. Thus the ongoing informal round of meetings among American, British, and French officials was standard practice: no formal arrangements to convene existed and none were particularly needed. Their extensive communications network was in evidence from the moment the British learned about the canal's nationalization. When news of Nasser's bold move was received during dinner on 26 July, Eden called a late-night emergency meeting at 10 Downing Street that included not only his inner cabinet and military Chiefs of Staff but also the American chargé d'affaires and the French ambassador.[49]

Third, and most important, despite the considerable efforts the allies made to communicate and coordinate their policies, divergent analyses of interests and objectives created insurmountable differences among them. No greater amount of consultation would necessarily have prevented the split within the alliance. The French and the British were dead set on using military force to stop Nasser. While Eisenhower would have preferred to sustain the solidarity of the alliance on which he believed the fate of the free world depended, he fundamentally opposed the allies' efforts to keep their colonial holdings in the Middle East. Furthermore, he was determined to uphold the nonaggression principles of the United Nations, not least because the American people would object to hasty military action. Eisenhower wrote about the paradox of Suez:

> I can scarcely describe the depth of the regret I felt in the need to take a view so diametrically opposed to that held by the British. Some in the British Cabinet were old friends of mine; indeed, several were comrades in the dramatic days of World War II and of the less exacting but still momentous times at NATO. . . . Yet I felt that in taking our own position we were standing firmly on principle and on the realities of the twentieth century.[50]

Though the American president did not feel similarly anguished by the prospects of crossing the French, with whom relations were never as close, his predicament was a stark measure of the limits of alliance.

In spite of Eisenhower's entreaties and the ongoing efforts to align the policies of the three principal NATO powers, the British and the French proceeded to prepare for war against Egypt. From 3 August onward, Anglo-French military planning took place under the overall command of British General Sir Charles Keightley, with French Vice Admiral P. Barjot as his deputy. General Sir Hugh Stockwell, the land forces commander, and his deputy, General André Beaufre, were assigned to hammer out the details of the invasion in a gloomy Whitehall basement.[51] The goal was integration of the Anglo-French forces on the wartime or NATO model.

Although the French accepted this arrangement as a matter of logistical necessity, they resented having to cooperate with the British, especially from what they perceived to be a subordinate position. Pineau later said that France, which possessed larger land forces, had only been willing to pool its resources because Britain had troop transport ships, heavy bombers, and the nearest invasion bases. Beaufre did try to limit the liabilities of integration under British leadership by establishing a separate task force for the operation. While one French team participated in integrated planning in London, Paris maintained a separate operational staff for its fighting units in Algeria.[52] This reluctance to participate in any formal joint command structure with other allies would be a recurring theme in French attitudes toward out-of-area activities. That they were willing to share at all in military planning for Suez confirmed the intensity of their determination to see Nasser defeated.

While the secret bilateral military planning got underway, American, British, and French officials met in London to discuss the appropriate response by the Tripartite Declaration signatories to Nasser's nationalization of the canal. Their public statements afterward revealed that neither the Europeans nor the Americans had been convinced of the merits of the other side's approach. On 3 August, French Prime Minister Mollet said, "The three have let Nasser know the rules he will have to bow to." He added, "All steps ought to be taken to make him submit. We will go all the way." Dulles, by contrast, commented mildly, "We do not want to meet violence with violence."[53] The three countries, however, did agree to invite twenty-four nations to a conference on restoring international authority over Suez on 16 August in London.[54] Eden wrote to Eisenhower that they could now "display to Nasser and to the world a united front between our two countries and the French."[55]

In addition to the three convening powers, the other NATO members invited were Denmark, the Federal Republic of Germany, Greece (which decided not to come at the last minute), Italy, the Netherlands, Norway, Portugal, and Turkey.[56] At the urging of Canadian Foreign Secretary Pearson, the NAC met in restricted session on 6 August with the intention of seeking out "some area of common agreement among the NATO members who were to participate in the Conference . . . and, at the same time, to underline the strategic importance of the Suez Canal to NATO."[57] Because neither the United Kingdom, France, nor the United States had any intention of having its hands tied in the Middle East by a NATO position, the meeting turned out to be a relatively meaningless exercise in superficial political consultation.

The London Conference opened on 16 August, with twenty-two nations in attendance.[58] Almost immediately, it split into two rival groups. Dulles led the "Big Three" bloc with the support of all the participants except Ceylon, India, Indonesia, and the Soviet Union. The statement devised by the United States, the United Kingdom, and France during their recent tripartite meetings formed the basis of a declaration supported by this eighteen-member coalition. It reasserted the principles of international control, recognized the sovereign rights of Egypt, guaranteed Cairo a fair return for the use of the canal, and proposed the negotiation of a new convention governing the canal's use. According to Lloyd, the West German representative felt that the "Conference had been a remarkable example of the solidarity of the Western Alliance," an assessment Lloyd also shared.[59]

The real impact of the conference, however, was that London and Paris were forced to postpone launching their military effort against Egypt for an entire month: first for the tripartite talks in early August; then for the conference itself; and afterward to allow Australian Prime Minister Robert Menzies to present the substance of the Western declaration to Nasser. Nevertheless, the argument advanced by some Suez analysts that the London Conference was solely an American diversionary tactic[60] is too narrow an explanation. The United States was genuinely and indeed passionately committed to finding a peaceful resolution to the problem, not least because Eisenhower found it awkward and painful to be at odds with his British colleagues and friends.[61]

The conclusion of the London Conference left the West at an impasse, despite the display of unity by the Big Three bloc. In the following weeks, Eisenhower and Eden exchanged several rounds of letters that revealed the intractable differences in their approaches to dealing with Nasser. Aware of the distance between their two countries' policies, the president and the prime minister nonetheless remained wedded to irreconcilable courses of action.

Eisenhower was particularly annoyed by accounts of ongoing British military preparations during this period. He recalled that in late August, when the British granted permission to the French to station troops in Cyprus, and both countries ordered the evacuation of their nationals from Egypt, Jordan, Syria, and Lebanon, "I was wondering at times whether the British and French governments were really concerned over the success or failure of the Menzies mission."[62] On 27 August, a letter from Eden gave Eisenhower the answer: "We have to continue our military preparations in conjunction with our French allies."

Eden also appealed again to the American body politic's fervent anti-Communism, writing in evocative prose: "I have no doubt that the Bear is using Nasser, with or without his knowledge, to further his immediate aims. These are, I think, first to dislodge the West from the Middle East, and second to get a foothold in Africa so as to dominate that Continent in turn."[63] While Eisenhower concurred in the British assessment of Soviet objectives, he vigorously disagreed with their determination to employ force to stop Nasser. In a 2 September reply to Eden, he repeated his unequivocal opposition to the British (and French) mobilization and his unwillingness to provide support for it:

> I must tell you frankly that American opinion flatly rejects the thought of using force, particularly when it does not seem that every possible peaceful means of protecting our vital interests has been exhausted without result. Moreover, I gravely doubt we could here secure Congressional authority even for the lesser support measures for which you might have to look to us.
>
> I really do not see how a successful result could be achieved by forcible means. The use of force would, it seems to me, vastly increase the area of jeopardy.[64]

Eden was disturbed by the substance of the president's message; it seemed to him that the United States was now backing down further by resisting the use of force at any juncture. Responding on 6 September, the British leader emphasized that the canal issue could not be separated, as Eisenhower advised, from the larger problems of Arab nationalism and Egyptian ambition that threatened Western interests in the Middle East. Drawing parallels between Nasser and Hitler, he argued, "The seizure of the Suez Canal is . . . the opening gambit in a planned campaign designed by Nasser to expel all Western influence and interests from Arab countries." Citing NATO's role in frustrating the Soviet grab for territory and influence in the late forties, Eden made the case that swift action could avert the more costly and difficult task of reversing Nasser's revolutions once they had swept the region. Eden concluded, "We have many times led Europe in the fight for freedom. It would be an ignoble end to our long history if we accepted to perish by degrees."[65]

Convinced that Britain's vital interests—and therefore the vital interests of the entire alliance—were at stake, Eden recommended that the NAC be convened again to consolidate opinion and coordinate action. The British had become so concerned about apparent allied disarray that they took the lead. Lloyd presided over the session, and although Dulles pointedly did not attend, all the other foreign ministers were present. Ironically, the meeting bolstered British resolve to stand up to Nasser's challenge. Lloyd recalled its impact:

> The discussion at the NATO meeting helped us to make up our minds. Luns of the Netherlands and Spaak took a robust line. If Nasser rejected the eighteen-power proposals, the NATO countries should refuse to recognise the seizure of the Canal; they should withhold the payment of dues, and the matter should be referred to the Security Council. . . . No American Minister was present, and the official representing the United States said very little.[66]

That the NAC assembled exclusively to discuss the Suez Canal situation vividly demonstrated that developments beyond the treaty area inevitably affected NATO even if it was not formally responsible for the defense of its members' out-of-area interests and commitments.

On 5 September, Nasser predictably rejected the proposed internationalization of the canal.[67] By then, however, Dulles had conceived of the Suez Canal Users' Association (SCUA). Although the association's purpose was left intentionally vague, the idea was to establish an organization of the eighteen London-proposal signatories that would work in conjunction with Egypt to ensure efficient operation of the waterway. The most significant difference between Dulles's concept and previous proposals was its implicit acknowledgment of Egyptian authority over the canal, something that had been carefully avoided in the past.

In his second letter to Eden in less than a week, Eisenhower endorsed the idea behind Dulles's SCUA proposal on 8 September, arguing that the organization would allow *"de facto* 'coexistence'" between the users and Egypt. He also revealed impatience with Eden's preoccupation with the Egyptian threat, admonishing that "you are making of Nasser a much more important figure than he is." Finally, Eisenhower repeated his warning about the potentially damaging consequences of a British resort to force: not only would it cause the

Arabs to support Nasser, but it "might cause a serious misunderstanding between our two countries."[68]

The United States communicated more details of the SCUA to the British and the French during bilateral meetings in Paris between the prime ministers and foreign ministers of the two countries on 10 September. Britain and France reluctantly agreed to support the American proposal. In Eden's view, this decision was one of the most crucial of the entire crisis, because it committed London and Paris to proceed with yet another protracted effort to negotiate a solution. Eden and Lloyd felt they had to go along with the Americans to uphold the pretext that they had exhausted all peaceful alternatives before going to war; moreover, the British (unlike the French) were driven by what Eden described as the fact that "cooperation with the United States had been a guiding principle throughout my political life."[69] The logic behind the French choice was more cynical: Pineau thought it best to wait out the results of the conference and thereby preserve a greater margin of maneuver for France.[70]

While Eden was defending the SCUA plan before an increasingly hostile House of Commons,[71] and just before the Second London Conference opened to establish the association, Dulles publicly appeared to undermine the entire proposal. Responding to press questions about a possible blockage of the canal, the American secretary of state asserted, "We do not intend to shoot our way through. It may be we have the right to do it but we don't intend to do it as far as the United States is concerned." After all, a plausible—albeit inconvenient—alternative to the canal route existed: diverting ships around the Cape of Good Hope. On the issue of Anglo-American coordination, Dulles commented that "each nation has to decide for itself what action it will have to take to defend and if possible realize its rights which it believes it has as a matter of treaty."[72]

Enraged by these comments, Eden claimed that the Americans had "knocked the teeth" out of the SCUA before it was born. More than any other event in the protracted crisis, the SCUA episode emptied the reservoir of good faith between London and Washington. The prime minister later described its negative impact on allied relations:

It would be hard to imagine a statement more likely to cause the maximum allied disunity and disarray. . . . The Users' Club was an American project to which we had conformed. We were all three in agreement, even to the actual words of the announcement. Yet here was the spokesman of the United States saying that each nation must decide for itself. . . . Such cynicism towards allies destroys true partnership. It leaves only the choice of parting, or a master and vassal relationship in foreign policy.[73]

Eden subsequently considered his acceptance of the SCUA proposal as the greatest mistake of his career.[74] British embitterment over this incident and, more generally, over American dissociation from the British effort to protect what London believed to be the interests of the alliance, reinforced their inclination to break with the United States and join the French in military action against Egypt.

Events had clearly bypassed the SCUA by the time the Second London Conference was convened on 19 September. Nasser had summarily rejected the entire concept. To make matters worse, on 2 October, the day after the creation of the organization was officially announced, Dulles made a highly antagonistic statement suggesting that the United States would not stand by its European allies if they went to war with Egypt: "This is not an area where we are bound together by treaty. Certain areas we are by treaty bound to protect, such as the North Atlantic Treaty area, and there we stand together and I hope and believe always will stand absolutely together. There are also other problems where our approach is not always identical. For example, there is in Asia and Africa the so-called problem of colonialism. Now there the United States plays a somewhat independent role." Then he struck another blow to the SCUA: "There is talk about the 'teeth' being pulled out of it. There were never 'teeth' in it, if that means the use of force."[75]

Eisenhower agreed with the basic substance, if not the tone, of his secretary of state's attempts to distance the United States from its allies' colonial commitments. While in several instances Dulles had imprudently fueled British and French expectations of American support, most notably in the case of the SCUA,[76] the president remained steadfast throughout the summer and early autumn of 1956 in opposing allied military action. Reflecting on the strains in Franco-American relations caused by differing perspectives on colonialism, Eisenhower observed:

> Difficulties compounded as the result of the emotional fear the French privately but constantly expressed of Nasser's influence in North Africa. They continued to drum on the argument that since we were allies in Europe we were bound to "stand by" them in any

situation they might encounter or create anywhere on the globe. While as a matter of sentiment, and in many cases as a matter of practicality, this was so, it could not apply in every conceivable circumstance. In the instant case, much as we valued our friendship with France, and as much as we desired solidarity with our principal allies, we could not encourage the unjustified domination of a small nation by foreign armies.[77]

In sum, the United States would not be bound by the interests or policies of its NATO partners outside of Europe if those engagements conflicted with the American foreign policy agenda.

Throughout October, the three countries were at cross-purposes. The total breakdown in communications alleged by some analysts[78] did not, in fact, take place, but the British and the French clearly censored their exchanges with the Americans. There were two different arenas of action and the United States was privy to information about only one. While in public—and in concert with the United States—Britain and France sustained the semblance of working toward a diplomatic solution, in private—and without the knowledge of the United States—they were polishing their plans to go to war.

Frustrated by the SCUA episode, the British and the French decided in early October to take the canal issue to the United Nations. American, British, and French leaders were therefore in constant contact in New York over the development of a United Nations Suez settlement plan, and there was no lack of opportunity for consultation during this period. Indeed, they agreed to hold private meetings and negotiations in addition to the Security Council sessions.[79] Although London and Paris had resorted to the United Nations without securing Washington's approval,[80] the United States supported a resolution tabled on 5 October by Britain and France that upheld the principles of the first London Conference. When this did not come to fruition, the three allies agreed to endorse the "Six Principles" of a settlement that had been developed by United Nations Secretary General Dag Hammarskjöld.[81] But the British and the French concluded the plan could never be effectively implemented, doubting there would be adequate means of enforcing its provisions for free and open transit through the canal. In moving ahead simultaneously to finalize their secret military designs, they revealed their profound lack of confidence in the United Nations effort that they had stimulated.

On 14 October, the day after the Hammarskjöld plan was adopted,

Eden met at Chequers at Prime Minister Mollet's request with secret French emissaries, including the acting foreign minister.[82] According to the British ambassador in Paris, by mid-October widespread French opinion held that "France had been let down by United States and that Great Britain, obsessed by need for Anglo-American solidarity and hampered by attitude of the Labour Opposition, had not adequately matched French determination to stand up to Nasser."[83] Disgusted with the lengthy delays caused by the Anglo-American minuet, the French now sought to involve the British in a clandestine alliance with the Israelis against Nasser. Although France and Britain had held discussions as early as July to coordinate their war plans, this was the first of a series of meetings that would confirm the details of their joint military action and of their collusion with Israel.

It was on the substance of these exchanges that the British, knowing full well the strength of the Eisenhower administration's opposition to the use of force at Suez, intentionally avoided keeping the Americans informed. In reply to an early query from the British ambassador to France about whether he might "take the U.S. Embassy here into our confidence" regarding the secret Anglo-French military planning, the Foreign Office replied, "So far we have said nothing about these conversations to the Americans here or in Washington, and we do not propose to do so."[84]

Eisenhower commented that as of 15 October, when intelligence information reported Israeli mobilization, a transatlantic "blackout of communications had been imposed" regarding these developments. There had previously been an almost complete sharing of intelligence judgments on the situation; "From this time on," he wrote, "we had the uneasy feeling that we were cut off from our allies."[85] Dulles sensed that something was going on but was not able to uncover any evidence. He commented that in the Middle East, "I don't think we have any clear picture as to what the British and French are up to there. I think they are deliberately keeping us in the dark."[86]

However, Washington did not lack for sources of information. As Richard Neustadt observed, "appropriately used—that is, to answer the right questions—these sources almost surely could have met most information needs."[87] One critic blamed the American intelligence services for failing to interpret heavy radio traffic between England and France and air reconnaissance reports of major military activity in the Middle East.[88] But a much more significant factor in the neglect of available intelligence information was what Eisenhower's biographer described as the effect of "strategic surprise": to the president, "it made no sense—indeed was self-destructive—for the British and French to attempt to seize and hold the canal . . . and it especially made no sense to him for Britain and France to attempt to act independently of the United States."[89] The ironic legacy of the intimacy of Anglo-American relations was that neither could clearly fathom the depth of the divide between them. The Americans could not believe that their allies would take action without them, and the British could not imagine that the United States would ultimately take action to harm them. Both sides had blinders on.

On 24 October, Britain, France, and Israel signed a secret accord at Sèvres, detailing their plans for joint military action against Nasser.[90] After an initial Israeli attack on Egyptian forces through the Sinai, and following the predicted rejection of a cease-fire and withdrawal ultimatum, Anglo-French military action would be initiated on the pretext of separating Israeli and Egyptian belligerents. Once aerial bombing had destroyed the Egyptian air force on the ground, Anglo-French troops would occupy the canal to protect the strategic waterway. Each participating government had its own agenda: for the British, the destruction of Nasser and reassertion of influence in the Middle East; for the French, revenge against the Egyptian leader and, indirectly, against the Algerian rebels; and for the Israeli, the pursuit of more secure borders. It was a marriage of convenience, and with the failure of the operation, the brief honeymoon in Anglo-French relations ended abruptly.

That neither the British nor the French chose to inform the United States of their planned attack reflected the profound disagreement among the three allies over Suez. Lloyd recounted his consideration of the issue with Pineau in their meeting on 23 October: "The question of discussions with the Americans was raised. It was not thought that any useful purpose would be served by talking to them as the French and ourselves had talked, owing to their pre-occupation with the election campaign, and the generally unsatisfactory nature of our exchanges with Mr. Dulles about U.S. action of any character."[91] Their respective motives for this break with Washington, however, differed: the French acted out of anger and frustration and in impatient spite of the United States, while the British resorted to collusion with resignation, weary of the effort to secure American support for their endeavor but wary of going it alone.

In taking action independent of its superpower guarantor, France sought the opportunity to reaffirm its identity as a great power. Defeated and occupied during World War II, routed in Indochina, faced with the prospect of civil war in Algeria, and member of an alliance in which it did not feel it was accorded equal status with the United States or, worse still, Britain, France had a serious self-image problem in the mid-fifties. Because of French dependence on the American security commitment to Europe, a good deal of spleen was vented at the United States. As one French observer commented, France's response to Suez was part of a larger phenomenon, "the first wave of extreme nationalism" since the thirties. A French politician put it more bluntly: "We have been cuckolded by the Americans, and we don't like it. We are not compelled to follow this one-way street any longer. We must pursue our national interests in our way, instead of tagging along on the coattails of the United States."[92]

French impatience grew as time dragged on and nothing was done. Pineau complained to Israeli Foreign Minister Golda Meir about dealing with the Americans: "Dulles has done everything to delay action. We must not put them in a position of having to say yes or no since they could only say no because of the oil lobby. That would get us into a much more difficult situation than if we hadn't consulted them."[93] Never having had a relationship with Washington like the one the British sustained with the Americans—a fact that in itself was a major cause of resentment—France would not try as Britain did to find some means of mollifying the United States.

The British based their decision not to inform Washington of the impending military action on a pair of conflicting premises, one assuming intimacy and the other acknowledging distance. The first was the expectation of American support. So fundamental was the assumption of cooperation that it was hard for either British or American policymakers actually to conceive of a damaging confrontation between them. In the end, Macmillan said, Eisenhower would "lie doggo" and let the British proceed. According to Macmillan, Dulles had reassured Eden earlier in the autumn that the British could always count on the "moral support" of the United States but that he did not want to know anything about further Anglo-French military plans. Eden recounted later, "One took great care not to inform him, officially or otherwise, when the time came."[94] Notwithstanding the secrecy surrounding the details of the final military blueprint, throughout the crisis there was certainly no lack of consultation; if anything, both sides knew each other's positions too well, but expected that their differences would be resolved in a gentlemanly manner, as they had been in the past.

The other factor underlying British behavior was their immense frustration with Washington since the canal had been nationalized. The Americans had taken every opportunity and used every ruse to delay action, and there was no apparent reason they would not try to do so again. Finally recognizing that the United States was not interested in playing a part in their scheme to overthrow Nasser, the British could no longer afford to be delayed by the special relationship. According to Lloyd, London therefore made "the judgement that Eisenhower would have been more offended if we had told him beforehand and then acted in spite of his opposition."[95] Macmillan echoed this view, arguing that "to be 'informed' rather than 'consulted' may be almost as wounding as to be kept in the dark."[96] That the British deliberately deceived their closest ally showed that they had exhausted all their options and could not bring the Americans aboard.[97]

Still, the leaders of the two countries remained in nearly constant contact. Eisenhower remarked on the steady stream of exchanges he had with Eden in late October and early November that the "exercise" was getting to be "a sort of transatlantic essay contest."[98] This enduring link explains in part why Anglo-American relations were speedily revived in the aftermath of Suez, while France's relationship with the United States progressively soured.

Military Action on a Short Fuse

Israeli forces attacked Egypt on 29 October, thrusting across the Sinai Peninsula toward the Suez Canal. As planned, on the following day the British and French issued an ultimatum to Israel and Egypt demanding a cease-fire and withdrawal to ten miles from the canal; simultaneously, the Anglo-French naval task force set sail from Malta. The United States again warned its European partners against fomenting a military showdown in the Middle East. Even before the news of the ultimatum reached him, Eisenhower sent Eden an urgent appeal for allied coordination:

> The possible involvement of you and the French in a general Arab war, seems to me to leave your government and ours in a very sad

state of confusion, so far as any possibility of unified understanding and action are concerned. . . . it seems to me of first importance that the U.K. and the U.S. quickly and clearly lay out their present views and intentions before each other, and that, come what may, we find some way of concerting our ideas and plans so that we may not, in any real crisis, be powerless to act in concert because of misunderstanding of each other. I think it important that our two peoples, as well as the French, have this clear understanding of our common or several viewpoints.[99]

Several more cables were exchanged during the day between the British and the Americans, but Eisenhower initially learned about the ultimatum when Dulles read him the story off a news ticker. Mollet was the first to officially inform the United States of the Anglo-French demand that Egyptian and Israeli troops be withdrawn and of France and Britain's intention to "temporarily" assume control of the canal.[100] Eisenhower's response to this charade was chilly. Addressing Eden as "Dear Mr. Prime Minister" (rather than with his characteristic "My dear Anthony"), the president admonished: "I have just learned from the press of the 12 hour ultimatum which you and the French government have delivered. . . . I feel I must urgently express to you my deep concern at the prospect of this drastic action."[101] The lack of advance consultation over the ultimatum was not due to any breakdown in communications. Rather, the allies understood each other's views and intentions all too well; indeed, they knew they were in profound and irreconcilable disagreement over how best to protect their individual—and collective—interests.

With the expiration of their contrived ultimatum, Britain and France implemented their plan to land troops in Egypt and to occupy the canal zone. On 31 October, British bombers launched an offensive against Egyptian airfields. Anglo-French forces steamed across the Mediterranean toward Egyptian ports. The United States deployed the Sixth Fleet, including two aircraft carriers and twenty thousand men, as well as a specially trained and equipped "hunter-killer" antisubmarine force with an additional carrier and five thousand more troops, to monitor Middle Eastern developments closely.[102] According to some accounts, this action was taken to inhibit the progress of the British and French armada. In a dispatch to the British Chiefs of Staff after the Suez operation ended, commander of the Anglo-French forces General Sir Charles Keightley commented that the American "move of the 6th Fleet, which is not so generally known, was a move which endangered the whole of our relations with that country."[103]

The United States introduced a cease-fire resolution in the United Nations Security Council on 2 November that urged all parties engaged in hostilities to agree to an immediate cessation of fighting. It also called on all members to refrain from introducing military goods into the area. The motion was approved sixty-four to five, with Britain, France, Australia, New Zealand, and Israel opposing, and Canada, South Africa, Belgium, Laos, the Netherlands, and Portugal abstaining. The abstention of several NATO nations reflected the divisiveness within the alliance of this confrontation among its most influential members.

The British and French governments, determined to proceed, defied the United Nations censure. Up to the last moment, it remained inconceivable to the British that the Americans would publicly humiliate their closest ally. Lloyd later wrote, "We felt that we might argue away like members of a family, but at the end of the day would never seriously fall out. Not having the Americans on our side, or at least benevolently neutral, was unthinkable."[104]

The publicly provocative attitudes of certain American officials and their ill-concealed pleasure in witnessing the decline of Britain's empire undoubtedly spurred the British onward in the execution of their battle plan. On 2 November, Vice President Nixon proclaimed: "For the first time in history we have shown independence of Anglo-French policies towards Asia and Africa which seemed to us to reflect the colonial tradition. This declaration of independence has had an electrifying effect throughout the world."[105] Eden informed Eisenhower on 5 November that despite his deep regret over the breach between them, he would not postpone the planned invasion to allow a United Nations force to implement the cease-fire proposals: "If we draw back now, chaos will not be avoided. Everything will go up in flames in the Middle East. . . . [W]e cannot have a military vacuum while a United Nations force is being constituted and transported to the spot."[106]

On 5 November, an airborne assault by British and French parachute regiments brought about the surrender of Port Said, the northern entrance to the Suez Canal. As Eisenhower won reelection in a landslide on 6 November, Anglo-French seaborne forces laid claim to the canal.[107] Eighteen hours later, their advance was abruptly halted twenty-three miles down the canal from Port Said. The British, succumbing to intense political and economic pressure from Washington, had ordered a cease-fire. Although outraged by London's weakness of will, the French—whose troops were under British command—had no choice but to follow suit and submit to the terms dictated by the Americans.[108]

During this period of diplomatic and military frenzy, a shocking series of events in Eastern Europe further complicated matters for the divided allies. To the enormous frustration of the Americans, developments in Hungary seemed to parallel those in Egypt: as the French and British armies were landing and occupying the canal zone, the Red Army reentered Budapest to crush the Hungarian rebellion.

The ironies of the situation were manifold. The two leading Western European military powers were so completely preoccupied with the situation in the Middle East that they virtually ignored the dramatic events in the European theater. The Hungarian situation created a profound policy dilemma for the United States, exacerbating Washington's displeasure with its allies' endeavors at Suez. Bolstered by the signs of liberalization in Poland earlier in October, Eisenhower's policy had been "to explore the chances of helping to assist centrifugal, disruptive currents in the Iron Curtain countries." Consistent with this approach, United States officials considered whether to employ military force to counter the Soviet offensive against Hungary.[109]

The Americans, however, were constrained by the actions of their two principal NATO allies. Although they vociferously opposed the Anglo-French plan of attack and its colonial undertones, they could not credibly criticize Russian imperialism in the Soviet sphere of influence while Britain, France, and Israel (the only Western-style power in the Middle East) were laying claim to Egypt. Central Intelligence Agency Director Allen Dulles complained to his brother, the secretary of state, "How can anything be done about the Russians, even if they suppress the revolt, when our own allies are guilty of exactly similar acts of aggression?"[110]

The Hungarian case remains a subject of considerable—if unresolved—speculation. Did the Soviet Union invade Hungary because of the apparent weaknesses and divisions in the Atlantic alliance at that critical moment? Were the allies unable to respond effectively to a crisis within Europe because of their out-of-area preoccupations? Had the Suez crisis not erupted, would NATO's response to Hungary have been different? Although there may never be definitive answers to these questions, they collectively underscore a central and enduring fact of life for the alliance: its resources can be stretched thin, its solidarity undermined, and its security diminished by the global commitments of its individual members.

In addition to their activities in Hungary, the Soviets made their presence felt during the brief period of military action in Egypt. When the British bombardment of Port Said began, loudspeakers announced that Soviet help was coming and that London and Paris had been bombed. Marshal Bulganin, chairman of the Soviet Council of Ministers, subsequently told the British, French, and Israelis that the Soviet Union was prepared to use force to "crush the aggression." In letters to Eden and Mollet, Bulganin ominously threatened to use a "rocket technique"—a veiled reference to nuclear missiles—against their two countries if peace were not restored. He also told Eisenhower, "If this war is not stopped, it is fraught with danger and can grow into a Third World War."[111] Although American intelligence sources concluded that the Soviets had neither the long-range missile capability nor the nuclear warheads to make good on their threat to attack Britain and France, Washington feared that Moscow might intervene directly in the Middle East.[112]

In reaction to their growing concern that the Soviets might exploit the chaotic situation in Egypt to their advantage, the Americans and the British put some of their differences behind them. Eisenhower and Eden resumed their frequent dialogue with remarkable alacrity.[113] Contemplating a meeting, the president commented to Dulles that the Soviet factor presented a critical challenge and that it should supersede any friction over Suez:

> When Eden comes, he will want to talk about what the Bear will do and what we should do in the face of the Russians' acts. There's no point now in making any recriminations against the British; what we need now is to prepare for whatever action we will take if Russia should enter the Middle East while British, French and Israeli forces remain there. We also need a coordinated Anglo-American intelligence effort in the region.[114]

An even more pressing threat motivating British cooperation with the United States was the imminent prospect of the United Kingdom's financial collapse. The pound was being traded at a discount on world financial markets, and there was mounting pressure on sterling reserves. These reserves had begun to fall during September, and

$279 million—15 percent of London's gold and dollar reserves—disappeared during November. Furthermore, on the evening of the cease-fire, Eden announced a 10 percent cut in oil consumption. With the canal blocked, all but one Syrian pipeline blown up, and Saudi Arabia refusing to sell to Britain and France, oil would have to be bought with hard currency.[115]

The Americans, however, pointedly refused to rescue the British from their financial predicament until hostilities had ceased and the Anglo-French forces were withdrawn. Eden, who desperately needed to bolster his own domestic political position in the aftermath of the Suez debacle, believed an early meeting with the American president would serve him well. On 8 November, the prime minister proposed an immediate rendezvous, suggesting that he and Mollet should fly to Washington that evening. Eisenhower agreed, observing that "after all, it is like a family spat."[116] A bit more surprisingly, Mollet also advocated a prompt meeting among the three allied leaders.[117]

This opportunity to mend fences turned into another irritant when Eisenhower cabled Eden later in the day that their meeting would have to be postponed. The president reneged on his initial acceptance largely at the instigation of his advisers, who believed that consultations among the three before the Suez embers had cooled would suggest that the Americans had, in fact, tacitly supported their allies' actions.[118] The prime minister, struggling for his political survival, continued to press for an early meeting in a series of telegrams to the president.[119] No such conference took place before he left office a broken man at the end of the year. Eden commented later that in the wake of the Suez fiasco this rebuff wounded him the most.[120]

In the aftermath of the military action, a United Nations Emergency Force (UNEF) was organized to defuse tensions in the canal zone. In spite of initial British and French disagreement, no major powers were permitted as members because the Americans did not want to create a pretext for Soviet involvement.[121] Two NATO allies—the Danes and the Norwegians—were among those providing troops, and because Nasser objected to Canadian participation, Canada donated support matériel and provided specialist troops as administrative personnel.[122] When the first peacekeeping contingents arrived in Egypt on 16 November, Britain and France still insisted that there were not enough guarantees to the security of the canal for their forces to be withdrawn completely.

But the economic pressures on Britain grew stronger with each passing day. To stabilize its finances, London desperately needed American support for the sterling. In the dead of winter, Western Europe was also running critically short of heating oil. The Americans had refused to shore up the pound or start emergency oil shipments until British and French forces departed the canal zone. On 28 November, British ambassador to Washington Harold Caccia urged London to bite the bullet in bargaining over withdrawal with American officials: "We have now passed the point where we are talking to friends. We are negotiating a business deal."[123] Creating momentum, Eisenhower authorized fifteen United States oil companies to help alleviate the European oil supply problem on 30 November.[124] On 3 December the British and French agreed to repatriate their forces in exchange for American promises of economic assistance. They completed their troop withdrawal on 22 December.

The Impact of Suez on Alliance Politics

Suez confirmed the shifts in the global distribution of power that had taken place in the previous decade. The crisis provoked a dramatic—if overdue—adjustment in the United Kingdom's perception of its own international position. It incontrovertibly established that the Americans controlled the Western policy agenda in the Middle East and that the future success of British policies in the region would depend on United States support. Reflecting the magnitude of the reassessment, on 9 December 1956 an editorial in the London *Observer* asserted that "the Suez crisis has shown that Britain has not got the resources to act as a Great Power in her own right, even in a traditional sphere of British interest. . . . where Great Power politics are concerned, we are dependent on America. We cannot assure our vital oil supplies by our own unaided efforts. We cannot defy Russia without full American backing. We cannot, therefore, 'go it alone.'"[125]

Suez reduced British influence in the Middle East and served as a stark reminder of the constraints on independent action, but it also reinforced Britain's determination to sustain a world role.[126] Concluding they could maintain influence over policy if they educated the Americans about the complexities and perils of the region, the British took on the role of teacher. The tutor's task, the Foreign Office observed, was often thankless: "If the Americans like any of our ideas they will appropriate them and claim them as their own (c.f. the Monroe Doctrine) and we shall have to accept this."[127] Middle East historian Albert Hourani explained why the British chose to channel their energies into shaping the contours of American policy from behind the scenes rather than simply to distance themselves from the United States: "The tension [between them] was partly held in check by the strength of the Anglo-American alliance in other regions of the world, and by the development of the idea of 'the West' as a political concept: to think of Western interests as a single whole, and of England as their guardian, was to give England a claim on American support, and to justify American inertia."[128]

Consequently, the British made every effort to reconstruct the Anglo-American special relationship. In a lengthy letter to Lloyd on 28 December, Ambassador Caccia articulated this pragmatic approach toward Washington: "I assume it to be our object to re-establish our relations on their previous footing and to recover all of our special position. While the Communist threat remains, nothing else makes sense, in dealing with a country whose power is likely to increase in relation to our own."[129] Prime Minister Harold Macmillan, who replaced Eden on 10 January 1957, concurred that the only way to maintain Britain's global influence was to rebuild a close relationship with the United States. If, as Suez had so brutally demonstrated, the United Kingdom could neither afford nor succeed in taking action alone, it would have to rely on extensive Anglo-American cooperation for the defense of its global interests.

Underlying Macmillan's personal determination to recement the bond was the profound and enduring partnership between the United States and the United Kingdom.[130] Despite occasional disagreements and conflicts of interest, the two nations shared a common outlook on the world—including their joint heritage, advocacy of democratic government, and opposition to Communist territorial or ideological expansion—that shaped their foreign policy objectives. Most important, since the establishment of NATO, American and British statesmen had seen it as their shared responsibility to define the alliance's security agenda. Thus in March 1957, less than four months after Suez, Eisenhower and Macmillan held tour d'horizon discussions in Bermuda to coordinate their foreign and defense policies.

A salient example of the post-Suez rejuvenation of the Anglo-American special relationship lay in the field of nuclear cooperation. In a shift the British government described as "the biggest change in military policy ever made in modern times," London decided in 1957 to increase its dependence on nuclear defense, thereby reducing expenditures on conventional capabilities.[131] In 1958, Congress amended the 1954 McMahon Act, which had essentially prohibited the sharing of nuclear information with other countries, to allow American nuclear assistance to Great Britain (this exception was never extended to France). As a result, the upgrading of Britain's nuclear forces was done with Washington's support and close cooperation. There was no little irony in this expanded relationship in that above all the debacle at Suez had triggered British disillusionment with conventional forces and increased emphasis on nuclear defense.[132] The outcome was continued reliance on the benefits of partnership with the United States, in spite of what proved to be the mounting political costs of such a course in Europe.

By autumn 1957, the wounds of Suez appeared almost totally healed. After meetings between Eisenhower and Macmillan in October, the two leaders issued a "Declaration of Common Purpose," which asserted that the task before their nations was to "provide adequate security for the free world."[133] The president and the prime minister also agreed to make a concerted effort to bolster the strained Atlantic alliance. They invited NATO Secretary-General Paul-Henri Spaak to participate in some of the October discussions, and the three men decided to upgrade the December NAC meeting to an unprecedented heads-of-government summit.[134] The British aggressively worked to counter the centrifugal impulses within the alliance, and they did so in characteristic fashion: by attempting to reinforce the security link between Europe and the United States.[135]

During the December 1957 sessions, Macmillan sought and received NATO agreement on the stationing of American intermediate range ballistic missiles on allied soil.[136] Ironically, Macmillan's attempt to reunite the alliance sowed the seeds of dissent. By increasing allied reliance on nuclear weapons, the strategy of massive retaliation also reduced the pressure on Europe to develop its own conventional defense capabilities. This fomented allied resentment by expanding the Europeans' dependence on the United States and thereby eroding their control over their security and their destiny.[137]

Suez had the opposite effect on France that it had on Britain, strengthening French aspirations for independent status and fueling their pursuit of an autonomous foreign and defense policy.[138] Paris began to pursue a strategy of maneuver on the margins of the alliance:[139] while maintaining formal membership in NATO, France pushed its national sovereignty to the limit. When Charles de Gaulle returned to power two years later, he capitalized on these deeply ingrained tendencies toward dealignment.

The experience at Suez further soured the French toward any form of allied cooperation beyond Europe. Reinforcing the lessons of Indochina, they concluded that reliance on allies not only constrained their action but could jeopardize or undermine the pursuit of France's global interests. Since the French held the Americans responsible for the failure of the Suez expedition, they subsequently sought to dissociate themselves from their membership in an alliance dominated by the United States, particularly with respect to developments outside the NATO area.

Suez also led the French to question the fundamental credibility of the American security commitment to Europe. Pineau commented acidly, "The principal victim of the Suez affair was the Atlantic Pact," adding, "If our allies had abandoned us in difficult, if not dramatic circumstances, they were capable of doing so again if Europe in turn found itself threatened."[140] Indeed, French statesmen still recall that when the Soviets threatened to rain nuclear missiles on London and Paris during the Anglo-French invasion, the United States did not seem particularly energized. By underscoring the questionable reliability of the American nuclear guarantee, the crisis emboldened those who believed that France should be prepared to defend itself with a nuclear capability of its own. At the end of 1956 the French government decided to build a plutonium reprocessing facility, enabling France to proceed to the production of nuclear weapons.[141]

After Suez, France began to turn toward a European vocation, believing that its leadership could create a counterbalance to the American superpower. Weakened by the failed Middle Eastern operation, the Mollet government pursued European unity both as an alternative to American hegemony and as a means of compensating for French impotence in Algeria.[142] Perceiving the establishment of the Common Market as a prime opportunity to gain political leverage within Europe, Paris also envisioned it giving its members the collective power to play a consequential role on the world stage. German Chancellor Konrad Adenauer remarked in a meeting with Mollet, "Europe will be your revenge."[143] Further complicating alliance politics, the French concept of Europe became exclusively Continental in the wake of Suez. Lloyd remembered France's antipathy toward any further cooperation with Britain: "The high hopes that it would lead to a new phase of a closer entente cordiale were dashed. The project had failed; many Frenchmen blamed us for it."[144]

For the United States, Suez heralded a changing of the guard. Henceforth, the Middle East would no longer be the preserve of the British but another playing field in the struggle between East and West on which the Americans would have a decisive role. While the principal interests of the United States and the United Kingdom continued to overlap, and though the Americans factored British concerns heavily into their decisions, Washington established itself as a major and independent force in the regional struggle for power.

This high American profile manifested itself most explicitly in the Eisenhower Doctrine, conceived by the president on the day of the Suez cease-fire, presented to Congress on 5 January 1957, exactly two months after the Anglo-French invasion, and signed into law on 9 March.[145] Eisenhower made the case that Middle Eastern security, long built around the power of several European nations, could no longer be guaranteed by them alone. Because of the region's geographic and economic value (in particular, its oil resources), the president predicted that the Soviet Union might manipulate the instabilities of newly independent regimes there to its advantage. Making an explicit connection between the interests of the Atlantic alliance and developments in the Middle East, he argued that if the Soviets were able to dominate the Middle East, "Western Europe would be endangered just as though there had been no Marshall Plan, no North Atlantic Treaty Organization."[146] The United States therefore had to assume greater responsibilities for the region.

The administration sought and received congressional approval for a three-pronged policy: (1) cooperation with nations in the Middle East desiring economic and development assistance; (2) the establishment of military assistance programs for any nations seeking such aid; and (3) if necessary, the employment of armed forces to help any nation or nations "requesting assistance against armed aggression from any country controlled by international communism."[147] With this commitment, the United States assumed an active role in the region. Although the British remained the dominant allied presence east of Suez for another decade, the Americans never again allowed their allies to control Western policy toward the area.

Just as the Suez crisis profoundly marked relations among the three principal NATO powers, it also affected the evolving definition of NATO's formal role in out-of-area crisis management. In this instance, as in most other developments beyond Europe that confronted the Atlantic allies, the formal NATO consultative mechanisms were not used. Instead, communications took place on an ad hoc basis between and among those allies whose direct interests were engaged in the particular dispute. The British and the French intentionally avoided consulting the other allies through official NATO channels about their Suez plans, although they informed individual allies on a bilateral basis and let it be known that the use of force had not been excluded as an option. They did not make an announcement in the NAC prior to the onset of military activity, as would have been standard practice.[148] While the NATO structure proved irrelevant, alliance issues remained dominant throughout the crisis. The NAC met repeatedly behind closed doors during the first week of November to discuss the situation. During these sessions, Britain and France were severely criticized for the lack of consultation and for the embarrassing coincidence of events in Egypt and Hungary.[149] The developments at Suez affected NATO not only because of what was at stake in the canal zone but because of their impact on alliance cohesion.

Throughout 1956, a committee of "Three Wise Men"—Halvard Lange of Norway, Gaetano Martino of Italy, and Lester Pearson of Canada—conducted a NATO-sanctioned study on the nonmilitary dimensions of the alliance relationship.[150] The impact on the alliance of events in Korea, Indochina, and the unfolding drama of Suez figured prominently in the motivations behind the project. Included in the questionnaire sent to all member governments in midsummer 1956 was the question, "Should consultation extend to problems outside the NATO area?"

Issued in December 1956, the "Report of the Committee of Three on Non-Military Cooperation in NATO" answered, "There cannot be unity in defence and disunity in foreign policy." In the alliance's first officially sanctioned acknowledgment of the importance of systematic consultation on matters of common interest not only within but beyond Europe, the report asserted:

NATO should not forget that the influence and interests of its members are not confined to the area covered by the Treaty, and that common interests of the Atlantic Community can be seriously affected by developments beyond the Treaty area. Therefore . . . they should also be concerned with harmonising their policies in relation to other areas, taking into account the broader interests of the whole international community; particularly in working through the United Nations and elsewhere for the maintenance of international peace and security and for the solution of the problems that now divide the world.

Significantly, it also addressed the issue of differentiation in allied interests and capabilities. This was of greatest concern to the smaller NATO powers, since the out-of-area entanglements of the principal allies were beyond their capacity to influence or control. Lending an institutional blessing to the already established pattern, the report recognized that the formation of ad hoc groupings based on mutual interest was an effective means of concerting policy.[151]

As such, the three wise men provided useful terms of reference and guidelines for the management of global challenges to alliance cohesion. As Suez had so vividly demonstrated, however, there was an endemic tension between individual national interests and collective alliance interests that, in extremis, could not be resolved. That NATO survived the worst intra-allied out-of-area crisis in its history attested to the members' overriding strategic interests in the maintenance of the Atlantic alliance.

Times of Turbulence: De Gaulle Confronts the Anglo-American Special Relationship, 1958–1961

The omnipresent Soviet threat to Europe kept the fundamental allied commitment strong throughout the fifties despite disagreements over the handling of developments beyond the NATO area. Ironically, because NATO was effective in deterring a potential Soviet attack on Western Europe, most of the military challenges affecting allied interests during this decade took place outside the European theater. From 1958 to 1961, disagreements over out-of-area crisis management strained alliance solidarity, much as they had at Dien Bien Phu and Suez. Furthermore, President Charles de Gaulle's return to power in France in 1958 dramatically changed the dynamics of alliance politics among the three principal NATO powers. While the Anglo-American connection was restored to its former warmth, the Franco-American and Anglo-French relationships continued to deteriorate, presaging difficulties that would plague the alliance during the 1960s.

Crisis Management in Lebanon and Jordan

The rapid resuscitation of the special relationship after Suez manifested itself in the concerted management of Middle Eastern developments. The Anglo-American partnership was largely symbiotic: it remained in the underlying interest of both parties to harmonize their activities. The Americans still preferred that the British take major responsibility for the defense of the region, thereby freeing United States resources for commitments elsewhere. And in retaining those duties, the British claimed the role of mentor and tutor to the American newcomers. This role allowed London both to shape and check United States policy.

As American policy toward the Middle East evolved, the British found some vindication for Suez. Selwyn Lloyd noted that Washington began to recognize that "the elimination of our colonial empire would simply add to American burdens" and that perhaps they had bungled the whole Suez affair.[1] In his diary entry for 13 May 1958, Macmillan noted, "Fortunately the Americans have learned a lot since Suez, and the Bermuda and Washington visits are beginning to show results."[2]

Since Suez, Nasser had caused increasing trouble in the Middle East for the NATO allies. In April 1957, only one month after Congress approved the Eisenhower Doctrine, the American president deployed the Sixth Fleet off the coast of Lebanon to deter threats to Lebanese sovereignty from pan-Arab agitators thought to be inspired by Nasser. The potential crisis was defused before any United States troops went ashore. But in January 1958, Egypt and Syria united to form a new nation, the United Arab Republic (UAR). To American and British officials, this was the opening gambit in Nasser's renewed campaign to assert control over Iraq, Jordan, Lebanon, and Saudi Arabia. Washington and London were also leery of the extent to which Moscow might exploit Nasser's gains.

Tensions mounted throughout the spring of 1958. Seeking self-protection, the two monarchies in the region, Iraq and Jordan, formed their own federation, the Arab Union. In a coup d'état on 14 July, rebel forces assassinated the Iraqi royal family, overthrowing the regime that the Western powers considered the main bulwark against Communist expansion in the region and that they had counted on to champion resistance to Nasser. American intelligence sources reported that a similar coup was planned for 17 July against King Hussein of Jordan.[3] President Chamoun of Lebanon and King Hussein promptly asked Washington and London to take military action. Eisenhower later recounted Macmillan's attempt to convey a coded message over an open telephone line: "We have had a request from the two little chaps."[4] Chamoun warned the American, British, and French ambassadors that if the West did not intervene within forty-eight hours, he would be assassinated and Lebanon would become a satellite of Egypt.[5]

The close and constant nature of Anglo-American consultations on the Middle East during the spring and summer of 1958 was an excellent example of effective informal out-of-area cooperation. As events unfolded, Eisenhower and Macmillan were in what the president described as "finger-tip" communication.[6] Their military staffs conducted contingency planning for force deployments in response to predicted crises in Lebanon and Jordan. Among plans devised for intervention was Operation Bluebat, which called for the joint deployment into Lebanon of two American Marine battalion landing teams and a British infantry brigade. Similarly, in an exercise code-named Combine II, the United States Marines, British Royal Marines, and Italian Navy were scheduled to practice joint landing operations off the coast of Southern Sardinia in the Western Mediterranean.[7]

In response to Chamoun and Hussein's appeal, the Americans and the British improvised a last-minute division of labor. Eisenhower decided against British participation in Operation Bluebat, concluding that United States forces would be adequate and that the British should use their 3,700 troops stationed on Cyprus for other purposes. Macmillan observed, "With regard to Lebanon, since the President had suggested that we might be wiser to preserve our forces, we were inclined to agree that this was the proper course, for they would certainly be needed elsewhere."[8] Thus United States amphibious troops landed at Khalde Beach near Beirut International Airport on 15 July; two days later, British paratroopers were flown into Jordan. Their somewhat ill-defined objective was to prevent any further upheavals on the Iraqi model. Several months later, when the situation in the Middle East appeared more stable, the allied forces were withdrawn.

De Gaulle was confronted with the prospect of Western involvement in Lebanon and Jordan shortly after he became president of France on 1 June 1958. He alleged that Washington and London not only rejected his offers of assistance in the Middle East but also failed to consult him about operating in Lebanon, where France had strong historical ties and responsibilities based on the Tripartite Declaration. French protestations about the lack of advance consultation to the contrary, Dulles and de Gaulle had in fact talked at length about the likelihood of American intervention in the Middle East during meetings in Paris on 6 July 1958. At that time the secretary of state rejected the French request to participate in any Western deployment; given France's previous colonial role in Lebanon, the Americans had concluded that a reintroduction of French troops would be a political liability. De Gaulle acknowledged this refusal with the mild comment, "If it becomes necessary to defend Western interests in the Levant, France will not be found absent."[9]

At the conclusion of their Paris meeting, Dulles and de Gaulle agreed that their governments should keep in close touch both with each other and with the British as the situation evolved.[10] The French president was therefore clearly aware of impending Western military activity in the Middle East, although he was only informed of the actual landings one hour before they took place.[11] Acknowledging that an extensive exchange had taken place, Foreign Minister Maurice Couve de Murville recollected, "Paris was advised simultaneously, whereas ten days before, the hypothesis of such a military intervention was discussed at length with Foster Dulles and it was understood that consultations would be pursued."[12]

Even though a private transatlantic understanding had been reached, the noisy public airing of differences, no matter how disruptive to Franco-American relations, proved useful in the French domestic political context. Thus French statesmen complained loudly that they were neither consulted nor informed in advance of the military action when in actuality both events had taken place. De Gaulle subsequently justified the minimal French contribution—sending the *Brest* to ensure the safety of French residents in Beirut—as an affirmation of French independence: "We held aloof from their joint expedition and sent a cruiser to Beirut to establish our separate presence."[13] The exclusion of France from the Anglo-American military action intensified French resentment of the special relationship and reinforced their growing inclination to loosen the Atlantic tie.

The Soviet reaction to the landings in Lebanon and Jordan further exacerbated French frustration with Anglo-American control over Western policies beyond Europe. Khrushchev sent de Gaulle, Eisenhower, Macmillan, and Nehru messages stating that the world was "on the brink of a military catastrophe" and that "the slightest imprudent move could have irreparable consequences."[14] Although there has never been any confirmation that Khrushchev intended to take further action, his communiqué nonetheless reinforced latent French anxieties that Anglo-American out-of-area exploits threatened France's national security.

The formal involvement of NATO in the crisis was limited to an ex post facto endorsement of the troop landings by the NAC, apprised of the military action only as the marines were going ashore in

Lebanon.[15] But NATO forces and infrastructure played key roles in the Anglo-American engagement. The European-based Twenty-fourth Airborne Brigade of the United States Army replaced the British in the execution of Operation Bluebat. United States air forces in Europe transported this NATO-designated battle group of sixteen hundred American army troops from its base near Munich, West Germany, to a NATO base in Adana, Turkey, for deployment to Lebanon. The airborne battle group, designated Force Alpha, arrived in Beirut on 19 July. Adana also served as the base for the formation of a Composite Air Strike Force, composed of B-57s and F-100s flown from the United States. The Marine Corps used Lajes air base in the Azores for refueling its aircraft en route to Beirut; other American transport planes were refueled in Rome. The Atlantic Fleet was also put on alert, as were all tactical and logistical units of the United States air forces in Europe.[16]

The unofficial power hierarchy that had existed in the alliance since its creation was reflected in the fact that the rest of the allies were summarily informed rather than consulted about the deployments and the use of their national facilities. The Americans and the British most often defined the interests of the West beyond Europe; the other NATO members had no choice but to acquiesce, since they relied on the deterrent power of the United States for their own security. The West Germans expressed the greatest alarm about United States actions and raised questions about the legality of using bases on their soil for the American airlift, but their influence over the out-of-area actions of the principal NATO powers was limited.[17]

Washington's purpose in orchestrating the Lebanon-Jordan interventions in the summer of 1958 was to establish the broader credibility of American security commitments. It was, therefore, aimed as much at Moscow as it was at Cairo. It was also designed to reassure those dependent on the United States—including the smaller NATO powers—that in a crisis Washington would make good on its promises of protection. Deputy Under Secretary of State Robert Murphy described Eisenhower's perspective: "He said that sentiment had developed in the Middle East, especially in Egypt, that Americans were capable only of words, that we were afraid of Soviet reaction if we attempted military action. . . . He wanted to demonstrate in a timely and practical way that the United States was capable of supporting its friends."[18]

On the Brink over the Offshore Islands

During the summer of 1958, another crisis was brewing in Asia. Beginning on 23 August, the People's Republic of China heavily bombarded the Nationalist-occupied offshore island groups of Quemoy and Matsu, a buffer zone between Taiwan and the mainland where Chiang Kai-shek had stationed one hundred thousand men, or one-third of the Nationalist ground forces. The barrage continued through the beginning of September and was supplemented by a successful seaborne blockade that prevented any resupply of the islands. Eisenhower and Dulles concluded that a Communist takeover of Quemoy and Matsu would lead to the collapse of Chiang Kai-shek's regime and that this would initiate a chain reaction throughout Asia. The United States therefore prepared to use its military might—including, if necessary, nuclear weapons—to protect these exposed territories against further aggression and Communist takeover.[19]

As a first step, American military capabilities in the Formosa Strait were enhanced. On 26 August, the Seventh Fleet was placed on alert; it was shortly reinforced by two aircraft carriers, one heavy cruiser, and four destroyers. An additional squadron of air force jet fighters was also deployed to the region. Then, on 4 September, Eisenhower formally announced that the United States would become actively engaged in protecting Quemoy and Matsu. Dulles warned that to break the blockade and resupply the islands the American navy would henceforth escort Nationalist convoys, and he hinted that the United States might use nuclear weapons to repel a Communist invasion. By 21 September the blockade had been broken, and a cease-fire was reached on 6 October.[20]

In explaining the rationale behind United States involvement, Eisenhower illustrated how the Americans believed they were acting in defense of the interests of the West writ large. He recalled, "The security of the western Pacific was essential but we were there not just to save the islands but also to demonstrate that force should not be used for aggressive purposes in the modern world."[21] As in the case of Lebanon, the message that the full repertoire of American power would be used to deter Communist expansion was aimed as much at Moscow as it was at the local enemy.

From the French perspective, however, American unilateral decision making regarding the possible use of nuclear weapons raised the specter that had haunted the allies in Korea: would the United States take on the People's Republic of China directly, and if so, would that not inevitably lead to World War III? Couve de Murville remembered, "Thus a potentially very serious crisis developed, whereas no concertation had been organized among the occidentals at least as far as France was concerned."[22] Employing what in diplomatic parlance is an extremely strong term, he later described the unilateral nature of American decision making regarding the management of the crisis as "unacceptable."[23] Whereas the British chose to air any differences they had over the handling of the situation privately and in any case not to allow them to hinder Anglo-American cooperation on issues of greater import,[24] de Gaulle used Washington's behavior during the summer of 1958 to reinforce his case for distancing France from NATO.

The Challenge of Charles de Gaulle

De Gaulle's return to power presented a potent challenge to Atlanticism. With French confidence in United States leadership of the Atlantic alliance at a low ebb, de Gaulle focused on developing European policies that could offset American power or that would at least allow the European members of NATO to participate in a more genuine way in shaping allied policies. Couve de Murville described the new French government's outlook: "France demonstrated its will for independence, which would refuse neither friendship nor alliances, but only subordination; its desire to play around the world, in the interest of peace, a role consistent with its calling."[25]

Since Prime Minister Pleven had unsuccessfully proposed the establishment of a three-power consultative body for global policy coordination among the Americans, the British, and the French in 1951, French officials had expressed grievances against United States dominance of the alliance. In de Gaulle's first meetings with American and British leaders after his accession to power in 1958, he raised again the issue of trilateral decision making on global security.[26] He told NATO Supreme Commander General Lauris Norstad that France wanted to play a central role in developing Western strategy around the world.[27] During discussions with Macmillan at the end of June and then again in meetings with Dulles on 5 July, de Gaulle made suggestions that foreshadowed the formal proposal he submitted for a three-power "Directorate" the following autumn.

In his exchange with Dulles, the French president warned that France would degenerate internally unless it perceived itself to be a "world power." Consequently, de Gaulle argued, issues of global security and nuclear deterrence should be coordinated at the highest level among France, Britain, and the United States. Since, in his view, Germany was not yet a major Western power, it should not be a member of this trilateral steering committee. De Gaulle also lobbied for extending the NATO guarantee to cover the Sahara and the Middle East, where France had vital interests at stake.

Dulles's reply was consistent with previous rebuffs by Washington: a formalized "world directorate" would be resented by other countries. Instead, the three principal allies should continue consulting each other informally on problems of common interest and coordinating their policies on an ad hoc basis whenever possible.[28] The timing of the Anglo-American nuclear cooperation agreement compounded this rejection: it was signed just one day before the encounter between de Gaulle and Dulles. This unfortunate coincidence reinforced French sentiment that an Anglo-American atomic condominium imposed its hegemony on the rest of the alliance.[29]

French sensitivity to the events of the summer of 1958 proved to be an early warning signal of the clash between Gaullism and Atlanticism in the decade ahead. Reopening the national wounds of Dien Bien Phu and Suez, the crises in the Middle East and the Formosa Strait emboldened de Gaulle in his quest to reassert France's independent margin of maneuver. De Gaulle concluded that, after nearly a decade in NATO, the status quo of the immediate postwar years no longer sufficed: neither American nor Anglo-American hegemony could be tolerated. Couve de Murville articulated the Gaullist perspective on the alliance commitment in a pointed critique:

> Only a fundamental reform of interallied relations would permit the attainment of real change. Either France would be narrowly associated with the United States, and of course also with Great Britain, for security related matters, beginning with the use of strategic arms, or she would be driven to reconsider her positions and notably participation in NATO that in fact commits her to follow America without being either really consulted, or as the case may be, in agreement.[30]

On 17 September 1958 de Gaulle sent Eisenhower and Macmillan a "Memorandum" detailing his formal proposal for a three-power

Directorate.[31] In his covering letter, the French president alluded to American preoccupations with the situation in the Far East, indicating that the timing of the offer was indeed related to French concerns about recent international developments.[32] In the Memorandum, which reached Washington on 25 September, de Gaulle asserted that the Atlantic alliance no longer corresponded to global political and strategic exigencies:

> The world being as it is, one cannot consider as adapted to its purpose an organization such as NATO, which is limited to the security of the North Atlantic, as if what is happening, for example, in the Middle East or in Africa, did not immediately and directly concern Europe, and as if the indivisible responsibilities of France did not extend to Africa, to the Indian Ocean and to the Pacific, in the same way as those of Great Britain and the United States.

French security needs, he continued, were therefore no longer being fulfilled by NATO. He proposed the establishment of an organization for the development of "world policy and strategy" composed of the United States, Great Britain, and France:

> It would be up to this organization, on the one hand, to take joint decisions on political questions affecting world security and on the other, to establish and if necessary, to put into effect strategic plans of action, notably with regard to the employment of nuclear weapons. It would then be possible to foresee and organize eventual theaters of operations subordinated to the general organization (such as the Arctic, the Atlantic, the Pacific, the Indian Ocean), which could if necessary be subdivided into subordinate theaters.

Although de Gaulle initially envisaged the Directorate as a tripartite steering group integrally linked to the alliance, his fundamental objective was the alignment of global—and specifically nuclear—policy among NATO's three principal powers. At the time, Macmillan made notes to himself that de Gaulle "suggested a world organization, under an Anglo-American-French triumvirate. NATO would be the European branch of this; other parts of the [free] world similarly."[33] De Gaulle emphasized the non-European dimension of the proposal in subsequent encounters with his American and British counterparts.[34] In late 1958, Couve de Murville confirmed de

Gaulle's focus: "Yes, in effect, it does amount to a veto on the use of nuclear weapons anywhere in the world." He elaborated by explaining that de Gaulle's intent stemmed from a particular concern about the employment of nuclear weapons in out-of-area contingencies: "If China attacks Taiwan, America may have to strike back with atomic weapons. This could lead to world war if Russia reacts. As your allies we would be plunged into war with you, without ever having been consulted or having participated in the chain of events. Do you think this is reasonable?"[35]

In the Memorandum, de Gaulle also advanced an explicit threat that differentiated the Directorate proposal from all previous discussions of a tripartite NATO steering group. Claiming the new arrangement was indispensable, he asserted that the French government would henceforth subordinate "to it as of now all development of its present participation in NATO," adding that he might provoke a revision of the treaty if France's demands were not accommodated. This warning was the "thunderbolt"[36] of the 17 September missive. De Gaulle had thrown down the gauntlet: he was prepared to distance France from the Atlantic alliance in order to reassert the nation's stature as a global, and hence great, power.

There is debate about whether de Gaulle was serious about the proposal—whether he actually expected the Americans to agree to worldwide shared control over nuclear weapons, and more broadly, whether he genuinely intended to bind French foreign and defense policy beyond Europe into a tripartite framework. On both accounts, the evidence suggests that de Gaulle never believed the Directorate proposal would be accepted or implemented.

Given the mistrust and mutual apprehension that had accrued since the early fifties between Washington and Paris, greater French authority over the use of American nuclear weapons was nothing short of inconceivable. De Gaulle also knew from previous exchanges with the Americans that they and the British opposed the creation of an official, formal hierarchy within the alliance on the grounds that any such arrangement would fragment NATO by reducing the incentive for participation and cooperation among the smaller members. Couve de Murville summarized the French strategy: "We never expected the United States to accept" the proposal; the Memorandum was "tactical."[37]

The fact that de Gaulle may have intentionally generated resistance to the Directorate among the weaker alliance members corroborates Couve de Murville's point. De Gaulle provided NATO Secretary-General Spaak with a copy of the Memorandum on the day before it reached Washington and London. Further, a résumé of its contents was passed to the West German and Italian ambassadors in Paris.[38] Spaak's reaction, as well as those of the German and Italian governments, was predictably negative.

Writing to de Gaulle on 15 October, Spaak harshly criticized the proposal. He disagreed with the premise that only the United States, the United Kingdom, and France had interests beyond Europe. Not only did the Netherlands, Portugal, and Belgium retain commitments spanning the globe, but more important, all the members of the alliance had shared interests in and might be led into conflict by developments outside the treaty area. Further, if the less powerful allies were deprived of the opportunity to discuss and consult about global concerns with the three principal NATO powers, they would lose their only means of defending their ideas and interests in the alliance and would be likely to take refuge in neutrality. Spaak thus argued against the creation of a tripartite global steering group for NATO, claiming, "One must take into account the fact that this conception, if it were realized, would signify the end of the Atlantic Alliance."

Spaak further warned that neither Italy nor West Germany would ever agree to such a plan and that "rather than submit to a global directorate from which they would be excluded, they would reclaim their total political independence, with all the dangers that such an act would represent both for Europe and the cohesion of the Western world."[39] West German Chancellor Adenauer was indeed angered by the scheme, believing that he had been duped since de Gaulle simultaneously had been extolling the virtues of Europeanism.[40] An Italian ambassador allegedly went so far as to suggest that "his government would be obliged to re-examine its entire foreign policy if America and Britain agreed to a tridirectorate."[41]

De Gaulle's orchestration of the Directorate's stillbirth was the opening gambit in a series of provocations designed to expand the French margin of independent action while continuing to reap the benefits of political and military partnership with the United States. De Gaulle was not so much insincere in his proposal as stubborn: he would proceed only on his own ideal terms. Since those terms were clearly unacceptable to the Americans and the British, and to the less powerful allies, he turned the offer's inevitable rejection to his advantage by using it as an excuse to pursue an autonomous course. He later confirmed this explanation: "I was trying to find a means of leaving the Atlantic Alliance and of reclaiming the freedom lost during the Fourth Republic at the time of the signing of the North Atlantic Treaty. Thus, I demanded the moon. I was sure that they wouldn't give it to me."[42] Eisenhower recalled the predicament of being on the receiving end of de Gaulle's inflexible appeal: "I would say to him, look, I'll do everything else. I'll consult you as you request. I'll promise to make no move and neither will the British unless we've all agreed that we'll do this thing by study, but let's don't proclaim it publicly as a three power directorate. But de Gaulle would have none of it, nothing less than his demands." He also recollected, "Our biggest argument as presidents came out of this idea he was sold on, to have a publicly proclaimed triumvirate."[43]

Eisenhower sent de Gaulle a written reply to the Directorate proposal on 20 October 1958. The president agreed that the threat to the free world was a global one and reminded de Gaulle that this fact had animated American foreign policy since the beginning of the Cold War. The creation of a network of regional security alliances had not only defended the participants but also had ensured the development of a critically important "habit of consultation" among them. The United States and France, Eisenhower pointed out, benefited from consultation on global issues in two such arrangements, NATO and SEATO. He argued that it was necessary to avoid doing anything that would destroy or set back "this developing intimacy among all the members of NATO and the closer bonds it forges." The impression must not be given to the rest of the allies "that basic decisions affecting their own vital interests are being made without their participation." The president explained that he foresaw serious problems "both within and outside NATO, in any effort to amend the North Atlantic Treaty so as to extend its coverage beyond the areas presently covered."[44] In an interview several years later, Eisenhower recalled his admonitions to de Gaulle about the potential impact of such a plan on other NATO members: "I'd say that I believe that in the long run we've got to have the support of West Germany, of Italy and of the rest of Western Europe, as well as France. Now, Mr. President, if we are going to just tell them that they are going to have to do such and such—while we are going to do so and so—why pretty soon they are going to say, now hold on there, you are making us second-class citizens and then they will desert us."[45]

The consistently negative American attitude toward a formalized Western three-power Directorate reflected historic resistance in the United States to alliance commitments any broader than absolutely necessary. It also reflected the conviction that global policy coordination among the principal NATO powers would be less frustrating to the weaker members of the alliance and less likely to provoke international suspicion if it took place unofficially, informally, and outside NATO channels. Eisenhower later recalled his reservations about the institutionalization of three-power planning: "I believed that any attempt to organize a coalition of the 'Big Three' NATO nations would be resented by all the others to the point that NATO itself might disintegrate. . . . What we should be seeking . . . was the substance and benefits of co-ordinations, not the facade of self-assumed authority among three great nations."[46]

Eisenhower did not, therefore, exclude the possibility of enhanced cooperation beyond Europe among the three principal NATO powers. Despite the strength of his opposition to any formal restructuring of alliance management of out-of-area issues, he promoted opportunities for ad hoc, informal coordination. To this end, he instructed Dulles to set up a subcabinet level "tripartite committee." Under this rubric Dulles proposed the initiation of three-power planning for Africa in December 1958. De Gaulle, who hoped that French interests in the region would benefit from allied support, welcomed the idea with one important caveat: "Of course, a common policy in North Africa would necessarily be a French policy."[47] Although the subject was discussed at irregular intervals for the next few years, the idea of routinized consultations on Africa did not bear fruit. An abortive series of meetings took place in Washington in April 1959, and de Gaulle never appointed a delegate to the proposed tripartite committee on Africa.

The British shared the American perspective on the disadvantages of an official three-power Western steering committee, albeit for somewhat different reasons. The special relationship was flourishing on a bilateral basis. Extending it to the French would have inhibited the intimacy of the Anglo-American rapport and diffused British influence over policy making. As Macmillan observed in contemporaneous notes to himself, no one had ever tried to "institutionalise" the exceptional relations between the United States and the United Kingdom and no one would try to do so.[48] Such formality would have been the antithesis of the private, flexible, and responsive bilateral dialogue on which the two countries relied.

The British were also concerned about the impact of the Directorate concept on other NATO members and, hence, on alliance cohesion. In his 21 October 1958 reply to de Gaulle's Memorandum, Macmillan proposed that he and de Gaulle meet to explore the problems that the British foresaw in the proposal, including its implications for the Federal Republic of Germany and for control over the use of nuclear weapons. De Gaulle was apparently noncommittal and indeed unresponsive to the request, letting London know that Washington was his real target.[49]

The last two years of the Eisenhower administration were marked by a growing distance between the United States and France. In March 1959, de Gaulle announced that the French fleet in the Mediterranean "would no longer be available to NATO in times of war." This "de-earmarking" of France's ships indicated that de Gaulle intended to act independently both inside and outside the NATO area and that he did not consider himself bound by the alliance commitment to refrain from doing so.[50] Subsequently, de Gaulle prohibited the introduction of American strategic nuclear weapons or their launchers in France.[51]

During this period, the French president repeatedly raised the issues of global cooperation and shared control over the use of American nuclear weapons in letters and meetings with United States officials. In so doing, he skillfully constructed the case for distancing France from the alliance. When Dulles made a special trip to Paris in July 1959 to defuse growing tension over the Directorate proposal, he attempted to placate de Gaulle by inviting the French to participate in tripartite military consultations. Recognizing that the three-power steering group for NATO was a dead letter, de Gaulle shifted ground. He advanced the argument that NATO itself should be expanded to cover the Middle East and at least all of Africa north of the Sahara, adding that the structure of the alliance should also be revised.[52] De Gaulle reiterated this new concept in a speech the following year, asserting that "France intends that the Atlantic Alliance should cover the whole planet so that the free world will be defended everywhere where there are free men."[53] Although his scheme for restructuring NATO by expanding the treaty area was as unrealistic as the original Directorate proposal, it generated additional ammunition for the battle to liberate France from American hegemony.

In August 1960, Eisenhower again endeavored to assuage de Gaulle, making another proposal "that would not contemplate formal combined staff planning, but rather talks among military representatives on all strategic questions of interest to France in various parts of the world, primarily outside the NATO area." De Gaulle did not respond to this offer; instead, he asked again for a meeting to deal with global problems and to reorganize the alliance. Eisenhower replied by inviting de Gaulle to elaborate his views on NATO in another memorandum.[54]

De Gaulle's only answer came in response to questioning at a press conference on 5 September 1960. He was queried about his attitude toward NATO and asked to explain the reforms he was demanding. Dwelling on familiar issues, he asserted that the limitation of the Atlantic alliance to Europe was no longer adequate. For the three principal NATO powers, something needed to be organized "from the point of view of the Alliance" with regard to their political and strategic activities beyond Europe. He asked rhetorically, "If there is not agreement among the principal participants of the Atlantic Alliance on subjects other than Europe, how will one be able to maintain indefinitely the Alliance in Europe?"[55]

The French president continued to insist on a tripartite Directorate within NATO even after Eisenhower and Dulles had made several offers to establish forums for the discussion of the issues that ostensibly concerned de Gaulle. Furthermore, de Gaulle never came forward with specific proposals for the reorganization of NATO. His refusal to acknowledge the American concessions and his unwillingness to respond seriously to such initiatives buttress the argument that the Directorate was a useful ploy rather than a realistic plan. The Eisenhower administration left office without resolving the problem.

De Gaulle and President John F. Kennedy discussed the question of tripartism in their first encounter in early June 1961, but the idea of a formal Directorate remained unrealized. During these meetings, Kennedy proposed high-level three-power military contingency planning for Laos, the Congo, and Berlin. Although de Gaulle said he would move to implement the plan, he never did so. The last time the topic of tripartism was raised specifically was in a letter de Gaulle sent to Kennedy in January 1962 in which he yet again advocated a permanent tripartite political planning group and common military staff to prepare "common decisions and common actions" and suggested that this group might begin by dealing with the "nonaligned nations."[56] The bottom line was that nothing short of his original and admittedly chimerical proposal would satisfy the French president.

The full potency of Charles de Gaulle's subsequent endeavors to diminish French dependence on NATO can only be understood against this backdrop. The seeds of France's growing estrangement from the alliance had been sown in Indochina and at Suez. During the late fifties, as Anglo-American cooperation intensified and de Gaulle's claims to great power status were rebuffed or ignored, France's alienation from NATO grew more acute. It became clear in the early sixties that competition between de Gaulle's vision of a European Europe and Kennedy's dream of a strengthened Atlantic partnership would severely strain the alliance. The endurance of NATO despite de Gaulle's formidable challenge to its solidarity attested to the overriding security interests its members shared.

CHAPTER FIVE

Grand Design or Troubled Partnership: Challenges to the Alliance, 1961–1968

The struggle between American-led Atlanticism and Gaullist-inspired Europeanism plagued the Atlantic alliance throughout the sixties. Harvard professor Stanley Hoffmann has depicted this conflict as one between those who believed in an Atlantic Europe in which NATO members would seek to influence the United States from within the alliance and those who envisaged a European Europe that would emancipate the allies from American predominance and give them a greater margin of independent maneuver.[1] These competing visions fostered dissension within the alliance over the handling of challenges beyond the treaty area.

This period also bore witness to a reversal of historic roles. Additional strains emerged among the allies over out-of-area crisis management as the United States grew stronger and more self-confident and assumed a greater share of responsibility for areas previously overseen by the Europeans. Capturing the spirit of this new era in American foreign policy, President Kennedy announced on 29 January 1961 that the United States was prepared to "pay any price, bear any burden" to protect freedom around the world.[2] American conduct of the Cuban Missile Crisis and the Vietnam War reflected the vast power and influence that superpower status conferred on Washington.

Although Washington urged its partners to maintain their global positions and participate in out-of-area engagements, the European members of NATO generally drifted toward Eurocentrism. Burned all too often by their overseas commitments, the allies were increasingly disinclined to sustain them; instead, they shifted their focus to the security of their own immediate boundaries. By the end of the decade, the British had entered a phase of retrenchment from the Middle East and the French had relinquished Algeria. Henry Kissinger captured the American perception of Europe's global perspective: "As a result of decolonization, our European Allies have ceased to think of themselves as world powers. . . . No European government, with the possible exception of the United Kingdom, is likely to be convinced that its security is jeopardized by events in another part of the globe."[3] During the Kennedy-Johnson era, a major source of friction between the United States and its NATO allies lay in competing views of Europe's global role and responsibilities.

Atlanticism versus Europeanism

Kennedy's vision of a closely integrated but Atlantic-oriented Europe—led by the United States and dependent on America's strength as a global superpower—was diametrically opposed to de Gaulle's vision of Europe. De Gaulle's Europe was to be unified politically under French leadership and ultimately to provide for its own defense. In 1961, France proposed that the Fouchet Plan for European integration serve as the basis for a union of Western European states.[4] The United Kingdom was caught in the middle of this struggle for leadership of the West. Macmillan originally conceived of the phrase "the Grand Design," but it became synonymous with Kennedy's Atlanticist model. Ironically, one of Macmillan's objectives in coining the term had been to convince de Gaulle to look on Britain as a partner in Europe and, more specifically, to accept British entry into the Common Market.[5] Reflecting on the United Kingdom's predicament, a de Gaulle biographer has written:

> The execution of de Gaulle's vast plan coincided with the launching of a vast American concept: Kennedy's proposal for an Atlantic partnership with Europe. In the middle was Great Britain, torn apart by conflicting commitments to America, Europe and its own Commonwealth. The uncivil war between de Gaulle and the Anglo-Saxons was about to enter its most bitter phase, "The Battle of the Grand Designs." The battlefield was principally Europe, but the conflict of interests spread around the world and involved the world.[6]

In setting forth his goals for the alliance, Kennedy emphasized that the United States viewed European integration as an essential element of expanded ties across the Atlantic. He made this case in a Fourth of July speech in 1962:

> We do not regard a strong and united Europe as a rival but as a partner. . . . We believe that a united Europe will be capable of playing a greater role in the common defense . . . and developing coordinated policies in all other economic, diplomatic and political areas. We see in such a Europe a partner with whom we could deal on a basis of full equality in all the great and burdensome tasks of building and defending a community of free nations.[7]

In exchange for a strengthened, integrated Europe transcending its internecine rivalries, Kennedy promised to allow a "full give-and-take between equals, an equal sharing of responsibilities, and an equal level of sacrifice."[8] This image of the partnership between the United States and Europe has been described as the "twin pillars" or "dumbbell" theory of alliance, in which a balance is struck between powers of equal weight.[9]

Through the Grand Design, the United States also projected an enhanced European role in managing out-of-area challenges to allied interests. When Kennedy spoke on 25 June 1963 at the Paulskirche in Frankfurt, the American message was clear: "We look forward to a Europe united and strong, speaking with a common voice, acting with a common will, a world power capable of meeting world problems as a full and equal partner."[10] Unfortunately, this scheme fueled rather than quelled frustration among European NATO members over the imbalance of power within the alliance. The American argument that the Europeans should unify in order to advance the collective global interests of the alliance was neither compelling nor convincing precisely because such interests were not always shared. Kissinger explained the misplaced rationale behind the initiative: "A decade and a half of hegemony have accustomed us to believing that our views represent the general interest."[11]

In establishing the precondition that European unity must precede the achievement of greater equality in the NATO hierarchy, Kennedy unwittingly emboldened de Gaulle in his crusade against American dominance. De Gaulle's vision of a united Europe with France at the helm was the antithesis of the entity that Kennedy viewed as a prerequisite to the success of the Grand Design: it was to be the foundation for the pursuit of a separate, European-oriented identity. In his efforts to foster the establishment of a political union in Western Europe, de Gaulle worked vigorously against the concept of the Grand Design and, indeed, he willfully destroyed it.

Torn between the United States and Europe, the United Kingdom found itself in a complicated predicament. Britain's search for an appropriate identity in the twilight of the Empire created a profound dilemma over which of several options to pursue: an intimate partnership with the United States, a reinvigorated role as leader of the Commonwealth, or a wholehearted entry into Europe.[12] Choosing a mixture, British foreign and defense policy in the first half of the decade was marked both by a significant shift toward Europe as well as by a continuing commitment to maintaining an independent world role in close cooperation with the United States. In trying to combine all three alternatives, however, Britain risked succeeding at none.

The April 1961 decision to apply for Common Market membership was a watershed, reversing decades—indeed centuries—of British foreign policy. Macmillan described it as "a turning-point in our history."[13] Not only did the United Kingdom hope that continental cooperation would provide a stimulus to British industry, but also it sought a new leadership position in Europe as the power and prestige of its imperial identity waned. Arguing that Britain's world influence would grow through participation in the Common Market, Macmillan instructed the House of Commons: "If there are little Europeans, and perhaps there are, is it not the duty of this country, with its world-wide ties, to lend its weight to the majority of Europeans who see the true prospective of events? I believe that our right place is in the vanguard of the movement towards the greater unity of the free world, and that we can lead better from within than outside.[14]

Other aspects of the British outlook on international affairs contradicted and indeed undermined this bold move toward Europe. In 1962, the British reaffirmed their commitment to sustaining a presence not only in Europe but in the Middle East, Asia, and Africa in the "Statement on Defence," the first comprehensive look at future policy since the five-year plan prepared in the aftermath of Suez. The statement actually downplayed the European component of the United Kingdom's defense responsibilities. Instead, emphasis was placed on the requirements of being a global power and, more specifically, on the upgrading of the British military commitment East of Suez at the expense of investment in Europe. With respect to NATO the statement stressed Britain's worldwide contribution to allied security: "We have to take account of the tasks we have to perform in other parts of the world, tasks which contribute to the containment of Communism and the maintenance of peace and order in areas whose stability is vital to the West."[15]

Furthermore, the United Kingdom's profound ambivalence about joining the Continent across the Channel derived in significant part from concern about whether Britain's entry into the Common Market would jeopardize its special relationship with the United States.[16] The outcome of meetings Kennedy and Macmillan held in Nassau in late December 1962 reflected the unresolved nature of Britain's European identity. The agreement the two leaders reached to substitute the new American Polaris submarine for the canceled Skybolt missile program linked the British nuclear deterrent to the United States for the foreseeable future. The Nassau arrangement stipulated that the submarines were to be provided for the purposes of defending the "Western Alliance" under the aegis of NATO, although in a situation of extreme peril, the British could choose to use them independently.[17] By moving toward further integration rather than greater independence in defense policy, the British government expanded the unique ties between London and Washington to the detriment of those across the English Channel.

The French interpreted this development as confirmation that British loyalty remained with the "Anglo-Saxons" rather than with the Europeans. A French defense official allegedly remarked after Nassau that Britain's agreement was "incompatible with choosing Europe."[18] From de Gaulle's perspective, the enhancement of the nuclear bond between London and Washington demonstrated that the Americans had no intention of permitting Europe to become self-sufficient in defense and that the British intended to exploit their privileged position to remain the dominant power in Europe. The French president was even more offended that the Polaris deal was offered to France only after negotiations had been completed between the United States and the United Kingdom. Not surprisingly, de Gaulle categorically rejected the proposition. British defense analyst Laurence Martin observed, "This development sharply differentiated British post-Suez policy from that of France and contributed to the exclusion of Britain from the political development of Europe."[19]

The United Kingdom's post-Suez calculus—that Anglo-American nuclear cooperation and the maintenance of British out-of-area commitments would enhance the special relationship and advance London's interests—prevailed through the mid-sixties. In spite of de Gaulle's disdain, the British continued to derive power and influence from their intimate association with the United States and from their extra-European responsibilities, most pointedly reflected in the ongoing and global nature of the Anglo-American dialogue. During the Cuban Missile Crisis of 1962, for instance, Britain was the only ally with whom Washington maintained regular communications; indeed, Kennedy was in daily contact with Macmillan. Following the Nassau meetings, American Secretary of State Dean Rusk reflected on the value of exchanges with the British: "We can't break with Britain. We have to be able to discuss world problems with someone. We can't discuss them with de Gaulle. We and the British don't always agree. But we discuss."[20] Significantly, when the United Kingdom finally scaled back its global commitments later in the decade, it would not do so because of some abstract commitment to Europe, but rather because its resources were no longer adequate to the task.

The Missiles of October

Cuba lies geographically beneath the Tropic of Cancer and even the waters surrounding it are beyond NATO's boundaries. Thus the emplacement of Soviet missiles on Cuba in October 1962 and the subsequent American naval blockade took place outside the treaty domain. However, in the age of nuclear parity and extended deterrence, the distinction between developments inside and outside the NATO area became increasingly blurred. The Cuban crisis revolved around the perceived direct Soviet threat to the territory of the United States—and, therefore, to territory covered by the NATO treaty. Under Secretary of State George Ball described the explicit challenge created by the stationing of Soviet missiles in Cuba: "There can be no doubt whatever that the intrusion of nuclear weapons into that unfortunate small country posed as much of a threat to Europe as to America. These missiles were to have been targeted on the strategic deterrent forces of the United States. In the last analysis the security of Europe and America alike—indeed of the whole free world—rests on the strength of that deterrent."[21] NATO's security was directly implicated during the crisis by the unprecedented high state of tension between the superpowers and by the active consideration of a linkage between Soviet withdrawal of the missiles in Cuba and American removal of NATO-designated Jupiter missiles based in Turkey. The Cuban crisis was thus a searing reminder for the European allies of how their security and, indeed, their destiny, depended on decisions and commitments made by American statesmen.

Following his 22 October speech to the nation revealing the discovery of the Soviet missile deployment, President Kennedy put American strategic nuclear forces at the highest state of alert in the history of the atomic era: DefCon 2, or full readiness for hostilities. A message went out to NATO Supreme Commander General Norstad, "warning him to be on the alert for possible trouble in the NATO area."[22] The United States imposed a naval quarantine on shipments of military hardware to Cuba, and more than five hundred American combat aircraft and one hundred thousand troops were rushed to Florida, the nearest staging area.[23]

But as preparations for an air strike and possible invasion were made, the group of senior officials convened by Kennedy to manage the crisis—the Executive Committee of the National Security Council (ExComm)—began to explore alternative means of defusing the crisis. As early as 19 October, Secretary of Defense Robert McNamara suggested that the only workable solution might be for the United States to relinquish its missile bases in Turkey and Italy in exchange for Soviet withdrawal of the missiles from Cuba.[24] The ExComm deliberations on a "trade" reached a critical point on 27 October. Soviet Premier Khrushchev, who in a missive on the previous day had indicated an inclination to settle the dispute without any American quid pro quo, baffled the ExComm members by sending a second letter through foreign ministry channels that proposed an explicit trade of missiles in Cuba for missiles in Turkey.[25] In their search for an appropriate response to the Soviet leader's confusing signals, the president and his advisers exhaustively examined the possibility of an exchange, focusing most of their discussion on the potential impact on the Turks and, more broadly, on NATO solidarity and morale. The proposal did not require a substantive concession by the United States or by NATO, since Kennedy had previously requested the removal of the Jupiter missiles from Turkey and they had already been withdrawn from Italy and the United Kingdom.[26]

The transcripts of the 27 October 1962 meetings reveal that the alliance implications of American actions loomed large, especially in the president's mind and in that of his national security adviser, McGeorge Bundy. Kennedy repeatedly suggested that a NAC meeting should be convened, observing, "I'm just afraid of what's going to happen in NATO, to Europe, when we get into this thing more and more, and I think they ought to feel that they've a part of it. Even if we don't do anything about the Turks, they ought to feel that they know."[27] Bundy emphasized the liabilities of a public trade, arguing that from the European perspective "it would already be clear that we were trying to sell our allies for our interests. That would be the view in all of NATO. It's irrational, and it's crazy, but it's a *terribly* powerful fact." Later in the day he added, "I think that if we sound as if we wanted to make this trade, to our NATO people and to all the people who are tied to us by alliance, we are in *real* trouble . . . that's the universal assessment of everyone in the government that's connected with these alliance problems."[28]

Kennedy's concern for the impact on the allies was tempered, however, by his clearheaded appreciation of the consequences of a superpower military confrontation. McNamara warned that if the United States attacked Cuba, the Soviets would most likely retaliate: "If we leave U.S. missiles in Turkey, the Soviets might attack Turkey. If the Soviets do attack the Turks, we must respond in the NATO area." The world would then be engulfed in war.[29] Although the president recognized that a trade would have negative consequences, he preferred them to uncontrollable escalation. Kennedy observed, "When we take some action in Cuba, the chances are that he'll [Khrushchev] take some action in Turkey, and they ought to understand that." Later on in the day's deliberations, the president called attention to the merits of a trade:

> I'm just thinking about what—what we're going to have to do in a day or so . . . all because we wouldn't take missiles out of Turkey, and we all know how quickly everybody's courage goes when the blood starts to flow, and that's what's going to happen in NATO, when they—we start these things, and they grab Berlin, and everybody's going to say, "Well that was a pretty good proposition." Let's not kid ourselves that we've got—that's the difficulty. Today it sounds great to reject it, but it's not going to, after we do something.[30]

Kennedy's logic dictated a two-track strategy for defusing the crisis. The United States government refused to link NATO's defenses with the Cuban situation and it insisted in all its public statements and its exchanges with the Soviet Union that there would be no explicit trade. The president also chose to sidestep Khrushchev's second letter. In what became known as the "Trollope Ploy," so named for the Victorian novelist's heroines who interpreted ambiguous gestures as offers of marriage,[31] Kennedy accepted the Soviet leader's initial vaguely worded offer to withdraw the missiles if Washington pledged not to invade Cuba. Underscoring the widespread public perception that the administration had steadfastly refused to contemplate an exchange, the *New York Times* reported that "though the Turkey missile base had no great military value, it was of great symbolic importance to a stout ally. To bargain Turkey's safety for the greater security of the United States would have meant shocking, and perhaps shaking, the Western alliance."[32]

At the same time, however, Kennedy undertook several discreet initiatives with respect to the Turkish missiles designed to deescalate the crisis. First, at McNamara's urging, he ordered the fifteen Jupiter missiles deactivated to retard any potential nuclear escalation in Europe, to show that the United States did not intend to use them, and to prevent their unintended use if the Soviets attempted to attack and capture them.[33] Second, he instructed his brother, Attorney General Robert F. Kennedy, to offer a private assurance to Soviet Ambassador Anatoly Dobrynin that if Khrushchev removed the Cuban missiles, the United States would take its missiles out of Turkey. McNamara recalled that the president gave specific instructions: "Bobby should inform Dobrynin that the Jupiters would be withdrawn, though he shouldn't conclude a public deal to that effect."[34] The bargain depended on absolute secrecy: its impact on alliance politics could only be managed if the arrangement was never consummated as an official trade. Kennedy emphasized the importance of discretion: "This was not the time for concessions that could wreck the Western alliance, seeming to confirm the suspicion Charles de Gaulle had planted that the United States would sacrifice the interests of its allies to protect its own security."[35]

In addition to protecting NATO from negative repercussions, this arrangement provided Khrushchev with a face-saving device. In private, he could reassure the Kremlin hard-liners and Moscow's allies, especially the Chinese (who at the time actively advocated the use of nuclear weapons to vanquish so-called imperialist forces), that he had extracted a key concession from Washington in exchange for the removal of the Cuban missiles.

Even more revealing of Kennedy's mindset was another secret arrangement only disclosed a quarter century after the crisis.[36] Although he was unable to reach a consensus among his advisers, the president concluded that it was not worth risking inadvertent nuclear war over fifteen obsolete missiles. Thus if the Soviets had not responded affirmatively to the Trollope Ploy in conjunction with the secret assurance, Kennedy was prepared to make a public trade. He set the machinery in motion through Dean Rusk. Rusk telephoned Andrew Cordier, until earlier that year a senior United Nations official, and dictated the text of a statement proposing the removal of both the Jupiter missiles and the missiles in Cuba. If Kennedy had decided to enact the plan, Cordier was to provide United Nations Secretary-General U Thant with the text so that he could publicly propose the deal. For face-saving reasons, it would have been easier for Washington to accept such an offer from the symbolic leader of the international community—an impartial mediator—than to accept the Soviet proposal directly. Since the secret communiqué reflected the substance of Khrushchev's second letter, the president assumed that Moscow would agree to it as well and that the crisis would be defused. Rusk recently recalled, "That step was never taken and the statement I furnished to Mr. Cordier has never seen the light of day. So far as I know, President Kennedy, Andrew Cordier and I were the only ones who knew of this particular step."[37]

On the morning of 28 October, Washington learned that on Moscow radio Khrushchev had announced his acceptance of the American reply to the initial Soviet proposal, and workers began almost immediately to dismantle the Cuban missile sites. Although Kennedy's fall-back option was never implemented, its significance was undiminished. In defusing the most menacing out-of-area crisis ever faced by the Atlantic alliance, the president calculated that NATO solidarity would best be preserved by avoiding nuclear war rather than by avoiding the appearance of trading away European security.

Seen from the European perspective, America's partners were caught in a double bind by the developments in Cuba. They faced two distinctly unattractive alternatives: being blackmailed by the Soviets into trading away symbols of their own security or being subjected to nuclear escalation. Secretary of the Treasury Douglas Dillon observed during the ExComm deliberations: "If you have a [NAC] Council meeting you'll probably get a strong reaction from a great many of the members of NATO against our taking any action in Cuba. They say, 'Don't trade,' but they also say, 'Don't do anything in Cuba.'"[38] The gravity of the situation, however, was reflected in the formidable display of allied unity in support of United States policy throughout the crisis.

Washington had little time, much less inclination, to consult its allies during the thirteen intense days after discovering the Soviet missile installations in Cuba. The sole exception was Britain, which was the first to be informed and the only country with which there was any regular communication about the situation throughout October. In what became the first of a series of daily telephone conversations with Kennedy, Macmillan gave the American president his full support. Writing in his diary on 4 November 1962, Macmillan noted, "We were 'in on' and took full part in (and almost responsibility for) every American move." He added, "Our complete calm helped to keep the Europeans calm."[39] Macmillan was adamant, however, that any deal that traded NATO assets for removal of Soviet missiles in Cuba would destroy the credibility of the American security guarantee to Europe.[40]

During the crisis itself, de Gaulle was uncharacteristically supportive of Washington. When former Secretary of State Acheson traveled to Paris on 21 October to brief de Gaulle on Kennedy's impending announcement of the blockade and quarantine of Cuba, the French president's initial response to Acheson's demarche was, "Are you consulting or informing me?" Although de Gaulle's instinct that the latter was taking place was correct, he nevertheless told Acheson that he clearly understood why the United States had taken decisions without consulting the allies: "You can tell your President that France will support him. . . . I think that under the circumstances President Kennedy had no other choice. This is his national prerogative and France understands."[41] In addition, de Gaulle made it clear that if the Soviets attacked the United States, France would immediately invoke article 5—the collective defense provisions—of the Atlantic treaty.[42]

On 24 October, as the ExComm explored its options, Rusk cabled the American ambassadors to NATO and to Turkey, asking for their assessments of the likely impact of a trade on the alliance and on bilateral relations between Washington and Ankara. A consensus emerged that the repercussions would be quite serious. Summarizing the case, a State Department memorandum asserted: "The Jupiters are not important as a military-strategic asset—but then, neither is Berlin. Yet both have elemental significance as symbols of the integrity of the Alliance and especially of our commitment to stand by the interests of each of its members."[43]

The Turks were never directly consulted about the removal of the Jupiter missiles. The ExComm members decided against discussing the issue with Ankara because they believed that doing so would shake Turkish confidence and that news of American consideration of a trade might leak, thereby weakening Washington's bargaining stance. George Ball warned the ExComm on 27 October: "If we talked to the Turks, they would take it up in NATO. This thing would be all over Western Europe, and our position would have been undermined. . . . Because immediately the Soviet Union would know that this thing was being discussed."[44]

Similarly, although Acheson had briefed the NAC after he met with de Gaulle, the NAC was neither consulted nor informed about any of the deliberations that followed the imposition of the blockade on 22 October. During the 27 October ExComm discussions, Kennedy repeatedly argued that NATO needed to be updated on the increasingly perilous situation. Since the crisis was defused within twenty-four hours, such an exchange never took place. Yet despite the closed nature of American decision making during this period, all the allied governments stood behind the United States.[45] Whatever their frustrations and fears, every NATO member knew that Western solidarity was vital during a superpower confrontation.

Notwithstanding this display of allied unity, the fact that Washington acted unilaterally and in so doing controlled the fate of Europe encouraged de Gaulle to distance France from the Atlantic alliance. The Cuban Missile Crisis was certainly not the principal cause of the French president's frustration with the United States, but it added to the balance sheet that he had already tallied: Indochina, Suez, Lebanon, the Chinese offshore islands, and the failure of the Directorate proposal. Moreover, the missile crisis confirmed his suspicion that the United States might well jeopardize European security to protect its own interests in a region of little import to the rest of the allies. The result, in de Gaulle's words, would be "annihilation without representation."[46]

In the aftermath of the missile crisis de Gaulle accelerated his effort to scuttle the Grand Design. This was blatantly evident in his efforts to obstruct British membership in the fledgling European Economic Community (EEC). On 14 January 1963, de Gaulle vetoed British entry into the Common Market, thereby demolishing the European pillar of Kennedy's vision for the alliance. He likened British participation in the Common Market to the entry of an American Trojan horse:[47] "In the end there would appear a colossal Atlantic Community under American dependence and leadership which would soon completely swallow up the European Community. . . . It is not at all what France wanted to do and what France is doing, which is a strictly European construction."[48]

De Gaulle's obstructionist tactics extended to the realm of security cooperation. To leave NATO, Couve de Murville recalled, France needed to have "free hands."[49] As soon as France's economic and military resources were no longer being drained by the Algerian war, NATO's significance to French security declined. Beginning in July 1962, French troops repatriated from Algeria to France were not reassigned to NATO and were instead maintained under national command. In June 1963, the French Atlantic fleet was removed from the NATO integrated military command, which led to the departure several months later of French officers from allied naval staffs.[50] There should have been no doubt in anyone's mind that it would only be a matter of time before de Gaulle would formally withdraw from NATO: France had already ceased to play its designated role.

Indochina Revisited

The Cuban Missile Crisis was not the only major out-of-area crisis of the sixties. During the early years of the decade, the Kennedy administration had discreetly but consequentially augmented the level of American involvement in Vietnam: in 1961, 692 United States military advisers were there; by 1962, that number had jumped to nearly 12,000.[51] Through the Tonkin Gulf Resolution of 7 August 1964, President Lyndon B. Johnson secured what he interpreted to be the full permission of the United States Congress to wage war in Indochina.[52] By early 1965, American ground troops had become directly engaged in the fighting; on 7 February, United States planes began bombing North Vietnam. In 1966, the number of American troops in Southeast Asia more than doubled, rising from 190,000 to 390,000; by 1968, the number had reached 500,000.

The Vietnam War had a significant long-term impact on NATO's effectiveness and cohesion. During the Johnson years, the United States diverted vast resources to Vietnam at the expense of NATO modernization—it is estimated that Washington spent $150 billion on the incremental costs of the war—and reduced both the quantity and quality of American troops in Europe to provide for the Indochina commitment. Robert Komer, under secretary of defense for policy in the mid-sixties, observed, "We robbed our NATO forces blind from 1965 to 1972." Compounding this, the post-Vietnam backlash against the use of military force led to deep cuts in American defense spending during the next decade, approximately 20 percent from 1971 to 1976.[53]

Although few specific figures have ever been made available, the existing evidence indicates that the war—and, more specifically, the way in which President Johnson attempted to wage the war in the face of eroding popular support—had a significant adverse effect on NATO readiness. The administration's decision not to mobilize new forces but, nevertheless, to expand those on active duty in Vietnam resulted in a serious deterioration of United States forces in Europe.[54] This choice was based largely on a calculation of American domestic political costs. The president foresaw that calling up the reserves would further undermine public backing for the war by connoting an emergency rather than a gradual build-up and by involving the middle and upper-middle classes in the fighting.[55] Reflecting the priority he assigned to victory in Southeast Asia, Johnson instead diverted first-quality assets intended for Europe—including both manpower and matériel—to Vietnam.[56]

In 1966, fifteen thousand American troops were withdrawn from the Federal Republic of Germany and sent to units in the United States that were being readied for duty in Vietnam.[57] Because of the desperate need for trained military manpower in Southeast Asia, the best of the Seventh Army's soldiers and an unquantified amount of equipment were removed from Europe and replaced largely by untrained or less highly skilled men, thereby reducing the combat readiness of United States forces in Europe. Furthermore, the logistics and support forces in Europe were cut back below the level considered necessary to provide adequate support for combat units there. The *New York Times* reported on 8 April 1966, "Over all, both numerically and qualitatively, the United States forces in Europe are at a lower level of strength than at any time since before the Berlin Crisis in 1961."[58] However, underscoring the Johnson administration's determination to pursue the war despite its apparent impact on other theaters, Secretary of Defense McNamara vehemently denied that NATO was being adversely affected. In congressional testimony on 21 June 1966 he insisted that "the U.S. is capable of maintaining its combat capability in Europe while continuing to meet planned troop deployments to Southeast Asia."[59]

The United States announced further cuts in its troop commitment to Europe in October 1967. In order to increase combat strength in Vietnam to 525,000, it diverted to Asia one of the five divisions normally earmarked for European reinforcement within the first sixty days of a major war.[60] By the final year of the Johnson administration, almost 60,000 American troops had been withdrawn from Europe.[61] European military strategists held that the diversion of forces normally earmarked for NATO wartime reinforcement would not seriously reduce allied security. The diminished strength, quality, and combat readiness of United States troops stationed on European soil represented a much more worrisome trend. Only the French, who believed that a nuclear war was the only war that would be fought over Europe, thought none of the cutbacks were significant.[62]

In addition to depleting NATO's defenses in Europe, the Vietnam War also engendered a long-resonating movement to reduce the American commitment to the Atlantic alliance. Senator Jacob Javits's comments in April 1966 exemplified growing American frustration with Europe: "We should remind them that we stood by them in their great hour of need when they might have gone down the drain. Why don't we press them on Vietnam? What is wrong with pressing them? Why are we so touchy and so fastidious?"[63] During a congressional hearing on 16 June, Senator Henry Jackson outlined the connection between the war in Southeast Asia and the American commitment to Europe: "I don't know of any question currently that is so much in discussion on Capitol Hill as the problem that I raised earlier—the question of a possible cutback in American forces in Europe. Many feel this should be done especially with the problem we face in Vietnam and in view of the fact that we have asked our NATO partners all through the years to make a greater contribution of ground forces."[64]

The notable absence of allied assistance in Vietnam, the French withdrawal from NATO's integrated military command in March 1966, and the general feeling that the United States was overcommitted and undersupported throughout the world fueled a series of legislative efforts to reduce substantially the number of American forces based in Europe. Championed by Senator Mike Mansfield, the first such resolution was introduced in the Senate on 31 August 1966—the day before de Gaulle delivered a blistering attack at Phnom Penh on American policy toward Southeast Asia. The resolution advised that a significant cutback be made in the number of American forces permanently stationed in Europe.[65] Although Mansfield's resolution was never adopted, its content gave voice to an increasingly powerful constituency that believed the burdens of Western defense were not being shared satisfactorily by the European allies.

As the United States became ever more preoccupied with the Vietnam War at the expense of its other global commitments, the European members of NATO—with the notable exception of France—were becoming increasingly parochial. They seemed to have neither the resources nor the will to play an active world role. In a *Foreign Affairs* article in 1965, British historian Alastair Buchan observed the portentous implications of this shift:

> Clear consideration of the relationship between NATO and the security of Asia and Africa has been bedeviled in recent years by what has been called "the reversal of roles" . . . But what has unquestionably been a courageous American acceptance of the responsibilities of its new power has been accompanied by an American doctrine that the United States will pay attention only to those European allies who are prepared to make a material contribution to extra-European security.[66]

American policymakers knew that they would have to wage the war in Southeast Asia without a large military contribution from the allies. They nevertheless assumed that the shared commitment to the containment of Communism, as had been the case in Korea, would ultimately motivate the Europeans to take action in support of the United States. In a speech in March 1965, Rusk exhorted the NATO members to look beyond their own regional security interests:

"Europe and the North Atlantic Community cannot preserve their security merely by holding a line across Europe. Their common security is involved also in what happens in Africa, the Middle East, Latin America, South Asia, and the Western Pacific. They have a vital common interest in the defeat of active aggression in Southeast Asia."[67]

Although the plea for European participation was addressed to all of the allies, the United States specifically stressed the importance of Britain's contribution to global security. Washington pushed for British assistance on two fronts: first, for material support for the war effort itself and, second, for the maintenance of a presence in other regions—especially in the Middle East—so that the Americans could concentrate their resources on Indochina. Skeptical of Washington's policies in Southeast Asia and strapped for resources, the United Kingdom tendered only lukewarm support for the American endeavor. Although this created an irritant to the Anglo-American relationship, it did not inhibit cooperation elsewhere. Continuing the established pattern, leaders of the two nations maintained a constant dialogue, and their differences over the substance and implementation of policy rarely turned into public rows.[68]

During the early years of the war, London used its commitment of thirty thousand troops to the defense of Malaysia in the 1963–1965 "confrontation" with Indonesia as an alibi for avoiding involvement in Vietnam.[69] The principal British pretext for not taking a more active role in the war, however, was that doing so would compromise Britain's position as co-chair of the Geneva Conference on Korea and Indochina and thereby make it difficult for the United Kingdom ultimately to play the role of mediator. This tactic, while precluding direct involvement, permitted London to demonstrate to Washington its potential contribution to the resolution of the conflict and to suggest British influence over American actions.[70] In a meeting in April 1965, Prime Minister Harold Wilson and President Lyndon Johnson reached what Wilson described as a "division of function," which served as the public rationale for the lack of a British military presence in Vietnam. Wilson recalled the terms of their agreement: "The American government would not be deflected from its military task; but, equally, he [Johnson] would give full backing to any British initiative which had any chance of getting peace-talks on the move."[71]

Nevertheless, Johnson still campaigned, albeit unsuccessfully, for a British military contribution. The importance of a public display of solidarity was a driving factor behind the president's demands for support. In February 1965, Johnson had told Macmillan, "As far as my problem in Vietnam we have asked everyone to share it with us. They were willing to share advice but not responsibility. . . . If you want to help us some in Vietnam send us some men and send us some folks to deal with these guerrillas. And announce to the press that you are going to help us." In July 1966, the American president, desperately seeking legitimation of the escalating military activity, inquired urgently about the possibility of a token force. He told the prime minister that a platoon of bagpipers would be sufficient; it was the British flag that Johnson needed.[72]

With rapidly expanding responsibilities in Southeast Asia, the United States also counted on the United Kingdom to maintain a Western foothold in other parts of the world. American arguments that Britain should maintain its overseas commitments, especially East of Suez, had deep resonance and were therefore considerably more persuasive than those pertaining exclusively to Indochina. The British continued to favor the retention of a global role, even at the expense of Europe. This was particularly true in light of de Gaulle's rejection of the United Kingdom's entry into the Common Market. In January 1964, before becoming prime minister, Wilson asserted that a thousand men East of Suez were preferable to another thousand in Germany.[73] In the latter half of 1965, the United States put substantial pressure on the British government to retain its presence East of Suez. Indeed, it has been alleged that the Americans threatened that their pledge to buy British military and aircraft equipment depended heavily on the United Kingdom's maintenance of its world role.[74] In an early 1966 comment to his cabinet colleagues, Wilson explicitly acknowledged the link between a continued British presence East of Suez and forthcoming American economic assistance: "Don't let's fail to realize that their financial support is not unrelated to the way we behave in the Far East: any direct announcement of our withdrawal, for example, could not fail to have a profound effect on my relations with L.B.J. and the way the Americans treat us."[75]

At the same time, larger economic realities gnawed away at British resolve. The 1966 "White Paper on Defence" observed that in the future the United Kingdom could not afford to sustain all of its overseas commitments. Arguing that Britain was suffering from global overextension, the government asserted: "To maintain all our current military tasks and capabilities outside Europe would impose an unacceptable strain on our overstretched forces, and bear too heavily both on our domestic economy and on our reserves of foreign exchange." Although the White Paper established that limitations needed to be imposed on the employment of military force outside Europe, it made only very general recommendations with respect to reconciling capabilities with commitments.[76]

Despite American entreaties, the United Kingdom relinquished the lion's share of its world role during the Vietnam era and limited its major commitments to Europe and the Mediterranean. Indeed, the ineffectiveness of the American war effort in Asia cast a long shadow on the value of sustaining the capacity to deploy force beyond the European theater and of doing so alongside the United States.[77] The devaluation of the pound in November 1967 dealt the final blow to any remaining hopes that the United Kingdom might be able to afford to sustain its global enterprise. In 1968 the British reduced their capability to take action outside the NATO area by evacuating Aden; reducing their forces in Malaysia, Singapore, and the Persian Gulf (and eventually abandoning their bases in the gulf); canceling the acquisition of fifty F-111A aircraft; and phasing out their carrier force.[78] By 1969, the die was cast. Reiterating and expanding on a statement made in the previous year announcing the future concentration of resources on Europe and the North Atlantic area, the British government asserted: "The basic aim of our defence policy is now fully established. It is to ensure the security of Britain by concentrating our major effort on the Western Alliance. . . . the task is irreducible; we can withdraw from East of Suez but not from our situation in Europe, on which our national security depends."[79]

The French, by contrast, were relentlessly and outspokenly critical of American involvement in and conduct of the Vietnam War, but they neither consequently nor significantly reduced their overseas commitments during the sixties. From the beginning of the Kennedy administration, de Gaulle made known his opposition to escalation of the Indochina conflict. During their late spring 1961 meetings, the French leader warned the new American president against becoming mired in the Southeast Asian imperial swamp: "France had tried it" and had learned its lessons, drawing the conclusion that a military solution was not possible.[80]

As the war escalated despite his admonitions, de Gaulle's message was clear and consistent: he did not intend to play Washington's global game, and, indeed, might intentionally frustrate American objectives outside of Europe. When France reestablished diplomatic relations with Peking in January 1964, it sent out a strong signal of its determination to remain autonomous of any "Alliance" policy in Asia.[81] In April, when the final declaration of the Southeast Asia Treaty Organization meetings in Manila lent unreserved support to United States actions in Vietnam, de Gaulle refused to associate France with the communiqué. Paralleling its stance vis-à-vis NATO, France then abstained from participating in subsequent SEATO meetings to protest American policy in the region.[82] In autumn 1964, de Gaulle paid visits to ten Latin American countries, encouraging them to take an independent stance with regard to the superpower to the north.[83]

The French affected a "holier than thou" attitude as the United States became increasingly entangled in Vietnam. Having painfully extricated themselves from Indochina in the 1950s and from Algeria in 1962, they were disdainful of the apparent inability of the United States to change its course. In a press conference on 9 September 1965, de Gaulle announced that France sought in Southeast Asia

> the effective end of all foreign intervention, and therefore the complete and controlled neutralization of the zone in which there is fighting. This is what France, for her part, subscribed to in 1954. This is what she then strictly observed. This is what she considers necessary, since the United States intervened in Indochina after the departure of France's forces. But it is all too obvious that this is not the road being followed.[84]

As the American bombings escalated, Paris found its warnings falling on deaf ears. Couve de Murville recounted that "it was clear that nothing could shake American determination."[85]

If 1966 was a climactic year in the Vietnam War, it was also the most turbulent period in Franco-American relations. Indeed, there appeared to be an element of schadenfreude in the French attitude toward the American predicament in Indochina. In late January, against the advice of the French and the British, Johnson decided to bomb Vietnam intensively. On 7 March, the French finally withdrew officially from the NATO integrated military command and demanded the withdrawal of foreign forces—referring to the Americans and Canadians—from France.

Announcing the withdrawal of French forces from the integrated military command, de Gaulle underscored how differences with the United States over out-of-area policies motivated his action: "We are not inclined to accompany the Americans in all the adventures into which they decide to throw themselves."[86] Some observers have emphasized the connection between the increasing bombings and the French departure from NATO's military wing,[87] but the escalation of United States military activity in Vietnam was more catalyst than cause. De Gaulle had been moving toward a more independent stance since acceding to power in 1958. The situation in Southeast Asia only reinforced his distaste for American hegemony. According to his foreign minister, the war was creating trouble around the world and "everything was poisoned by it."[88]

Although the substance and timing of the decision displeased the United States, France's withdrawal shocked no one. Even Couve de Murville noted the "relative serenity" with which Johnson received the decision.[89] In addition to the extensive advance warning he and his predecessors had received from de Gaulle,[90] the American president chose to avoid a major intramural alliance crisis while his energies and attentions were otherwise engaged. The Johnson administration therefore actively downplayed the significance of the French departure.

This response was not unwarranted: despite its exodus from the integrated military command structure, France planned to continue to subscribe to the North Atlantic Treaty and independently to maintain its treaty obligations. In a 25 March letter to the *New York Times*, de Gaulle affirmed France's commitment "to fight at the side of her allies in case one of them is the object of unprovoked aggression."[91] During subsequent congressional testimony, Secretary of State Rusk emphasized that France intended to remain a part of the Atlantic alliance and would respond to an attack on NATO territory as indicated in article 5 of the treaty.[92] Notwithstanding this concerted public relations effort, a blow had been struck to the partnership and, more pointedly, to the prestige of the United States at a vulnerable time.

Later that year, de Gaulle's critique of United States policy toward Vietnam became vituperative. In his 1 September speech in Phnom Penh, he insisted that only a complete American pullout would permit peace negotiations and the neutralization of Indochina. Moreover, he asserted that France would not associate itself actively with any mediation process until all American forces were repatriated.

Distancing himself even further from United States global initiatives, he announced: "Yes, France's stand is taken. It is taken by the condemnation that she harbors for the present events. It is taken by her determination not to be, wherever it may be and whatever may happen, automatically implicated in the eventual extension of the drama and, in any event, to keep her hands free."[93] American policymakers, aside from being annoyed with the substance of his discourse, correctly interpreted de Gaulle's Cambodian trip as the beginning of an effort to maneuver himself into the role of mediator for the Indochina conflict.[94]

This determination to break away from any association with American policy was, like the NATO withdrawal, based on de Gaulle's calculation that he could emerge at the helm of a third force, between the two superpowers, beholden to neither bloc. The public dissociation from Washington's activities in Asia was designed to confer on de Gaulle independent political credibility, especially in the developing world. His message was clear: when the United States spoke of and for the interests of the West, it really only represented the Anglo-Saxons.[95] Those who were not included should look instead to de Gaulle as their leader.

France, however, contributed to the security of the West in its own unorthodox way. The French maintained their responsibilities in Africa, the Pacific, and the Indian Ocean during this period. Their presence in the Indian Ocean was small at the time, but given the British withdrawal and the American unwillingness to replace the United Kingdom's forces, the French position in Djibouti, for example, became more important. By rejecting formal cooperation with other NATO members—especially the United States—France reinforced dependence on informal channels for the management of out-of-area developments.

For the rest of the NATO allies, the Vietnam War was a difficult period of waiting and warily watching as the leader of the Atlantic alliance, on whom they depended for their security, sank deeper into a quagmire. Although the less powerful allied governments almost never publicly criticized United States policy in Indochina, their silence was indicative not of agreement but of acquiescence.[96] Individual NATO members contributed only medical aid and some educational assistance to South Vietnam; among other United States allies, only Australia, New Zealand, and South Korea provided troops.[97]

As the war's toll climbed, popular opposition mounted in Europe. By May 1967, approximately 80 percent of Western European public opinion opposed what the Americans were doing in Vietnam.[98] The French, scornful of European cowardice vis-à-vis the United States, maintained that the other allied governments were too afraid of getting into disagreements with the Americans to speak their minds.[99] There was some truth to the French perception: the Europeans were generally reluctant to create more tensions in an already strained alliance and to expend their limited political capital on an issue over which they knew they had marginal, if any, influence. Indeed, some allies accused France of damaging NATO by criticizing the United States.[100]

NATO as an institution remained mute on the subject of the war. Rather than seeking to resolve the intractable differences in allied perspectives, it chose—at least in its public stance—to avoid the Vietnam issue. Significantly, there was not a single mention of the conflict in any NAC or Defence Planning Committee (DPC) communiqués during the sixties, reflecting the fact that the allies could not collectively find a common denominator on Southeast Asia. The only oblique reference to the divisiveness of the war appeared in the Harmel Report on the Future Tasks of the Alliance. Named after the Belgian foreign minister who had suggested in 1966 that NATO undertake a broad analysis of the challenges ahead, including the management of threats to alliance security beyond the European theater, the report was approved by the NAC in December 1967.

The conclusions of the Harmel Report hinted at the difficulties the alliance was experiencing in coordinating the out-of-area policies of its members, acknowledging that the "North Atlantic Treaty area cannot be treated in isolation from the rest of the world. Crises and conflicts arising outside the area may impair its security either directly or by affecting the global balance." The report's recommendations emphasized, however, that "as sovereign states the Allies are not obliged to subordinate their policies to collective decision," and therefore that "the Allies or such of them as wish to do so will also continue to consult on such problems without commitment and as the case may demand."[101] As such, the Harmel Report officially sanctioned the ad hoc approach to the management of out-of-area crises that had become the accepted pattern among the Atlantic allies. Secretary of State Rusk observed that in so doing, the report encouraged

NATO or its individual members to cooperate in dealing with security crises arising outside the treaty area, but it "does not require the convoy to go at the speed of the slowest ship."[102]

In the two major out-of-area crises of the sixties, Washington defined Western interests as its own, and vice versa. American handling of the Cuban Missile Crisis and the Vietnam War confirmed that, despite its rhetoric about a partnership of equals, the United States assumed it had the right and the duty to set the security agenda for the Atlantic alliance, particularly with respect to developments beyond Europe. The Cuban experience underscored the extent to which security had become indivisible in the nuclear age. This posed a problem independent of the substance of policy: even if the European allies agreed with American objectives, their lack of influence over events deprived them of control over their destiny. The Vietnam trauma proved that while superpowers may be muscle-bound, they also face resource constraints. This raised doubts about the credibility of the American commitment to Europe and the wisdom of American leadership of the alliance. Indeed, the Vietnam era brought about the breakdown not only of the postwar foreign policy consensus within the United States but within the West as well.

Yet in Southeast Asia, NATO survived the longest running and, in terms of its impact on European defense, most significant out-of-area problem in its history. The alliance endured because it continued to satisfy the vital security interests of its members. As the *Wall Street Journal* observed during the war, "Indeed, it is the deep underlying conviction that American power will keep Russia at bay which makes European politicians feel safe enough to engage in considerable nose-thumbing."[103]

Retrenchment and Renewed Commitment: From the Nixon Doctrine to the Carter Doctrine, 1969–1979

The retrenchment of the United States and the United Kingdom from major global commitments in the early seventies constituted what has been aptly described as "a tale of two withdrawals."[1] The American disengagement from Southeast Asia and the British departure from positions East of Suez reflected the emergence of a new world order over which the NATO allies had diminished control. In the United States, Vietnam was perceived as a humiliating failure; commenting on the war's legacy, George Ball argued that it "marked the end of an uncritical globalism that reflected our postwar preeminence."[2] In Southwest Asia, Britain's abandonment of most of its remaining positions in the Persian Gulf completed the course begun at Suez and ushered in a decade of change and upheaval: the October 1973 Middle East war, the oil crises of 1973–74 and 1978–79, the disintegration of an Iranian regime considered the major regional ally of the West, and, finally, the Soviet invasion of Afghanistan in December 1979. By the end of the decade, these events, coupled with America's recovery from the paralyzing legacy of the Vietnam War, brought out-of-area issues to center stage.

The Legacy of Vietnam

Although United States activities in Southeast Asia would not cease for more than six years, Richard M. Nixon's arrival at the White House in January 1969 heralded the beginning of the end of the Vietnam era in American foreign policy and the initiation of a period of contraction of American power. The new administration's "Vietnamization" scheme also established the outlines of its broader regional security strategy: the devolution of direct responsibility for security onto allies.[3]

The president first presented the principles that came to constitute the Guam Doctrine or, subsequently, the Nixon Doctrine in an informal background briefing for the press on the island of Guam in July 1969.[4] Later that year, in a nationally broadcast speech on Vietnam, Nixon established that henceforth the United States would "look to the nation directly threatened to assume the primary responsibility of providing the manpower for its defense."[5] In contrast to President Kennedy's commitment to "pay any price, bear any burden," the Nixon Doctrine's central premise reflected the mood in America at the end of a long and divisive war: "The United States will participate in the defense and development of allies and friends, but . . . America cannot—and will not—conceive *all* the plans, design *all* the programs, execute *all* the decisions and undertake *all* the defense of the free nations of the world. We will help where it makes a real difference and is considered in our interest."[6]

This new policy, though part of the process of disengagement from Vietnam, was not a radical break with the past. Since the Truman Doctrine, the United States had built up friends and allies so that they could defend themselves; such a goal had been the original intent of NATO. With respect to Asia, Secretary of State Acheson observed in 1950 that American policy could only be effective if the peoples in question supported their governments with determination and loyalty.[7] The full weight of his message had become apparent with the passage of two decades and the spillage of no little blood.

Changing the Guard in Southwest Asia

As the Americans extricated themselves from Vietnam, the British proceeded with the planned withdrawal of the majority of their forces from positions East of Suez. United States policymakers, however, had no intention of substituting American troops for the departing British contingents. A senior American official told Congress in 1972 that the "withdrawal of British military forces from the Persian Gulf has, in our opinion, left no vacuum in the usual sense of the word" and that the "United States has assumed none of the former British military role or functions and has no intention of seeking or appearing to replace the British presence in the gulf."[8] Instead, the United States would cultivate and support regional powers in areas of interest or concern.

Thus Iran and, to a lesser degree, Saudi Arabia became the beneficiaries of the Nixon Doctrine. In 1969, a National Security Study Memorandum on "Future U.S. Policy in the Persian Gulf" (NSSM 66) established the framework for American relations with the region. It concluded that Iran could perform the role that the United Kingdom had played if the United States supported the Shah's regime militarily and economically.[9] Henry Kissinger, then national security adviser, later offered the background to this decision:

> We could either provide the balancing force ourselves or enable a regional power to do so. There was no possibility of assigning any American military forces to the Indian Ocean in the midst of the Vietnam war and its attendant trauma. Congress would have tolerated no such commitment; the public would not have supported it. Fortunately, Iran was willing to play this role. The vacuum left by British withdrawal, now menaced by Soviet intrusion and radical momentum, would be filled by a local power friendly to us.

In addition, since the Shah was willing to pay for the relevant military equipment out of his oil revenues, the American financial burden appeared to be minimal.[10] At the conclusion of meetings in Iran on 30–31 May 1972, Nixon summed up the arrangement with Teheran in two words to the Shah: "Protect me."[11]

Through the Nixon Doctrine, the United States expected to maintain influence at a reduced cost in Southwest Asia. The policy reflected a reordering of priorities for the post-Vietnam era. As mentioned above, the Vietnam War had both preoccupied American policymakers and diverted United States resources to Southeast Asia at the expense of other commitments, most notably NATO. Between 1963 and 1970, one hundred thousand United States troops had been withdrawn from Europe.[12] By the early 1970s, American officials had begun to worry about the health of the alliance. Reflecting this concern, Ronald J. Spiers, director of the State Department's Bureau of Politico-Military Affairs, argued in congressional testimony against pressing NATO governments to do more in the Indian Ocean region because it "might adversely affect the commitments they have to NATO defenses closer to home."[13]

The October 1973 Middle East War

When the Egyptians and Syrians—condoned and supplied by Moscow—attacked Israel on 6 October 1973, the threat of war, not only in the Middle East but between the superpowers, loomed large. According to Kissinger, who had by then become secretary of state as well, the situation was "murderously dangerous."[14] American management of this out-of-area crisis and the European response to it created severe strains within the alliance, leading to what some observers described as a "Suez in reverse."[15] The sources of allied disagreement were threefold: the military resupply of Israel, the handling of the relationship with the Soviets, and the looming prospect of an oil embargo against the West.[16]

During the initial phase of the war, the Egyptians and Syrians inflicted severe casualties and loss of equipment on the Israelis. Within the first week of fighting, the Israeli air force lost nearly half of its American-supplied Phantom jet-fighters. Responding to desperate pleas from Israeli Prime Minister Golda Meir and stung by apparent Soviet efforts to exploit the situation to their own advantage, the Nixon administration decided to mount a massive airlift of planes and matériel to Israel.

The first problem in alliance relations created by the war revolved around Washington's plan to use Western and Southern European air bases to facilitate the American resupply of Israel. The United States took the view that its provision of arms and equipment to Israel "is just as much in the vital interest of West Germany and the other NATO allies as it is in our interest."[17] In general, however, the European NATO members attempted to dissociate themselves from American actions, fearing that their access to oil would be jeopardized by Washington's alliance with the Arabs' enemy.

All the geographically relevant NATO allies, with the exception of Portugal and, at the outset, the Federal Republic of Germany, directly or indirectly refused to facilitate the American airlift and banned American planes from flying over their territories to resupply Israel. The principal partners of the United States—those who traditionally played a role in the Middle East—rejected the American plan of action outright. On the first day of war, Britain and France refused to support the American proposal for a United Nations cease-fire resolution. France demonstrated its pro-Arab policy by continuing to ship tanks to Libya and Saudi Arabia during the crisis. While American policymakers expected a certain degree of French intransigence, they were infuriated when the British made it known that they did not want their bases in England or on Cyprus to be used either for the airlift or intelligence collection. Indeed, British Prime Minister Edward Heath privately requested that if United States reconnaissance planes used bases in the United Kingdom, he should be absolved of responsibility. Kissinger was so enraged by Heath's demand for a "cover story" that he declared a temporary ban on the exchange of intelligence information between the two countries.[18]

Other NATO allies also denied access to bases along the crucial Mediterranean route. On 10 October, as Israeli forces were sustaining serious losses on both the Golan and Suez fronts, Turkey informed Washington that Incirlik Air Base and other American facilities on Turkish territory were "for the security and defense of the North Atlantic Treaty area and have been set up solely for defense cooperative purposes of Turkey." The bases therefore could not be used in connection with the conflict in the Middle East. Three days later, on the first day of the full-scale American airlift to Israel, Greece announced that "U.S. bases have nothing to do with the Arab-Israeli war." Italy also refused the United States the use of its bases.[19]

The Federal Republic of Germany did not object at the outset to the American use of its facilities to resupply Israel, perhaps because the United States had not yet provided Bonn with specific information about the airlift. The *New York Times* reported that "Washington simply decided not to raise the question of landing and flight rights, hoping its allies would look the other way."[20] During the first days of fighting, United States Air Force cargo planes flew from the American military logistics and supply center at Ramstein carrying small arms, munitions, and tanks to Israel. Israeli ships loaded American weapons in Bremerhaven. It has also been alleged that the Americans removed aircraft from their NATO-designated squadrons based in Germany in order to resupply Israel. However, once Bonn discovered these movements of military matériel, it requested that Washington halt airlifts and sea shipments via Germany.[21]

The only ally providing facilities to the Americans for the duration of the war was Portugal, and this only after blatant diplomatic arm twisting. Initially, the Portuguese government claimed that it did not have any interest in antagonizing the Arabs. Further, Lisbon announced that in exchange for providing the requested access, it wanted Washington to promise to supply military equipment for

Portugal's colonial wars in Mozambique and Angola. Kissinger responded by drafting a letter from Nixon to Portuguese Prime Minister Marcelo Caetano that "refused military equipment and threatened to leave Portugal to its fate in a hostile world unless he complied immediately with the U.S. request."[22] This veiled threat to withdraw the NATO defense guarantee had its intended effect: within a day, the Portuguese gave the United States unconditional transit rights at Lajes Air Base in the Azores. The only other ally to support United States policy unconditionally was the Netherlands, but it was not geographically relevant to the airlift.

The widespread denial of facilitative access in Western and Southern Europe forced the United States Navy and Air Force to develop an alternative plan for getting matériel to Israel that avoided overflying certain countries along the supply route.[23] American cargo planes based in Germany were obliged to make a detour of two thousand miles to reach their destination. They flew out to the Atlantic, skirting France and Spain,[24] entered the Mediterranean at Gibraltar, and then headed straight to Israel. Navy A-4 Skyhawks coming from the east coast of the United States landed in the Azores to refuel and then refueled again by tanker aircraft off the carrier *John F. Kennedy* stationed near Gibraltar. They stayed overnight in the Mediterranean on the carrier *Franklin Delano Roosevelt* and refueled in the Eastern Mediterranean in the air near the carrier *Independence* on the last leg of the journey. In order to avoid using Greek bases for the delivery of the F-4 Phantom fighter-bombers, the air force flew them via the Azores to the eastern Mediterranean, where they were refueled in the sky by air force tanker planes. Kissinger noted later that the "Soviet Union had been freer to use NATO airspace than the United States, for much of the Soviet airlift to the Middle East overflew allied airspace without challenge."[25]

By the third week of October, the situation seemed to be escalating out of control. As the Americans continued their airlift to Israel, the Soviets were infusing Cairo and Damascus with massive amounts of military equipment. Three Russian airborne divisions in Eastern Europe had been put on alert. Israeli troops, contravening the first United Nations call for a cease-fire, reached the outskirts of the town of Suez and effectively trapped the Third Corps, the best fighting force in the Egyptian army. On the night of 24 October, Washington received an ultimatum from Moscow warning that unless the Americans joined them in immediately dispatching troops to the

Middle East to impose a settlement, the Soviet Union would be "faced with the necessity urgently to consider the question of taking appropriate steps unilaterally."[26]

Washington's reaction to the Kremlin's communiqué precipitated a second dimension of the crisis that both fed on and exacerbated tensions between Europe and the United States. Within hours of receiving the Soviet message, Kissinger put the global forces of the United States on nuclear alert. Around the world that night, American units were ordered to DefCon III, the highest stage of readiness in peacetime conditions. Under such circumstances, troops are placed on standby and await further orders. The Sixth Fleet, which was already cruising the Mediterranean at DefCon II, remained poised to attack.[27]

There was no advance consultation with the NATO allies despite the potentially dramatic implications of the American decision.[28] The British were informed a little over an hour after the command was given. The alert included three United States Air Force bases in the United Kingdom and the Polaris submarine base in Scotland. Although apprised before the rest of the allies, the British were nonetheless presented with a fait accompli rather than consulted in advance. Kissinger commented that the exchange of information with London's ambassador in Washington "was a classic example of the 'special relationship' with Britain as well as of the limits of allied consultation."[29] The NAC was not told until the following morning. By then, however, news of the alert was being broadcast on television. Kissinger insisted that he had not consulted the allies in advance to ensure that news of the alert did not leak prematurely to the Soviet Union and thereby diminish its intended impact: "We chose this timing above all because we knew that to obtain allied support we would have had to give reassurances of the limits of our commitment; we preferred that these not reach Moscow via our allies until the Politburo had made at least a preliminary decision."[30]

During the crisis, the United States government took upon itself the responsibility, as Kissinger later described it, of acting as "custodians of Western security."[31] It was precisely this role that had frustrated and frightened the Europeans since the Korean War. NATO officials expressed anger about the "lack of real consultation" in October 1973 and observed that the episode was an uneasy reminder that the United States and the Soviet Union dealt with such situations over the heads of the European allies.[32] In addition to fearing a

Soviet-American condominium, the Europeans were justifiably nervous about the immediate dangers of a superpower confrontation. More broadly, they were concerned about the tenuousness and volatility of the superpower relationship. The Nixon administration's strategy of linking détente to Soviet regional behavior could, if rigidly applied, destroy the benefits of détente that the Europeans were enjoying during the early seventies. Finally, the European NATO members were highly vulnerable to retaliation because of their dependence on Middle Eastern oil and therefore did not want to be identified with the United States and its ally, Israel.

Contending with the Arab Oil Embargo

A third and more protracted source of tension for the Atlantic allies emerged as the boundary between the resolution of the October 1973 war and the looming energy crisis became increasingly blurred. Although the military confrontation in the Middle East was defused shortly after the American nuclear alert, a serious new threat to Western solidarity and security manifested itself during the third week of October. The Arab members of the Organization of Petroleum Exporting Countries (OPEC) declared an embargo against the United States (and eventually the Netherlands). Just prior to the October 1973 war, Western Europe depended on imported oil from the Persian Gulf for 70 percent of its domestic consumption, while the United States imported only 5 percent of its requirements.[33] Despite the wide divergences in levels of oil dependency, the underlying economic interdependence between the United States and its European allies meant that all were vulnerable to supply disruptions and price increases.

The embargo effectively split the alliance into three groups. France and the United Kingdom, which sought to respond independently by making direct bilateral deals with Arab oil-producing nations, were essentially exempt from the embargo. Paris insisted that each state should conduct its negotiations with the producers separately and that there should be no consumer cartel. The other EEC members, including West Germany and Italy, were subject to progressive monthly oil supply reductions of 5 percent. The Federal Republic spearheaded the push for a coordinated European response. The United States, along with the Netherlands, was totally embargoed, and it lobbied for wider cooperation among all oil-consuming states. Whatever strategies allied governments employed to cope with the supply shortage, the quadrupling of oil prices placed a severe economic strain on all oil-dependent industrialized countries. The major international oil companies allocated the approximately 7 percent world petroleum shortfall that year on a pro rata basis. As a result, even France suffered supply reductions similar to those of its European neighbors.[34]

In an effort to smooth over the fissures created by the embargo and develop a united Western approach, Kissinger convened an allied Energy Conference in Washington in February 1974.[35] The meeting's much publicized squabbles highlighted the clashes of policy among the Europeans as much as it did those between Europe and the United States.[36] Finally, the allies reached agreement—despite France's refusal to participate—on an American proposal to create the International Energy Agency (IEA). The conference's affirmation of "the need for a comprehensive action program to deal with all facets of the world energy situation by co-operative measures,"[37] however, only papered over profound differences of attitude and interest. This was manifested in 1978–79 when the Iranian revolution brought that country's oil production to a complete halt and the oil-consuming countries did not resort to the cooperative plans they had endorsed in 1974.[38]

In the months preceding and following the Washington Energy Conference, the schism in the alliance, and in particular between France and the United States, expanded. French Foreign Minister Michel Jobert sought to widen the rift by using the EEC as a forum. In the wake of the October war, the Community members had issued a declaration urging Israel's withdrawal from the territory in the Sinai, Jordan, and Syria that it had occupied since the 1967 Six Day War and calling for international guarantees of a peace settlement to be negotiated by the United Nations.[39] Subsequently, French President Georges Pompidou called for a summit conference of the EEC members, which was convened in Copenhagen in December 1973. This meeting became noteworthy when several Arab foreign ministers appeared during the proceedings, allegedly at the behest of the British and the French.[40] These events foreshadowed the 4 March 1974 decision by the EEC leaders to establish an autonomous Euro-Arab dialogue within the framework of European Political Cooperation (EPC).

Not much ever came of the Euro-Arab dialogue, however, or of the efforts on the part of the Community to play a role in the Middle East peace process.[41]

In spite of European differences with the United States over Middle East policy, the French effort to promote the Euro-Arab dialogue placed the majority of the NATO allies in an awkward position and inevitably created further strains in the alliance. This was compounded by the harshly unenthusiastic American response to the initiative. Reflecting the extent to which the administration expected the Europeans to play a subordinate and acquiescent role, Kissinger told German Foreign Minister Walter Scheel, the president of the EEC Council of Ministers, that the "United States will not accept this procedure in the long run without its having a great effect on our relationship."[42]

The Non-Year of Europe

Henry Kissinger had intended that 1973 be devoted to rejuvenating the Atlantic partnership. In a major address on 23 April, he announced that "1973 is the Year of Europe because the era that was shaped by decisions of a generation ago is ending. . . . The revival of Western Europe is an established fact, as is the historic success of its movement toward economic unification." Instead of giving credence to the emerging power of Europe, however, he went on to argue that the "United States has global interests and responsibilities. Our European allies have regional interests." Although the national interests of the members of the alliance were not automatically identical, a solution had to be found "for the management of their diversity, to serve the common objectives which underlie their unity. We can no longer afford to pursue national or regional self interest without a unifying framework. We cannot hold together if each country or region asserts its autonomy whenever it is to its benefit and invokes unity to curtail the independence of others. . . . We need a shared view of the world we seek to build."[43]

Kissinger assumed that as leader of the alliance and as its only member with the global interests that would warrant such an all-encompassing vision, the United States would define this collective outlook. More specifically, in order to wage détente with the Soviet Union, he counted on European support for American policies both within and beyond the NATO area. Thus Kissinger dealt directly with the Soviet Union on all the major issues, notably the handling of the October war, assuming the allies would give Washington a blank check for the conduct of their foreign relations. Hence the irony in the phrase "Year of Europe"—a concept in which Europe was to be relegated to a supporting role.[44]

In the wake of the October war, Kissinger delivered a speech to the Pilgrims Society in London, complaining that "the attitude of the unifying Europe seems to elevate refusal to consult into a principle defining European identity." Despite Kissinger's assertion, "We do not accept the proposition that the strengthening of Atlantic unity and the defining of a European personality are incompatible," the unresolved tension between a more integrated Europe and the Atlantic partnership—the same dilemma that divided Kennedy and de Gaulle in the early sixties—surfaced again.[45] Through the Year of Europe, the United States tried to will away the contradiction between the two in order to establish a common front on areas considered by Washington to be of vital import. But if the appeal of Europeanism was only nascent in the early years of de Gaulle's tenure, by the early seventies a more self-confident Europe challenged the assumptions made by an overbearing superpower ally.

While 1973 turned out to be a very bad year for the alliance, 1974 ushered in a period of healing. The simmering standoff among allied leaders was resolved largely by domestic political changes in the key European countries during the first half of the year. In late February, British Prime Minister Heath was replaced by Harold Wilson. In conjunction with his new foreign secretary, James Callaghan, Wilson endeavored to patch up Britain's strained relationship with Washington. In early April, French President Pompidou, the inheritor of de Gaulle's legacy, died, and so the prickly Michel Jobert departed the Foreign Ministry. The new French government under Valéry Giscard d'Estaing was decidedly less antagonistic toward the Atlantic relationship and, specifically, toward the Americans. By June, German Chancellor Willy Brandt had been supplanted by Helmut Schmidt, who as finance minister had espoused a more conciliatory stance toward United States policy throughout the energy crisis.[46] On the occasion of the twenty-fifth anniversary of NATO in June 1974, the NAC produced a "Declaration on Atlantic Relations" that reflected the symbolic rapprochement between the United States and its European partners. It announced that the allies were resolved to carry out "frank and timely consultations" on matters relating to their shared interests as members of the alliance, "bearing in mind that these interests can be affected by events in other areas of the world."[47]

Protecting Alliance Interests in the Persian Gulf

Despite this period of reconciliation, the 1973 war and its aftermath presented the alliance with an out-of-area problem qualitatively different from any experienced in the past. The evidence of its legacy was incontrovertible: Western and, more specifically, European access to Persian Gulf oil was critical to the continued economic viability and hence political stability of the European members of NATO, and so, too, to NATO's very existence.

For the rest of the decade, however, little was done to promote a coordinated alliance strategy toward Southwest Asia. The United States continued to rely heavily on the Shah of Iran to protect Western interests in the region throughout the Nixon and Ford administrations. In the five-year period between 1972 and 1977, more than $10 billion worth of military equipment was sold to Iran. Southwest Asian security analyst Gary Sick recalled that as a result of almost exclusive reliance on the Shah, the Americans "lay strategically naked beneath the thin blanket of Iranian security."[48]

After President Jimmy Carter took office in January 1977, the United States considered the development of alternative means of exerting influence in the Persian Gulf. The new administration's first major review of the Soviet-American strategic balance, Presidential Review Memorandum 10, predicted that the Persian Gulf would be the most likely arena of confrontation between the United States and the Soviet Union. It identified the Persian Gulf as "a vulnerable and vital region, to which greater military concern ought to be given."[49] In midsummer 1977, National Security Adviser Zbigniew Brzezinski advocated the creation of a force capable of rapidly deploying into areas where American forces were not permanently stationed; in August, Carter approved the general plan as part of Presidential Directive 18. With his decision, the president confirmed that the United States needed to improve its capability to project power to distant areas of the world and, specifically, to the Persian Gulf region.[50]

Both the Pentagon and the State Department resisted the rapid deployment concept, thereby slowing progress to a practical stand-still. The military argued that it would divert resources from Western Europe, and the diplomats felt such an intervention force would be politically provocative. Thus despite the presidential order, almost no progress was made in the Defense Department toward fulfilling its goals. Instead, the Carter administration fell back on the Nixon-Ford strategy of reliance on Iran until the Shah's regime disintegrated in 1979.[51]

The Genesis of the Carter Doctrine

In November 1979, Iranian militants seized the United States Embassy in Teheran and held more than fifty Americans hostage, demanding the return of the Shah and his wealth. The taking of American hostages in Iran and the Soviet invasion of Afghanistan one month later provoked a dramatic reappraisal of United States policy. With the Shah's fall, the United States had lost its main instrument of leverage in the region, and American officials became painfully aware of how few military options were available to them in their effort to secure the release of the hostages.[52] These unpleasant circumstances forced Washington to develop a new approach toward protecting Western interests in Southwest Asia.

In the early days of the hostage crisis, American policymakers sought allied support for economic and diplomatic sanctions against Iran. This campaign met with only limited success. In consultations with NATO foreign ministers in early December 1979, Secretary of State Cyrus Vance believed he had gained support for an American effort to persuade the United Nations Security Council to approve international sanctions against Iran. He also thought the allied leaders had agreed to impose sanctions even if the Soviet Union vetoed the United Nations resolution. But the Europeans reneged on the commitment, arguing weakly that without United Nations authorization there were no legal grounds for the imposition of sanctions. In truth, the British, French, and West German governments feared that taking sanctions against Iran would provoke an anti-Western response in the Middle East and thereby again threaten oil exports.[53]

The allies consistently warned Washington not to take any military action against Iran. European officials recommended instead that the United States continue to seek a negotiated release of the hostages, even if the process of doing so was frustratingly long and slow. David Watt, director of Britain's Royal Institute of International Affairs, commented, "This is a case when a great power simply has got to take it."[54] The American administration's assessment of the allies' attitude was that "at each stage they reluctantly took only what they considered to be the minimum steps necessary to prevent the United States from moving to a military solution."[55]

The Soviet move into Afghanistan on the night of 25 December 1979 dramatically augmented concern in the Carter White House about the strategic situation in Southwest Asia. The invasion proved to be the catalyst for an almost complete revision of President Carter's estimate of Moscow's intentions. Cumulatively, the developments in Iran and Afghanistan revealed the hidden cost of the Nixon Doctrine: United States interests in Southwest Asia were exposed and vulnerable to both local instabilities and Soviet adventurism.

In his State of the Union address on 23 January 1980, Carter described the stakes in Southwest Asia:

> The region which is now threatened by Soviet troops in Afghanistan is of great strategic importance: it contains more than two-thirds of the world's exportable oil. The Soviet effort to dominate Afghanistan has brought Soviet military forces to within 300 miles of the Indian Ocean and close to the Straits of Hormuz, a waterway through which most of the world's oil must flow. The Soviet Union is now attempting to consolidate a strategic position, therefore, that poses a grave threat to the free movement of Middle East oil.

Departing from the policy of his predecessors, and reversing the decade of decline in direct Western involvement that had begun with the British withdrawal from East of Suez, the president asserted, "An attempt by any outside force to gain control of the Persian Gulf region will be regarded as an assault on the vital interests of the United States of America, and such an assault will be repelled by any means necessary, including military force."[56]

This proclamation of American interests in Southwest Asia became known as the Carter Doctrine. With it, access to oil became, more than six years after the first oil crisis, a national security priority. By committing the United States to the preservation of Western interests in Southwest Asia, the president filled the vacuum created by the two withdrawals that had marked the beginning of the decade.

CHAPTER SEVEN

Stretching the Limits of Alliance: NATO in the 1980s

The Carter administration's commitment to the defense of Southwest Asia forced the out-of-area debate onto center-stage in the eighties. The previous decade, which had begun with the British withdrawal from the Persian Gulf and ended with the Soviet invasion of Afghanistan, compelled the United States and its European allies to reassess the strategic significance of out-of-area developments, especially those in Southwest Asia, to alliance security. Developments outside the treaty area clearly had the potential not only to weaken the alliance's political cohesion but to undermine the economic stability and military security of its members.

Beginning in 1980 the United States made out-of-area cooperation a high priority on the alliance agenda. Washington pursued this objective through two separate but related processes, which can be distinguished as the formal and informal approaches to out-of-area management. The first was a novel and often contentious effort to use NATO institutional and consultative mechanisms for the discussion and limited coordination of policy toward Southwest Asia. Through this formal approach, the American government sought allied political sanction, financial compensation, and military contributions for its efforts to defend Western interests in that region.

The second, informal dimension of United States policy had similar goals, in that Southwest Asia was its primary focus, but the means of policy implementation were noticeably different. It built on the firmly established pattern in alliance politics that those allies with global commitments and the capability to protect and advance them would, where possible, coordinate their strategies. Although based on shared interests and responsibilities as members of the Atlantic alliance, such efforts did not take place under NATO auspices. The significance of this informal network of bilateral and multilateral exchanges has often been underestimated or overlooked precisely because the interallied dialogue took place on an ad hoc basis. Since NATO's creation, it has been the informal rather than the formal mechanisms that have played the greatest role in the management of out-of-area concerns.

The Legacy of the Carter Doctrine

In January 1980, without consulting any of the NATO allies, President Carter announced his decision to make Southwest Asia a strategic commitment on the same level as Europe, Japan, and Korea. American planners had not considered the Carter Doctrine's implications for the individual allies or for NATO's collective security. The 1979 Pentagon analyses supporting the decision to raise the American military profile in the region did not contemplate cooperative contingency plans, but rather addressed the issue of how the United States could meet the challenge to Western interests alone.[1]

The first effort to gain formal allied support for the new American commitment to Southwest Asia was triggered by the search for an appropriate response to the Soviet invasion of Afghanistan. From the outset, there was disagreement between the United States and its European allies over the nature of the challenge to Western interests posed by Moscow's military action and over the most appropriate means with which to counter it. France, in particular, was initially ambivalent, and its government carefully avoided overtly criticizing the Soviet Union. In its first statement following the invasion, the French cabinet affirmed that "France does not, for its part, propose to renounce its quest for détente which is of reciprocal interest and the alternative to which is a return to the Cold War."[2] Shortly thereafter, President Carter revealed his frustration with the rapidly changing French attitude toward the Soviet attack:

> They've had at least five different public positions: first saying that this was no threat to Western Europe; then a . . . public statement by Valéry [Giscard d'Estaing] condemning the Soviets and saying this was a threat to détente; then Giscard's visit to India,

where he issued a noncommittal statement with Mrs. Gandhi; then his meeting with Helmut [Schmidt] and a very strong (and supportive) communiqué they issued; and then more recently saying that they could not attend any meeting that did not contribute to friendship between us and the Soviet Union. I don't know what's going on in France.[3]

In fact, the vagaries of the French reaction reflected the broader European inclination not to jeopardize relations with Moscow and thereby raise tensions within Europe over a development beyond NATO's borders.

One example of the resultant interallied bickering was the much publicized argument over participation in the 1980 Moscow Olympics. In an effort to punish the Soviets for their aggression and to induce them to withdraw their forces, the United States declared that its athletes would not participate in the summer Olympic games. Washington expected and actively sought allied support for the boycott. However, the only three NATO countries that joined the protest were the Federal Republic of Germany, Canada, and Norway. Although the British, Italian, and Dutch governments offered verbal support for the boycott, they left their Olympic committees free to make the final decision. Not surprisingly, the committees decided to allow their athletes to attend, alongside teams from France, Belgium, Portugal, Greece, and Denmark.[4] In the months following the Soviet invasion, similar arguments also took place among the allies over cutting off high technology exports to the Soviet Union and imposing trade sanctions.

In the wake of Afghanistan, American military analysts finally began to examine the implications of the commitment to the defense of Southwest Asia for security in other theaters. Specifically, the Carter administration's decision to develop a worldwide rapid deployment force—stimulated by the perceived need for an upgraded intervention capability in the Persian Gulf—forced the issue into the NATO domain. When it officially came into being, the Rapid Deployment Joint Task Force (RDJTF) had no troops assigned to it. Instead, it was to draw on the existing pool of forces assigned to the various American unified commands. Although most of its actual planning and training focused on Southwest Asia, the RDJTF concept would rely heavily in time of crisis on forces assigned to NATO. This potential diversion of manpower and matériel from Europe compelled

American policymakers to seek consensus within NATO on the strategic importance of Southwest Asia to the security of the alliance.

In March 1980, the United States consequently spearheaded a two-phase effort to define an alliance-wide response to the Soviet invasion of Afghanistan. NATO's Defense Planning Committee concurred that the alliance should develop a program to accelerate already agreed-on defense commitments in order "to send a signal to Soviet decision makers that Soviet actions outside of NATO but against NATO's interests would not go unanswered."[5] In May, NATO's defense ministers acceded to a series of short-term defense goals designed to enhance force capabilities *within* the NATO area. Labeled "Afghanistan Phase One," these measures were to be fulfilled by each ally individually.[6]

In April 1980, while the Afghanistan Phase One initiatives were being considered, American Secretary of Defense Harold Brown sent allied defense ministers a supplemental plan. It recommended additional measures that were specifically designed to offset the potential depletion of NATO's defenses should United States forces that were normally designated to reinforce Europe be deployed to Southwest Asia. These "Afghanistan Phase Two" proposals were adopted at the DPC meeting in December.[7]

Two of these measures were particularly significant. The first was the expansion of military assistance to Portugal and Turkey. American policymakers hoped both NATO countries would make a significant contribution toward facilitating any deployment of forces to the Persian Gulf by providing access to their air bases. The second was a call for the accelerated provision of additional reserve units for ground combat in Europe. Pentagon planners calculated that these allied troops could "fill in" for American reinforcements should United States forces be diverted elsewhere.

Because American policymakers recognized that NATO could not respond directly to the Soviet invasion of Afghanistan, most of the Phase One and Phase Two measures were not focused on the crisis in Afghanistan itself. Instead, Washington used Afghanistan as a catalyst to motivate the allies to enhance defense and mobilization readiness in Europe. The goal was simultaneously to strengthen conventional capabilities within the treaty area and free United States resources for use in other places.[8]

During 1980, the functional term *out-of-area* made its formal entry into the lexicon of alliance politics. The United States embarked on a broad diplomatic campaign to raise the level of awareness within NATO about out-of-area threats to its interests and about the corresponding need to be prepared to meet such challenges. As part of this endeavor, American policymakers actively sought NATO's formal blessing for consideration of out-of-area issues and their impact on alliance security. At the outset, Washington focused mainly on the inclusion of language in NAC and DPC communiqués acknowledging the significance of out-of-area problems. The first DPC communiqué after Afghanistan reflected the initial success of the American initiative:

> The stability of regions outside NATO boundaries, particularly in the South West Asia area, and the secure supply of essential commodities from this area are of crucial importance. Therefore, the current situation has serious implications for the security of member countries. The altered strategic situation in South West Asia warrants full solidarity and the strengthening of Allied cohesion as a response to the new challenges. . . . It is in the interests of members of the Alliance that countries which are in a position to do so should use their best efforts to help achieve peace and stability in South West Asia.

The key phrase—"countries which are in a position to do so"— reflected the pattern that had been evident since the creation of the alliance: only certain members had the will and the capability to act beyond the European theater.

The defense ministers also officially validated Washington's campaign to address out-of-area issues in the NATO context, observing that the commitment of the United States to defend Southwest Asia "could place additional responsibilities on all allies for maintaining levels and standards of forces necessary for defence and deterrence in the NATO area."[9] This offered the less powerful alliance members an opportunity to contribute by bolstering their capabilities in Europe so that American resources could be employed elsewhere if necessary.

The June 1980 NAC communiqué was more reticent, asserting with respect to Afghanistan only that "ministers agreed that the international crisis caused by the Soviet intervention calls for a resolute, constant and concerted response on the part of the Allies." It demurred on the delicate question of NATO out-of-area cooperation, welcoming actions taken by individual nations "in a position to make a contribution to peace and stability in the region."[10]

By the end of 1980, there was an even greater discrepancy between the DPC and NAC positions. The American campaign to increase allied awareness of the implications of the RDJTF for alliance defense planning had met with substantial success on the military level. This was reflected in the substance of the December DPC communiqué. Acknowledging that Afghanistan "demonstrated that events outside NATO boundaries can bear directly on the security of all member countries," the defense ministers "agreed that it would be essential to prepare against the eventuality of a diversion of NATO-allocated forces the United States and other countries might be compelled to make in order to safeguard the vital interests of member nations outside the North Atlantic Treaty area." In this official acceptance of Afghanistan Phase Two measures, they also noted the importance of "transit facilities being available" as well as "host nation support to facilitate the reception and employment of reinforcement forces."[11] Conversely, the December 1980 NAC communiqué was restrained in its endorsement of formal allied out-of-area cooperation with respect to Southwest Asia. Its careful and cautious wording indicated the difficulty of reaching consensus at the political level: "Members of the Alliance are prepared to work for the reduction of tension in the area and, individually, to contribute to peace and stability for the region, while protecting their vital economic and strategic interests."[12]

The significant divergence in tone between the DPC and NAC positions had several causes. The defense ministers on the DPC took a military perspective. They were keenly aware both of the implications for NATO of the United States commitment to Southwest Asia and of the potential benefits of a coordinated strategy. By contrast, the NAC foreign ministers generally resisted policies relying on the use of force in favor of diplomatic alternatives. Further, they were less willing to be perceived as signing a blank check for American global activities since they bore the political responsibility for commitments made on their watch. In addition, the French—who since 1966 had not been members of NATO's integrated military command—did not participate in the DPC, although they remained on the NAC. Their view that the out-of-area issue did not exist since NATO's responsibilities were limited to Western Europe placed a damper on NAC discussions and communiqués.

Such divergences of opinion at the political level made the military channel all the more significant as a means of out-of-area policy coordination. It quickly became clear that there would be little for-mal, visible political support for American policy but that there would be substantial informal military cooperation with those allies who had the inclination and the ability to take action. As a conse-quence, NATO's political forum remained largely irrelevant as a tool for the management of alliance out-of-area concerns. Indeed, in retro-spect most of the post-Afghanistan measures endorsed by the NAC appear to have been largely rhetorical; the commitments they en-tailed were not binding and produced few substantive results.

During the last year of the Carter administration, United States policymakers came to recognize that in terms of military and diplo-matic strategy the United States not only could not, but should not, go it alone in Southwest Asia. This recognition, however, was never translated into a coherent conceptual framework for engaging the allies in planning for the defense of the region.[13]

The Reagan Administration Wish List

Specific definition of the kinds of out-of-area assistance the United States wanted from its allies emerged only after President Ronald Reagan moved into the White House in January 1981. The Reagan administration's case for enhanced NATO cooperation in Southwest Asia was based on four premises. First, American military planners asserted that a deployment of the RDJTF would affect the availability of manpower and matériel reinforcements for NATO even though no United States forces already stationed in Europe were scheduled to be diverted to the Persian Gulf in a crisis. Second, they insisted that the American capability to deploy and sustain forces in the region required overflight rights and access to European bases and facilities. Third, they argued that European military contributions in the region could augment Western strength and, as a corollary, its deterrent value. Fourth, American policymakers believed that it was symbolically important to engage the European members of NATO in the defense of common interests beyond the treaty area. Much as Britain and France had sought to expand American global commit-ments in the decade after NATO's creation, Washington hoped that European participation in out-of-area endeavors would force more allied governments to take broader views of their security interests.

The effort to secure specific allied contributions toward the de-fense of Southwest Asia began within a month of Reagan's arrival in the Oval Office. Indeed, the incoming assistant secretary of defense with responsibility for Southwest Asia, F. J. West, Jr., published an article in late January 1981 that argued for the creation of a "NATO naval force" linking the alliance to the Persian Gulf.[14] He was apparently persuaded, however, to pursue a less ambitious and more realistic strategy once he entered the government. On 21 February, United States Deputy Secretary of Defense Frank Carlucci told a conference of Western military experts in Munich that the administration sought an allied response to challenges to NATO's interests beyond Europe. He did not suggest the creation of a NATO force per se, instead advocating "individual, but complementary, efforts by the members of our Alliance" to improve their ties with the gulf and to deploy forces in the region.[15]

Simultaneously, officials in the State Department's Bureau of Politico-Military Affairs were developing a list of guidelines identifying what the United States sought in allied support for Southwest Asian contingencies. There were three broad categories for general reference, and within each, a more detailed account of specific requests. These included (1) compensation, or "filling in behind" for United States forces and equipment likely to be diverted elsewhere; (2) facilitation, including the provision of overflight rights, access to bases, and European air and sea lift for American and/or European forces to Southwest Asia; and (3) participation, involving the maintenance of peacetime presences in the region, the provision of regional economic and security assistance, and force commitments for potential deployments.[16]

The State Department coordinated this list with the Pentagon in preparation for a speech that Under Secretary of Defense for Policy Fred C. Iklé was to give at NATO headquarters. Iklé presented the American request for out-of-area support in a classified address before the permanent representatives to the NAC in October 1981:

> The Reagan Administration regards contributions from our European Allies as critical to the protection of our common interests in the region. Since the deployment of the RDF to Southwest Asia could weaken the capabilities of the alliance—particularly in the Southern Flank and in the Mediterranean—force improvements by our Allies in these areas are essential. In addition, we have to call on our Allies to facilitate our force projection to the Gulf region by providing logistics support and transit arrangements.

After insisting on the necessity of allied support for the American strategy in Southwest Asia, Iklé then described six specific areas in which the allies could make their contributions, echoing the list put forward by the State Department.

Iklé's recommendations, which went significantly beyond the Afghanistan Phase One and Phase Two requests for compensation in Europe, henceforth constituted the agenda for the out-of-area debate within NATO. First, he asserted, "We value a *peacetime military presence*," including naval and air deployments, joint exercises with regional states, the offer of military advisers, and the expansion of training programs. Second, he urged an increase in *"economic and security assistance* to key countries." Third, and according to Iklé possibly the most important of all, he requested the provision of *"overflight rights and en route access."* Fourth, he emphasized the importance of *"strategic mobility,"* especially in the event of simultaneous deployments to two theaters. Allied civil wide-body aircraft and sea lift support—principally roll-on/roll-off ships and large cargo and intratheater airlift—would be needed to reinforce Europe. Fifth, and most controversial, he called for *"military participation,"* although he acknowledged, "Planning can, of course, be accomplished on a bilateral basis outside NATO." Finally, he reiterated the importance of compensatory measures, or an *"increase in defense capabilities within the territory of our Alliance."*[17]

In response to American pressure for greater institutional recognition of the connection between NATO's security and developments in Southwest Asia, the NAC made its first explicit reference to out-of-area concerns in December 1981. Its communiqué acknowledged, "Those allies in a position to do so will be ready to take steps outside the Treaty area to deter aggression and to respond to requests by sovereign nations for help in resisting threats to their security or independence."[18]

During the following year, the Americans scored several symbolic successes in their campaign to secure formal support within NATO for increased cooperation outside the treaty area. The December 1982 DPC communiqué highlighted the compensatory and facilitative measures the allies might take, noting that "individual allied nations, on the basis of national decision, would make an important contribution to the security of the Alliance by making available facilities to assist such deployments."[19] The NAC statement issued in December 1982 was the most direct yet: "The allies recognize that certain events outside the Treaty area may affect their common interests as members of the Alliance."[20] The use of the term *common interests* was unprecedented in this context: until then, the NAC had referred to the interests in question as those of individual members of the alliance.

In 1982 the allies also agreed to undertake a South West Asia Impact Study (SWAIS) to address the implications of the American RDJTF deployment for European security and to identify possible individual allied compensatory measures within Europe. As part of this process, in June 1983 American Defense Secretary Caspar Weinberger urged the NATO defense ministers to develop sound contingency plans for bolstering European defenses should United States forces be diverted to Southwest Asia. The DPC noted in its December 1983 ministerial communiqué that the implications of the American "rapidly deployable forces" for the defense of the NATO area would be dealt with in the defense planning process, "the next stage of which is the adoption of force goals" in 1984. Prepared by the NATO International Military Staff, and formally entitled "Study on the Implications for NATO of the US Strategic Concept for South-West Asia," the SWAIS attempted to define the levels and specific types of compensation that each NATO member could contribute. Based on its recommendations, the NATO defense ministers agreed in December 1984 on a new set of biennial force goals for Europe to offset potential United States deployments to Southwest Asia.[21]

Although the SWAIS was not vested with the authority to oblige any ally to make the resource commitments it recommended, the study did force the allies, both individually and collectively, to focus on the impact a potential American engagement in the Persian Gulf would have on European security. The study's nearly exclusive emphasis on compensation, however, reflected growing American awareness that the United States would have to secure more direct forms of support for its Southwest Asian undertaking outside the formal NATO framework.

While NATO was working on the SWAIS, the United States moved forward with the planning and implementation of its independent strategy for projecting force into Southwest Asia. The Reagan administration gave the RDJTF increased funding and programming priority, and on 1 January 1983, it was elevated in status to the United States Central Command (USCENTCOM), a unified command with its own specific geographic responsibilities.[22] In February 1983 the United

States Congressional Budget Office published a report entitled "Rapid Deployment Force: Policy and Budgetary Implications." This study asserted unequivocally that a RDJTF mobilization of 220,000 troops or more would have a consequential impact on American reinforcements available to NATO in the initial sixty days of a conflict in Europe. It also concluded that a major deployment of the RDJTF would substantially tilt the balance of forces in the European theater in favor of the Warsaw Pact.[23]

As the American commitment became more reality than rhetoric, the European allies were confronted with its repercussions for their own security. Responding to the conclusions of the SWAIS, the allies agreed to factor the December 1984 ministerial guidance into their national force goals.[24] The European members of NATO, however, disagreed both with Washington and among themselves about the appropriateness and effectiveness of the strategy of the United States for Southwest Asia. More specifically, many remained skeptical about the role the allies would be expected to play should the Americans choose to use force in the region. Thus despite dire predictions like those made by the Congressional Budget Office, NATO members generally resisted doing more than they were already doing to offset the potential impact in Europe of the American plan.

NATO's lukewarm response inevitably affected American attitudes toward the alliance. Indeed, by 1982 the degree of allied support for Washington's global foreign objectives had become a contentious political issue in the United States. In the face of the rising federal deficit, there was increasing domestic pressure to trim the defense budget and, specifically, to reduce expenditures on NATO. On Capitol Hill, burden sharing became the buzzword for a heated debate about the benefits that accrued to the United States relative to the costs of its European commitments.[25]

In a reprise of Senator Mansfield's earlier efforts, Congress demanded to see tangible evidence that the allies were bearing their "fair share" of the defense burden—particularly with respect to the Persian Gulf—in exchange for the continued provision of the military funding necessary for NATO's security. Senator John Glenn advanced the congressional perspective during hearings on "NATO Troop Withdrawals":

The basic problem is that the NATO allies will not look beyond the NATO area in any of their considerations, and the world has changed and they are not changing with it. They are still talking about whether they have their conscription at home and that kind of stuff or not, while we are taking on the whole Persian Gulf on their behalf, and our behalf too, of course. And they will not budge one iota on their interest outside the NATO area as a way of saving money.

It is a good ploy, but I do not think we ought to be letting them get away with it. We ought to be pushing much harder.[26]

Attempting to pressure the NATO allies, legislators on both sides of the aisle advanced an implicit threat: a failure to play a greater role in defending access to oil in the Persian Gulf would lead to a diminishment of security in Europe. Senator William S. Cohen explained that the Europeans would be held responsible one way or another:

U.S. policymakers must continue to disabuse their Western European counterparts of this desire to have it both ways. The Europeans cannot expect the United States to unilaterally defend vital Western interests in the Persian Gulf and at the same time not draw down on the American forces on the Central Front. West Europeans must do more in areas outside of Europe, such as the Persian Gulf, or be ready to commit more of their own resources to the defense of the Continent.[27]

The European Perspective: Britain, France, Germany, and Italy

The American campaign on behalf of increased allied support for United States global initiatives triggered an extensive debate and widely diverse reactions in Europe. In general, the Europeans affirmed a strong disinclination toward the formal, institutionalized cooperation under NATO auspices that the United States had been promoting with respect to Southwest Asia. The allies expressed concern that American policy, and particularly that of the Reagan administration, relied too heavily on military solutions instead of diplomatic initiatives and polarized regional crises by injecting an East-West dimension into them. Underlying this concern was the ever present fear—one that first surfaced during the Korean War—that the United States would drag Europe into an unwanted conflict beyond the NATO area or inadvertently bring war to Europe. Nonetheless, the principal alliance powers maintained their established pattern of coordinating out-of-area policies informally, demonstrating the effectiveness of this approach through their complementary efforts to protect freedom of navigation in the Persian Gulf in 1987–88.

London

Within the context of their special relationship in the postwar period, the United Kingdom and the United States consistently held wide-ranging consultations on global developments. Further, the British never viewed out-of-area issues as exotic or obscure problems beyond their ken. Challenges emanating from beyond Europe were constant if not central concerns on London's postwar foreign and defense policy agenda, even though there seemed to be an ever increasing disparity between Britain's interests and its available resources. The 1982 Falklands campaign reversed the trend in the reduction of British overseas commitments that had been triggered by Suez and that continued through the late seventies. The war with Argentina underscored the importance of maintaining the capacity to respond to threats to perceived interests beyond Europe and emphasized the value of being able to both give support to and receive support from allies.[28]

The British reaction to the American out-of-area propositions of 1980 and 1981 was conditioned by the time-honored precept that London and Washington should support one another's endeavors whenever possible. A senior Foreign Office official summed up the British perspective: while there was no formal obligation outside the treaty area to concert policy, there was, in the interest of allied "solidarity," a "moral obligation" not to undermine one's colleagues.[29] This inclination was reinforced by the shared worldview of Prime Minister Margaret Thatcher and President Reagan. In response to the Reagan administration's initiatives, Thatcher publicly extolled the virtues of both formal and informal out-of-area cooperation. She endorsed the concept of an allied defense strategy that reached beyond NATO boundaries in early 1981, stating, "We must prevent Soviet encroachment in regions vital to the interests of the members of the alliance and to the economies of the world."[30]

This predilection to support the United States was dramatically reinforced by the Falklands War in the spring of 1982. The conflict between the United Kingdom and Argentina proved to be a potent reminder of the limits of formal cooperation inside NATO and the value of informal allied cooperation beyond Europe. The British did not consult NATO before taking action, but informed it about the change in the disposition of its forces—70 percent of the Royal Navy was committed to the Falklands[31]—so that the necessary adjustments could be made in Europe to compensate for the deployment to the South Atlantic. London, however, urgently requested American assistance through bilateral channels, which, after some delay, it received. The *Economist* described the extent to which the United Kingdom ultimately depended on support from the United States: "The British operation to recapture the Falklands could not have been mounted, let alone won, without American help." Pentagon officials confirmed that the United States provided critical intelligence information, 12.5 million gallons of aviation fuel from United States defense stockpiles, hundreds of Sidewinder missiles, airfield matting, thousands of rounds of mortar shells, and other equipment.[32] The fact that the French, Spanish, and other members of NATO publicly dissociated themselves from the British side of the conflict further strengthened London's inclination to coordinate directly with Washington rather than to seek broader allied sanction.

Beneath its broad support for the American initiative to engage the allies in the protection of global Western interests, the United Kingdom was generally skeptical of efforts to formalize allied cooperation beyond the treaty area and instead advocated informal collaboration outside NATO channels. In keeping with established precedent, British officials preferred to act independently but in parallel with the United States. In addition, London was adamant about differentiating among the wide variety of potential global threats and about devising appropriate responses. Consequently, the Thatcher government articulated a three-pronged British approach that covered the full spectrum of contingencies.[33]

The first dimension of the policy consisted of military assistance and training in Third World countries, with the specified goal of helping each to consolidate its own defense capabilities. This included short-term consultative visits to approximately twenty-five countries per year, and the loan of service personnel and training teams involving between 600 and 750 people in thirty countries such as Oman, Kuwait, and Zimbabwe. The ties were discreet but deep: for example, the Omani navy was led by a British admiral and had other British sailors on secondment or direct contract. Up to 4,000 military personnel from non-NATO countries visited the United Kingdom on an annual basis. In 1986–87, over 3,700 students from non-NATO countries were trained at British defense establishments. With respect to Southwest Asia, at mid-decade Britain maintained approximately 400 servicemen in the Persian Gulf, spread out in every country but Iraq and Iran, with almost 200 people in Oman alone.[34]

The second dimension of British out-of-area policy consisted of maintaining the capacity to deploy and sustain forces beyond Europe on a protracted basis. This permitted the United Kingdom to establish a military presence in a chosen country or region, such as Belize, Cyprus, the Indian Ocean, Kenya, Malaysia, or the Persian Gulf, and to exercise alone and with the forces of allies and friends. In 1987, there were approximately 1,400 men in Belize, 4,900 troops on Cyprus, one naval party and one marine detachment on Diego Garcia, several ships in the Indian Ocean, a garrison of 1,500 men in the Falklands, and exercises being held around the world, including in Kenya, Malaysia, the Middle East, and the South Atlantic.[35]

The third aspect of British out-of-area policy focused on developing the capacity to deploy an intervention force to any crisis situation within or beyond Europe. The White Paper published in December 1982 recommended that the United Kingdom not only increase its defense expenditures but develop a rapidly mobile capacity to respond in multiple contingencies.[36] Consequently, the Fifth Infantry Brigade was given an expanded capability, particularly with respect to overseas operations, and was transformed into the Fifth Airborne Brigade. Although not specifically earmarked for use in Southwest Asia, the Fifth Airborne Brigade had the capacity to participate as an independent force alongside the United States and others in the region.[37]

With respect to the formal American effort to involve NATO in the defense of alliance interests in Southwest Asia, the British repeatedly urged that such planning be pursued, as was done during the Falklands War, through bilateral channels rather than under the aegis of NATO. The British did endorse the compensatory measures designed to enhance NATO's conventional deterrent and improve its strategic mobility. These measures would offset any potential depletion of NATO's defenses should American forces be deployed to the Persian Gulf. London, however, argued that Washington incorrectly based its calculations on a worst-case hypothesis involving the forces required to combat a full-scale Soviet invasion of the Persian Gulf through

Iran.[38] In such a dire scenario, the United States would have needed to deploy seven divisions—or approximately 440,000 troops—to Southwest Asia, with obviously dramatic consequences for American reinforcement of Europe. British Foreign Office and Defence Ministry officials believed that overt Soviet aggression was the least likely challenge to regional security, and they asserted that Western interests were more likely to be threatened by internal instabilities and interstate rivalries, perhaps fomented by proxies. They also insisted that it was unwise to make compensation for such an extreme and improbable contingency into a test of NATO solidarity.

Additionally, British officials argued that the United States would have been more astute to present the RDJTF as a force designated for all purposes—including use in the European theater—rather than specifically for use in Southwest Asia. This was how Britain—and France—framed their efforts to enhance their national power projection capabilities. Had it done the same, Washington could have avoided creating the doubly negative perception that the RDJTF simultaneously diminished European security and represented a Western menace to Southwest Asian sovereignty. A British Defence Ministry official commented, "Our contribution to stability may require a certain distancing from the muscular expression of power by the United States." A Foreign Office official added, "We don't want to get the British military capability out-of-area tarred with the Rapid Deployment Force brush."[39]

Instead, based on their ability both to facilitate and to participate in joint operations in the Persian Gulf, the British conducted contingency planning with the Americans through bilateral channels outside NATO auspices. With respect to facilitation, the United Kingdom coordinated to the fullest extent possible with the United States. Its most significant contribution to the RDJTF was the provision of support facilities at Diego Garcia, which became the main American staging base in the Indian Ocean.[40] Britain also made it known that its sovereign bases on Cyprus and positions in Oman could play supporting roles in a joint deployment.

Finally, the British dismissed the concept of a Southwest Asia force under NATO auspices on the grounds that it would be politically counterproductive. As one senior Foreign Office official observed, in Southwest Asia, "The worst flag to fly under would be the NATO flag." They instead advocated low-key, low-profile involvement by individual states modeled after their training role in Oman. London also promoted the notion of "carving up the cake," or dividing up responsibilities for the region according to historical ties and strategic advantage.[41] Their perspective did not preclude participation alongside the United States; indeed, in practice it enhanced Anglo-American out-of-area cooperation. Britain's contribution ensured that the Reagan administration's efforts to protect and advance Western interests in Southwest Asia did not create unnecessary divisions within NATO or inadvertently undermine stability in the Persian Gulf region.

Paris

As previously noted, throughout the postwar period there was an inherent paradox in France's attitude toward cooperation with the Atlantic allies in the world beyond Europe. The French conception of an acceptable alliance was one that did not require diminished sovereignty and yet provided additional security. In the eighties, the Mitterrand government offered an updated version of this constant theme. When it came to power in 1981, its stated policy of "independence and solidarity" toward the Atlantic alliance reflected the perpetual determination to have it both ways. Defense Minister Charles Hernu explained the government's concept in late 1982:

> France is the master of her political and military decisions, largely thanks to her nuclear power. But, as a result of her geostrategic position, the ensemble of her values, her democratic institutions, she stands with the occidental world and is seriously concerned with the security of her European partners. In effect, for us, independence and solidarity are not antithetical concepts, but the contrary.[42]

Much more pointedly than the British, the French resisted formal, institutionalized alliance cooperation on global issues. This only enhanced the value of informal, bilateral channels of communication between France and its principal partners and, hence, the possibility of effective coordination of out-of-area responses among them. The French argued publicly that discussions of Third World crises had to be disengaged from military approaches and brought back into the realm of the political. In practice they did the contrary: they were unwilling to talk in political forums about allied cooperation outside the treaty area and instead coordinated on a military-to-military basis with relevant alliance members.

The pretense of separating the political and military dimensions of security problems had been the cornerstone of French relations with NATO since the mid-sixties. This evolved as a result of France's departure from the alliance's integrated military command structure in 1966. Although France remained a participant in the political dialogue conducted by the NAC, it gained independence in the military domain. This stance vis-à-vis NATO permitted Paris the maximum margin of maneuver. In discussions of NATO strategy, the French refused to contemplate any action that implicitly assumed their military compliance. Paradoxically, the autonomy the French gained from their nonintegrated military posture freed them to cooperate at the military level.

In fact, it was precisely this public distinction between political and military cooperation that allowed the French Ministry of Defense to coordinate on a wide range of security issues with NATO members both inside and outside the treaty area. There was widespread popular support in France for a global military role; unlike most of its NATO neighbors, France had no neutralist, pacifist or anti-nuclear movement of any consequence in the eighties. Socialist President François Mitterrand advanced a high-profile commitment to enhancing France's defense capabilities within and beyond Europe with the formula, "Pacifism is not peace."[43] Conversely, because France remained a member of the political branch of the alliance, and because politicians in France were vulnerable to public disapproval of any decision that compromised French independence, cooperation in the diplomatic arena was a much more sensitive domestic issue.[44]

Consequently, throughout the Reagan era the French consistently opposed any institutionalization of out-of-area cooperation at the political level. François de Rose, former French permanent representative at NATO, advocated Western coordination of contingency plans to respond to global Soviet threats menacing vital European interests, but he insisted that such efforts should be undertaken in "the least official and least structured manner possible."[45] A Quai d'Orsay official echoed his position: "Politics is symbols," and therefore France is "hostile to all systematic and formal co-operation."[46] Paris therefore maintained that policy coordination on out-of-area problems should take place on an informal, ad hoc basis, and outside NATO channels. During the debate over formal alliance support for the American commitment to the defense of Southwest Asia, the French literally refused to talk about out-of-area issues in the NATO context. The slogan that French foreign ministry officials coined for the topic was "hors zone, hors sujet" (out-of-area, off the subject).

In addition to their procedural opposition to any NATO-centered responses to out-of-area problems, French diplomatic and military analysts shared the British view that the main threat in Southwest Asia lay in local instabilities and regional rivalries rather than in Soviet designs. They argued that a conspicuous military presence on the part of a superpower would be counterproductive. Prime Minister Pierre Mauroy made this case in his annual defense policy speech on 20 September 1983: "In the belief that the Soviet menace has become planetary, the temptation to a correspondingly planetary response is manifesting itself. That is not France's view. The extension of the area of East-West confrontation outside the Atlantic area imposes Manichaean choices on other countries. Besides, a strictly East-West reading of all conflicts does not appear realistic to us."[47] The French government's effort to separate regional problems from the bipolar superpower framework coincided, not accidentally, with its ongoing endeavor to conduct an independent foreign policy. This provided another rationale for its consistent opposition to the formulation of an "Alliance policy" with respect to out-of-area issues.

Because France was not a participant in the military branch of the alliance, it was not asked to compensate within Europe for the potential deployment of American forces to the Persian Gulf or to facilitate or participate formally in any joint military activity in Southwest Asia. Yet despite its resistance to formal out-of-area cooperation, France maintained a wide range of global commitments and played a significant role in protecting interests consonant with those of the alliance, especially in Africa and the Indian Ocean. Indeed, the French contribution to the promotion of Western interests often appeared to be in inverse proportion to the vociferousness of their public opposition to allied coordination. The more the French government criticized its superpower ally, the greater its domestic credibility. With such popular support, Paris was free to deal discreetly and constructively with Washington.

During the eighties, the French advocated and pursued a two-dimensional approach to the informal management of developments beyond the NATO area. The first dimension was based on the principle that each ally had different strengths that should be exploited in dealing with regional instabilities. To this end, France maintained discreet supportive relationships and semipermanent presences around the world. As of mid-1987, French forces were positioned in a variety of places, predominantly in Africa and the Indian Ocean, including 1,600 in the Central African Republic, 2,500 in Chad, 4,000 in Djibouti, 600 in Gabon, 500 in the Ivory Coast, 1,750 in Lebanon, 1,250 in Senegal, and 40 in the Sinai. The French also maintained 3,300 troops in an interservice command on La Réunion and Mayotte, their dependencies in the southwest quadrant of the Indian Ocean. In addition to stationing over 10,000 troops in sub-Saharan Africa, the French injected $2.5 billion in aid (the largest international contribution), trained about 200 African officers in France, and sent approximately 1,000 French officers to advise African armies in 1987.[48]

The second dimension of French global policy was based on the pattern of bilateral and multilateral allied coordination outside the formal NATO framework that had evolved over the course of the postwar period. A prototypical example of this kind of informal, ad hoc crisis management took place when the United States and France coordinated resistance to the Libyan occupation of Chad in 1983–84 and again in 1986–87. During the first phase of fighting there were numerous disagreements between the two allies, both procedural and substantive, but Paris and Washington ultimately evolved a suitable division of labor in which the Americans provided critical military assistance as a complement to the leading role played by the French. They also exchanged essential intelligence information about the situation on the ground in Chad and about Libyan activities. The sustained French presence, their military support for the Chadian government forces, and the emergency aid and equipment provided by the United States, served as a deterrent to Libyan expansion. It led, in the spring of 1987, to the most important Chadian rout of Libyan forces in the history of Colonel Muammar el-Qaddafi's efforts to annex Chadian territory.[49]

Another manifestation of such informal coordination among France and its allies was discreet military-to-military cooperation in the Indian Ocean. The French maintained the largest allied presence there with, in addition to troops in Djibouti and on La Réunion and Mayotte, the naval command ALINDIEN, which in 1987 had ten to fifteen ships and 1,800 troops on deck.[50] The American, British, and French navies in the region coordinated their movements on a bilateral basis. Although France resisted trilateral naval coordination, a French Defense Ministry official described the existing arrangements as "beautiful," commenting, "Nobody wants to change them and nobody wants to talk about them." Indeed, NATO's Supreme Allied Commander Bernard Rogers is said to have embarrassed French officials when in May 1983 he publicly praised the "extremely close cooperation and co-ordination" that existed with the French ministry. One example of this relationship was "Link Eleven," a highly sophisticated communications system that since the mid-seventies has connected American and French ships in the Indian Ocean, in the Persian Gulf, and, for a time, off the coast of Lebanon. The British subsequently began to fit their ships with compatible technology.[51]

Complementing the French role in informal out-of-area cooperation, the Mitterrand government took action to enhance France's global power projection abilities. In fact, the movement toward enhanced conventional capabilities had begun under President Giscard d'Estaing, who believed that France's interests in Africa and the Mediterranean were not being properly defended due to the disproportionate emphasis of previous governments on the nuclear deterrent.[52] Mitterrand's Military Programming Law for 1984 to 1988 heralded the creation of a quick intervention capability, the Force d'Action Rapide (FAR). It was assigned 47,000 combat troops to be organized into five divisions, three of which already existed and two of which were to be newly created, and was to be composed of marine infantry, airborne, air-mobile, alpine, and armored units.[53] The FAR was designed both to reinforce French forces in Germany in the advent of a crisis on the Central Front and to be deployed overseas to protect French interests beyond Europe.

The FAR's dual designation signaled a softening of the rigid Gaullist resistance to binding alliance commitments that had characterized French foreign and defense policy since the late fifties. The change in attitude was particularly marked with respect to crisis management in the NATO area. In June 1983, the French hosted the first NAC meeting in Paris since de Gaulle withdrew France from the integrated military command in December 1966. On the eve of the sessions, the French government indicated that it intended to live up to all its responsibilities as an ally.[54] General Jeannou Lacaze, the armed forces chief of staff, asserted that the new FAR units allowed France the possibility of "participating earlier alongside the alliance" in a European battle.[55] Defense Minister Charles Hernu subsequently acknowledged that the use of the FAR within Europe would naturally require coordination among the Atlantic allies and that any deployment would have to be agreed on with the NATO command.[56]

Taking this approach one step further, the French and West German governments reached an agreement in 1986 to strengthen their defense cooperation, including the development of detailed plans for the use of the FAR to defend the Federal Republic against attack.[57] In 1987 the French parliament approved a major five-year rearmament program that was integrally linked to the concept of closer military collaboration with West Germany and other European allies.[58]

This series of steps committed France to go beyond its traditional doctrine of sanctuary, or frontier defense, and to coordinate on the military level with other NATO members to protect France's interests beyond its national borders. This new direction inevitably affected French attitudes toward allied cooperation beyond the European theater. Cumulatively, the developments of the eighties formed a trajectory in which the French, having clearly established their independence, moved—albeit with caution—toward enhanced cooperation within the framework of the Atlantic alliance.

Rome

Since the creation of NATO, there had been a wide qualitative and quantitative gap between the global interests and capabilities of the British and the French and those of the other European members of the alliance. In the late seventies, however, Italy began to demonstrate in both rhetoric and deed that it sought a new role within NATO. In exchange for political credibility and clout, the Italians were willing to assume responsibility for a larger share of the military burden outside of Europe.

Until 1979, Italy supported NATO loyally, but it did not count among those who made key contributions to Western security. This was largely the legacy of the terms of the Italian defeat in World War II and of the unique relationship established between the United States and Italy in the early postwar period. For almost thirty-five years, Italian foreign policy was aligned with the United States in exchange for a defense guarantee. As part of the bargain, Italy absolved itself of responsibility beyond the NATO area.

The definition and perception of Italy's role began to change under Defense Minister Lelio Lagorio in 1979. Lagorio and his chief political-military adviser, Brigadier-General Luigi Caligaris, developed a new national security concept focused on the enhancement of Italy's capacity to take military action, an imperative if the country was to be taken seriously by its allies. Caligaris described the effort as an attempt to remedy the problem that the "relationship between military credibility and political effect is not always understood in Italy."[59] The endeavor was underwritten by the armed forces' 1975 decision to embark on a ten-year (subsequently stretched to fifteen-year) restructuring and modernization program.

The underlying impetus for this "new international image" was Italy's longing to be treated as a principal partner by the United States, Britain, France, and Germany. A senior Foreign Ministry official commented that a stimulus for change had been Italian frustration at not being included in the Guadeloupe Summit in 1979. In addition, the Italians were faced during that year with a critical security choice: they had to decide whether to deploy American cruise missiles on their territory.[60]

The novel Italian strategic concept was complementary—indeed integrally connected—to the NATO commitment. NATO's 1979 "dual-track" decision to modernize intermediate range nuclear forces (INF) in Europe presented the first real test to the credibility of Rome's new defense policy. The public debate over INF modernization became a catalyst for national interest in defense issues, and the country's decision to accept the new weapons signaled the emergence of a domestic consensus over an increased international role for Italy.[61]

In 1980, Lagorio established three goals that demonstrated Italy's commitment to a new international role. The first was developing an increased capability in the Mediterranean; the second was ensuring the neutrality of Malta; the third was participating in the international peacekeeping force in the Sinai.[62] In the years that followed, Italian defense analysts devoted substantial attention to the potential contribution their forces could make to NATO southern flank security and Mediterranean stability.[63] The Italians, however, remained ambivalent about a Mediterranean vocation; the idea conjured up memories of Fascist proclamations of *mare nostrum*. Critics of the approach also argued that if Italy was ever to achieve equal status with its European partners, it could not confine itself or be confined to a Mediterranean presence. A senior foreign ministry official observed that an exclusively Mediterranean role for Italy "would imply the concept of an Alliance with different levels of importance and of security assigned to its different geostrategic sectors, a concept that is simply unacceptable."[64]

The decision made in January 1982 to participate in the Sinai

Multinational Force and Observers (MFO) was one of Italy's most significant foreign policy choices since its accession to the Atlantic alliance. For the first time since World War II, Italian soldiers set foot on soil outside the NATO area. As of 1987, ninety Italian troops were stationed in the Sinai. Since Italy had opposed the Camp David approach to a Middle East settlement, its involvement in the MFO demonstrated the strength of its desire for a new international image. A senior Foreign Ministry official candidly described the motivation behind this unprecedented deployment: "Out-of-area participation in the guise of peacekeeping was intended to provide Italy with access to major power status in the Alliance."[65]

Italy's subsequent contribution of more than two thousand troops to the allied Multinational Force (MNF) in Lebanon from September 1982 to February 1984 was also a portentous gesture. It was the first postwar deployment of Italian forces overseas without United Nations cover, and it was considerably more dangerous and politically controversial than the MFO. After the MNF was withdrawn, the Italians continued to provide a small contingent of troops to the United Nations Interim Force in Lebanon (UNIFIL).[66]

In April 1981, the Italian government announced the creation of an interservice intervention force to fulfill Rome's new military commitments. It was designated as a small deterrent power to meet threats to Italian, European, and Mediterranean security. Though plagued by insufficient funding and interservice rivalries, this force supplied the manpower and matériel for the Italian contingents in the international peacekeeping expeditions.

Informal out-of-area cooperation in peacekeeping missions with the Americans, the British, and the French grew out of the Italian ambition to be counted among the leading powers of NATO. At the same time, the Italians remained highly sensitive to American pressure to expand their international commitments and worried about the prospect of being "graded" on their out-of-area behavior. They consequently argued against the establishment of any formal out-of-area doctrine for the alliance, advocating instead a division of labor that allowed each ally to contribute based on its individual capabilities.

Reaffirming its determination to play a greater role in NATO, the Italian government in May 1988 agreed—despite significant domestic political costs—to provide new basing facilities for seventy-two American F-16 fighter-bombers. During negotiations the previous year, Spanish Prime Minister Felipe González had demanded that these planes, which had been based at Torrejon Air Base outside Madrid, be removed. The Italians immediately insisted that the aircraft remain on the southern flank of NATO. After securing an official request from NATO that Italy should take responsibility for the homeless jets, Rome agreed to harbor the 401st Tactical Fighter Wing when it leaves Spain in 1991.[67] This commitment again demonstrated that despite their chronic governmental instability, the Italians have been and are determined to remain reliable and dependable allies.

Bonn

The out-of-area debate touched the two most sensitive nerves in contemporary West Germany. The first was the legacy of Germany's central role in bringing about two world wars in the twentieth century. Its residue included extreme sensitivity to other people's sensitivities about any revival of German nationalist behavior and, more specifically, about seeing German soldiers "on the march" again.[68] A strong disinclination toward a great power role for the Federal Republic was therefore been deeply embedded in the conscience of this generation's leadership. As a result, Bonn resisted any military involvement outside Europe.

The second exposed nerve was the residual intra-German predicament. Bonn officials argued that the application of a Cold War yardstick to Third World conflicts would strain East-West relations and therefore raise tensions along the internal German border. They claimed this would be exacerbated if West Germany was perceived to be directly aiding Washington by playing a military role in the developing world. They also maintained that they needed to concentrate their efforts on ensuring stability on the Central Front, and that any more extended commitment of their resources would detract from that effort and thereby diminish the security of NATO as a whole. West German Defense Minister Hans Apel insisted that activities like the American rapid deployment force "must not jeopardize the balance of forces in Europe. For Europe, the stability of East-West relations is the foundation of its security. The global commitment of the United States and regional stability in Central Europe must be harmonized with each other."[69] In sum, the debate over Bonn's contribution to the protection of Western out-of-area interests was caught up in the broader struggle between the Federal Republic's longing for normalized relations with East Germany and its staunch commitment to the Atlantic alliance.

As a consequence of these sensitivities, the Federal Republic neither was nor aspired to be a significant player beyond Europe. According to the Basic German Law, the Federal Republic's armed forces can only be used for purposes of self-defense, or in the context of NATO responsibilities within the European theater.[70] This constitutional limitation defined the parameters of all public discussions of a potential German role beyond the treaty area. These often cited legal restrictions—which could certainly have been modified if the Germans had chosen to do so—were a convenient excuse for the underlying fact that Germany was not prepared to assume a greater international role. As a result, in the Federal Republic, as in France, although for profoundly different reasons, a distinct line was drawn between the political and the military dimensions of the out-of-area debate. Indeed, the issue of alliance cooperation beyond Europe was intentionally kept off the political agenda.

Instead, requests for German activity beyond NATO's boundaries were dealt with in a limited military context. Specifically, the security implications for Germany of planning for the RDJTF, and the related American request for compensatory actions, provoked the development of a Federal Republic policy on out-of-area contributions.[71] Given the historic constraints on a German military presence outside Europe, it was logical that the Federal Republic should avoid requests for participation and instead focus on compensation and other measures of support within Europe.

The issue of compensation, however, proved to be extremely thorny, compounding German demographic constraints. Before the completion of the SWAIS, the Federal Republic had already made a substantial effort to improve reserves and restructure its forces for a crisis. In resisting American requests for more troops to compensate for the possible redeployment of NATO-designated forces to Southwest Asia, Bonn emphasized its projected military manpower shortage. Washington's demands also spawned anxiety about the possible weakening of security in the central region as a result of the commitment of the United States to defend the Persian Gulf. Similarly, despite French designation of the FAR for use inside the NATO area as well as outside, the Germans worried that the FAR might draw troops away from Europe.[72]

With respect to facilitation, German Foreign and Defense Ministry officials emphasized that while in principle they would provide logistical support and overflight rights in the event of an American deployment to Southwest Asia, such actions could not take place automatically. They insisted on the importance of "timely consultations," especially in the wake of the 1973 Middle East war. Nevertheless, in an effort to assist the United States in its military preparations for a variety of contingencies, and specifically to provide adequate support on German soil for American reinforcements, Bonn signed a Host Nation Support Agreement with Washington in 1982.[73]

Ironically, the Germans were unwilling to participate in out-of-area military deployments for the precise reason that the United States sought their involvement: it would have been perceived as a first step toward a larger German international role. For example, in distinct contrast with Italy, the Federal Republic resisted providing troops for international peacekeeping forces in the eighties. Foreign Ministry officials recalled that there had been a theoretical discussion about whether Germany should make an exception to its Basic Law for peacekeeping operations. The government concluded that participation in peacekeeping would have diminished German resolve not to get involved outside the treaty area by awakening Germany's consciousness about its global opportunities—a consciousness that had remained conveniently repressed since the end of World War II. Participation in a Middle Eastern peacekeeping force would also have aroused other German sensitivities. Specifically, the Germans did not want to put themselves in the position of having to fire on Israelis.[74]

Instead, the Federal Republic used economic assistance as its principal foreign policy tool in the Third World. Defense Minister Apel made this case at the 1982 Wehrkunde Conference:

> Development aid and diplomacy are the decisive means of political action available to us in the Third World.
>
> Avoiding and controlling conflicts in the Third World, and averting dangers that threaten to disrupt the flow of raw materials to the Western industrial nations is thus largely a political problem, at least not only a military one.[75]

Bonn contributed to strengthening the alliance's perimeter defenses through the provision of aid to key NATO southern flank countries such as Greece, Turkey, and Portugal. In the mid-eighties, its development assistance expenditures consumed 2.6 percent of the federal budget (more than double the percentage in the United States) and included contributions to Egypt, the Sudan, and Pakistan.[76] The Germans thereby played a role in advancing Western interests beyond Europe without unraveling the fragile tapestry of their postwar identity.

Reactions in Other Capitals

At the beginning of the eighties, American military planners hoped to count on two other NATO allies—Turkey and Portugal—to make significant, although very different, contributions to the defense of alliance interests in Southwest Asia. In a crisis, American strategists hoped to secure access to bases in the eastern part of Turkey as staging areas for projecting power into the Persian Gulf region. In November 1982 Washington and Ankara signed a memorandum of understanding permitting the United States to modernize ten existing Turkish air force bases and establish an undisclosed number of new ones. Payed for out of NATO infrastructure funds, these improvements included the upgrading of runways and support facilities in eastern Turkey at Erzurum, Batman, and Mus that considerably enhanced NATO's deterrent posture in the region.[77]

Although a Soviet attempt to move into the Persian Gulf would have threatened Turkey's vital interests, both in terms of physical security and access to oil, Turkish officials did not agree to grant permission to the United States Central Command to utilize these or other Turkish bases in the event of a Soviet incursion in the Middle East. Further, the Turkish government officially committed itself only to the facilitation of NATO-approved actions.[78] The Turks feared that any other agreement would be provocative to the Soviet Union and might lead to a preemptive attack on the facilities in question. In addition, they worried that it would complicate Turkey's ties with the Islamic world. Moreover, maintaining control over use of the bases strengthened the Turkish bargaining position vis-à-vis the United States over further American military and economic assistance.[79]

Portugal, by contrast, extended critical facilitative assistance to United States forces at Lajes Air Base in the Azores as it had done since the early days of NATO. Despite the extreme pressure to which Henry Kissinger subjected the Portuguese over the use of Lajes during the 1973 Middle East war, Lisbon continued to permit American

planes to refuel there. Such cooperation, subject to Portuguese concurrence on a case-by-case basis, was recodified in a bilateral agreement with the United States in 1984.[80] Consequently, use of the base
did not require any NATO blessing of the kind insisted on by Turkey.
Given the general uncertainty about timely access to other European
facilities, the Portuguese were therefore in a position to play a key
role in supporting a deployment to Southwest Asia.

Beyond making compensatory contributions within Europe, the
rest of the allies played relatively minor military roles outside the
treaty area during the eighties. For those countries with neither
the capability nor the desire to support American global initiatives,
participation in United Nations activities offered an alternative opportunity to make a limited contribution to international stability.
For example, in keeping with their long tradition of support for
United Nations peacekeeping forces, the Canadians provided a contingent of approximately 225 men for the United Nations Disengagement Observer Force in the Golan Heights (UNDOF), and 140 men for
the MFO in the Sinai. The Netherlands provided about 800 troops to
UNIFIL in southern Lebanon until the middle of the decade and subsequently retained approximately 105 troops in the MFO. Norway maintained a force of about 860 in UNIFIL. As of early 1987, Belgium,
Denmark, Greece, Luxembourg, Portugal, Spain, and Turkey had no
sustained military presences outside the European theater.[81]

Test Case: Allied Cooperation in
the Persian Gulf, 1987–1988

The most significant result of the effort by the United States to
secure formal support for its commitment to Southwest Asia from
NATO was increased awareness of the limitations of such a formal
approach. The official alliance structure proved a restrictive, cumbersome, and generally unsatisfactory mechanism for policy coordination beyond the treaty area, except, perhaps, for exploring compensatory measures.

Recognizing the inhibitions to progress within NATO, the Reagan
administration slowly began to shift its emphasis away from the
endeavor to gain NATO's official sanction for out-of-area actions. As
the decade progressed, American officials returned to the established
pattern, pursuing cooperation on an informal basis in both bilateral

and multilateral forums. This did not mean that the United States ceased to appeal to NATO for support, but rather that it concentrated its efforts on contingency planning outside the NATO framework. Revealingly, this traditional and more practical means of policy coordination with relevant allies was being used to manage a variety of developments while the formal approach was pursued.

The most salient example of this kind of coordination took place with respect to bilateral contingency planning for a crisis in the Persian Gulf. In a series of meetings on both sides of the Atlantic, the Americans and the British, and, separately, the Americans and the French, endeavored to identify potential threats and appropriate responses. But these efforts, which took place over the course of the five-year period from 1982 through 1986, lacked the sense of immediacy and the sharp focus that a crisis would impose.

The escalation of the seven-year-old Iran-Iraq war in late 1986 and early 1987, and the commensurate increase in attacks on shipping traffic in the Persian Gulf, created that crisis atmosphere. Iraq continued to attack ships within its self-declared exclusionary war zone and vessels serving Iranian ports and oil-loading facilities, and Iran stepped up its retaliation against nonbelligerent shipping in international waters. Specifically, Iran targeted its attacks on Kuwaiti vessels in retaliation for Kuwait's logistical and financial support for Iraq. In late December 1986, the Kuwaiti Oil Tanker Company approached American officials to express interest in reflagging its ships in exchange for protection from United States naval forces in the area. Shortly thereafter, on 13 January 1987, the United States learned that the Soviets were prepared to reflag Kuwaiti ships and provide them with protection. Washington decided during the first week of March to reflag all eleven Kuwaiti vessels in question, thereby limiting the Soviet role to chartering three long-haul tankers to Kuwait. In attempting to explain the reflagging policy to Congress, Defense Secretary Weinberger argued, "Moreover, should we not be responsive to Kuwait's request for help, the Soviets will be quick to supplant us, thereby positioning themselves to become the protector of the Gulf."[82]

Following the allegedly accidental Iraqi attack on the American frigate *Stark* on 17 May, the United States decided to seek allied support for an expansion of its efforts to protect Western access to oil in the Persian Gulf. Weinberger solicited individual allied contributions during DPC meetings in late May. Although he pressed the European members of NATO for "any assistance that we would be able to get," he apparently stopped short of specifically requesting a collective response. French cooperation was sought outside NATO channels entirely. At the conclusion of the DPC sessions, NATO Secretary-General Lord Carrington emphasized that the call for assistance should be considered outside the formal NATO framework: "What happens in the Gulf has a very considerable effect on the members of the alliance. But when you get to doing anything about it in military terms, or in planning terms, then that has to be done either in a different forum or bilaterally."[83]

Throughout the months of June and July, all but one of the European members of the alliance resisted the American entreaty. In general, the allies were uneasy about the wisdom of Washington's reflagging policy and feared that it might lead to a further escalation of the conflict in the Persian Gulf and to increased terrorist attacks on European citizens. More specifically, the revelations about the Reagan administration's secret plan to trade arms to Teheran in exchange for the release of American hostages and to funnel the proceeds of the sale to the Nicaraguan Contras fostered doubt and mistrust about Washington's strategy and tactics in the region. Only the Netherlands agreed in principle to send naval vessels to help protect gulf shipping should conditions there worsen. The Dutch also announced that they would take compensatory measures within the NATO area should gaps be left in alliance defenses because of deployments to the gulf.[84]

Despite their skepticism about the American plan to reflag and escort Kuwaiti tankers through the Strait of Hormuz and into the Persian Gulf, the British and the French maintained and indeed enhanced their presences in the region during the late spring and summer of 1987. By early August, 20 percent of the Royal Navy had been deployed to the area. Although the British did not escort their commercial vessels through the gulf, their warships shadowed British oil tankers. This meant that while the Royal Navy did not lead the way for the commercial ships, it discreetly followed them along their route. In midsummer, the French increased their gulf patrols to twice a month, and they too began unofficially to accompany, or shadow, their merchant ships. In late July, Paris also dispatched an aircraft carrier group to the Gulf of Oman at the mouth of the Persian Gulf.[85]

Notwithstanding the significant British and French contributions, American legislators fiercely criticized the allies for failing to do more in the Persian Gulf. Congressman Les Aspin, chairman of the House Armed Services Committee, insisted that the administration should be "relentless and uncompromising" in demanding allied support: "If we end up with American boys losing their lives in the Persian Gulf because of strikes like the Stark, and you've got cars in Europe zooming down the autobahn using up the gas, that is just going to set this country off like a tinderbox."[86]

London and Paris continued to spurn Washington's requests for greater assistance until the threat to their own shipping had grown demonstrably. On 24 July, the reflagged Kuwaiti tanker *Bridgeton* hit a mine. National Security Adviser Frank Carlucci then traveled to Europe to secure allied contributions of minesweepers on behalf of the American convoy effort in the gulf. Initially, the allies with minesweeping capabilities—the British, French, Italians, West Germans, and Dutch—rejected the American request, although all but the French acknowledged that they might consider doing more at another time.[87]

Within two weeks, however, the British and the French had reversed their positions, paving the way for other allies to do the same. On 10 August, an American-operated tanker struck a mine off Fujayrah in the Gulf of Oman, about eighty miles south of the entrance to the Persian Gulf. No mines had previously been found in this area, which both London and Paris used as a staging base to prepare their forces for transiting the gulf. This provided both allies with an opportunity—and a rationale—to deploy minesweepers in defense of their own shipping interests and of international freedom of navigation rather than exclusively to protect the American convoy operation.

Almost simultaneously on 11 August, France and Britain announced that they would be sending minesweepers to meet this new military threat. Both emphasized, however, that their minesweepers would operate separately from the United States naval force in the gulf and would be used to reinforce the British and French flotillas already patrolling the region. French Defense Minister André Giraud commented, "We do not foresee carrying out any combined operations." Characteristically, Prime Minister Thatcher sounded more comfortable with the likely interaction among allied forces in the region, observing that the several navies in the area, although not operating under a joint command, were coordinating their efforts and that "I think that is what they will increasingly do." In keeping with past patterns, the three principal powers of NATO therefore worked in parallel to protect Western interests rather than under a formal regime of cooperation.[88]

This development stimulated a response among the smaller NATO powers who did not want to be perceived as disloyal allies once the British and French had reversed course. The Netherlands, which held responsibility for minesweeping within NATO, began to explore the prospects for a cooperative European effort under the auspices of the Western European Union (WEU). Long dormant, the defense organization that had been the predecessor to NATO was in the process of being revived as a forum for the consideration of European security issues.[89] Dutch Prime Minister Ruud Lubbers, who held the rotating WEU presidency, spearheaded the effort to organize allied participation in a minesweeping force. He convened senior diplomatic and military officials of the seven WEU nations in The Hague on 20 August to work out the details.

By early September, the outlines of a coordinated European response to the mining of Persian Gulf and Gulf of Oman waters began to emerge. Under this plan, the Dutch and the Belgians each deployed two minesweepers and shared a Belgian command and support ship. The British agreed to provide protection for this combined force, and Luxembourg paid for part of the flotilla. The Italians at first resisted the concept of cooperation under the WEU umbrella for fear that it might connote colonialism or limit their independence. After an Italian container ship was fired on in the gulf on 8 September, however, Rome dispatched an eight-vessel task force, including three minesweepers, three frigates, and two support ships. This operation was the Italian navy's biggest combat undertaking since World War II. Italy was also the only country other than the United States to escort its merchant shipping all the way to Kuwait. Finally, the West Germans took an unprecedented step toward out-of-area cooperation. Although they emphasized to their WEU colleagues that they could not deploy military force outside of Europe, they sent four warships to the western Mediterranean to take over the NATO duties of other allied vessels diverted to the gulf. The Norwegians deployed ships to the English Channel for similar purposes.[90]

By the autumn of 1987, the allies had assembled the largest concentration of Western naval power since the Korean War. The United States and Western Europe each had nearly forty ships in the Persian Gulf region. All seven members of the WEU were participating either directly or indirectly in the minesweeping effort. While there was no formal agreement to coordinate, the allied navies in the gulf inevitably worked together to maximize their effectiveness and minimize the risk to their forces. As Dutch Defense Minister W. F. van Eekelen observed, "On a naval level, if you don't have close coordination, you are mad."[91]

For the Dutch and the Belgians, who would have preferred to operate under United Nations auspices, the WEU umbrella provided essential political cover. It also gave the less powerful members of NATO a means of cooperating with the United States without being dominated by or explicitly identified with Washington. Finally, by choosing to conduct their coordinating efforts through the WEU, its members enhanced the WEU itself. In so doing, they promoted the gradual emergence of a European defense identity that was separate from but complementary to NATO.

In early 1988, the six NATO members with forces in the Persian Gulf agreed to expand their cooperation through the establishment of an informal unified command for minesweeping. They planned to maintain five minesweepers operating in the gulf at any one time and to follow a coordinated pattern that would keep shipping lanes relatively secure throughout the affected area. With this organized division of labor, they reduced the number of minesweepers each individual ally needed to retain in the region. In late April 1988, meeting under the auspices of the NATO Nuclear Planning Group, American, British, Dutch, Belgian, and Italian officials agreed to further expand their cooperation in order to avoid wasteful and duplicative searches for mines. The French were expected to participate in this enhanced program, although they did not attend the NATO meetings and characteristically maintained that their minesweeping forces operated independently.[92]

As the American, British, and French forces patrolled the Persian Gulf, they were confronted with the larger question of how they would respond should they be in the vicinity of an attack on an allied or neutral ship. The French set an important precedent in January 1988 by coming to the assistance of a Liberian-registered chemical tanker that was engaged in a firefight with Iranian gunboats. In April, the Americans expanded the rules of engagement for their forces in the gulf to include responding to distress assistance requests from vessels not flying the United States flag. Based on this extended commitment, an American warship fired a warning shot near Iranian gunboats that had attacked a Danish-flagged supertanker on 2 July. The British never formally expanded their coverage beyond their own vessels and the Dutch and Belgian minesweeping unit, although their broad commitment to keeping the gulf sea lanes open for Western shipping suggested that they would not allow an attack on an allied vessel to go unchecked. Reflecting the extent to which the informal bond among allies reached beyond the treaty area, the captain of the American guided missile frigate USS *Jack Williams* observed the British destroyer HMS *Gloucester* nearby as they convoyed their ships through the Strait of Hormuz and commented, "Diplomatically I guess it has been difficult to get all these countries to agree to coordinate their policies. But we keep in touch out here and I certainly would not sit by and watch if any aircraft attacked the Gloucester."[93]

As the immediate threat to international shipping declined due to the effectiveness of the minesweeping effort and the growing prospect of an end to the Iran-Iraq war, the allies began to consider bringing some of their forces home from the Persian Gulf. This did not mean, however, that they intended to abandon their role in ensuring freedom of navigation through the strategic waterway. Indeed, in the late summer of 1988, the United States and the European members of the minesweeping team entered into discussions about a coordinated mine-clearing operation to remove the remaining mines and debris from the Persian Gulf.[94] Thus the successful effort undertaken in the Persian Gulf in 1987 became a prototype for future allied out-of-area endeavors.

The Americans, the Europeans, and the Atlantic alliance re-learned some old lessons from the Persian Gulf experience. Despite its early enthusiasm for formally involving NATO in Southwest Asia, the Reagan administration discovered that the established pattern of informal, bilateral dialogue on out-of-area issues among the principal partners produced greater tangible results. The Europeans focused on the unpleasant fact that American resources—both military and fiscal—were not limitless, and that Europe's security could be affected, either directly or indirectly, by developments beyond the treaty area. Together, the members of the alliance found that they had the capacity to organize and implement a plan to protect their mutual interests beyond Europe that simultaneously respected their individual sovereignties and capitalized on their collective power.

Conclusion

The Atlantic alliance was established to contain Soviet expansionism in Europe. Yet the allies soon found themselves confronted with developments outside the NATO treaty area that threatened their interests and their security. Looking back across forty years, out-of-area crises have played a prominent role in the history of the alliance. The allies have turned to one another during these crises for support and reassurance, and alliance relationships have been reaffirmed or redefined by the way challenges beyond Europe were handled.

In managing out-of-area crises, if the allies sought agreement on action within the formal alliance framework they ran the risk of overburdening their collective agenda, provoking disagreements that would damage allied solidarity, and overextending NATO's commitments. Instead, they evolved the practice of informal consultation and coordination among those members with common interests in an area or a problem beyond Europe and the capability to protect those interests. Developments outside the treaty area have thus been handled on an ad hoc basis, ensuring that NATO's political consensus and military resources were not stretched too thin by challenges beyond its official domain of responsibility. This process gave birth to what is, in effect, a shadow alliance. The shadow alliance constitutes one of the unrecognized strengths of the Atlantic partnership.

As the alliance enters its fifth decade, it confronts momentous changes in the international system. These derived at least in part from NATO's very success. The postwar containment doctrine, cornerstone of American and allied policy, had seemingly worked, and President Bush declared that it was time to move "beyond containment."[1] For the first time since the creation of NATO, there was serious debate among the allies about what the world would look like after the Cold War receded.

In the late eighties, Soviet President Mikhail Gorbachev had embarked on a massive reform of the Soviet economy and, as part of that effort, appeared to be overhauling Moscow's international role. Within Europe itself, the Iron Curtain gave signs of eroding as some Warsaw Pact countries moved toward a more open and democratic status. The Russian leader launched arms control and troop reduction initiatives designed to reduce economic burdens within the Soviet Union while simultaneously alleviating pressure on the Continent. In addition to the prospect of change in the superpower relationship within Europe, there was also a possibility of change in the nature of the East-West competition in the Third World. Around the globe, Soviet adventurism seemed to be on the decline, as indicated by the withdrawal of troops from Afghanistan and Soviet cooperation with Western efforts to bring about an end to the conflicts in Angola, Cambodia, and Namibia.

The other major evolutionary change affecting allied relations testified to the success of American efforts to promote a secure, strong, and united Western Europe. The outcome of the Marshall Plan and NATO was a viable, economically competitive Europe playing an increasingly independent international role. Indeed, the move toward European economic integration in 1992 was the embodiment of the long-standing American commitment to European unity. The European allies, however, were thereby positioned to play a separate global game in pursuit of commercial and diplomatic advantage, increasing the prospect of competitive or divergent policies in the developing world. NATO would have to adapt to reflect this shifting balance of power.

Some analysts argued that these two changes heralded the beginning of the end of NATO. But at a meeting of NATO heads of state and government in Brussels in May 1989, allied leaders concluded that even if the Cold War were to become a memory and the European allies were to achieve a degree of unity and a greater degree of autonomy in the foreign policy domain, the allies would still share a broad range of common interests, both within and beyond Europe. Addressing the changing world in which NATO would have to operate, they focused on global challenges to alliance security, outlining a broad out-of-area agenda: "Worldwide developments which affect our security interests are legitimate matters for consultation and, where appropriate, co-ordination among us. Our security is to be seen in a context broader than the protection from war alone." The leaders went on to enumerate a list of problems for allied consideration: "Regional conflicts continue to be of major concern. . . . We will seek to contain the newly emerging security threats and destabilizing consequences resulting from the uncontrolled spread and application of modern military technologies. . . . we will increasingly need to address worldwide problems which have a bearing on our security, particularly environmental degradation, resource conflicts and grave economic disparities. We will seek to do so in the appropriate multilateral fora, in the widest possible co-operation with other States."[2] Thus in addition to dealing with regional threats like instability in the Persian Gulf, NATO members agreed to consider a broad range of global problems. Such an agenda might appropriately include the destruction of the ozone layer, nuclear proliferation, overpopulation, and terrorism.

If the superpower dimension of regional instability diminishes, a good deal of conflict would be defused, but as NATO's leaders recognized, a myriad of challenges to Western interests would also remain. Significantly, many of the crises beyond Europe examined in this book were not exclusively generated by the competition between the United States and the Soviet Union. The East-West contest has been a constant undercurrent throughout the postwar period, but regional rivalries and nationalist stirrings challenged Western interests as much as Soviet expansionist designs. Such was the case in Indochina in the early 1950s, at Suez in 1956, in Lebanon and Jordan in 1958, in Vietnam in the 1960s, in the Middle East in 1973, in the Falklands in 1982, and in the Persian Gulf in 1987. This kind of regional and local threat to allied interests will inevitably persist.

Looking toward the twenty-first century, it is possible to envision a world in which the Cold War is not the dominant dynamic in the international system. Should NATO be restructured or, more radically, disbanded, there would consequently be an even greater reliance on the informal mechanisms established over the history of the alliance for the management of out-of-area challenges. In such a world, the habit of consultation, not the obligation, would become all the more important, and the lessons learned during the crises of the postwar period all the more valuable. Allied leaders would increasingly rely on the shadow alliance to meet predictable as well as unforeseen global challenges to Western security.

Appendix

Articles of the North Atlantic Treaty of 4 April 1949 referred to in this book:

ARTICLE FOUR

The Parties will consult together whenever, in the opinion of any of them, the territorial integrity, political independence or security of any one of the Parties is threatened.

ARTICLE FIVE

The Parties agree that an armed attack against one or more of them in Europe or North America shall be considered an attack against them all and consequently they agree that, if such an armed attack occurs, each of them, in exercise of the right of individual or collective self-defence recognised by Article 51 of the Charter of the United Nations, will assist the Party or Parties so attacked by taking forthwith, individually and in concert with the other Parties, such action as it deems necessary, including the use of armed force, to restore and maintain the security of the North Atlantic area.

Any such armed attack and all measures taken as a result thereof shall immediately be reported to the Security Council. Such measures shall be terminated when the Security Council has taken the measures necessary to restore international peace and security.

ARTICLE SIX

For the purpose of Article 5 an armed attack on one or more of the Parties is deemed to include an armed attack on the territory of any of the Parties in Europe or North America, on the Algerian Departments of France,* on the occupation forces of any Party in Europe, on the islands under the jurisdiction of any Party in the North Atlantic area north of the Tropic of Cancer or on the vessels or aircraft in this area of any of the Parties.

ARTICLE SIX (modified on the accession of Greece and Turkey on 22 October 1951)

For the purpose of Article 5, an armed attack on one or more of the Parties is deemed to include an armed attack:

i. on the territory of any of the Parties in Europe or North America, on the Algerian Departments of France, on the territory of Turkey or on the islands under the jurisdiction of any of the Parties in the North Atlantic area north of the Tropic of Cancer;
ii. on the forces, vessels, or aircraft of any of the Parties, when in or over these territories or any other area in Europe in which occupation forces of any of the Parties were stationed on the date when the Treaty entered into force or the Mediterranean Sea or the North Atlantic area north of the Tropic of Cancer.

*Insofar as the former Algerian Departments of France were concerned, the relevant clauses of the treaty became inapplicable on 3 July 1962.

Notes

INTRODUCTION

1. Stanley Hoffmann, "Persistent Problems in the NATO Alliance," in *American Defense Policy, Fifth Edition*, ed. John F. Reichart and Steven R. Sturm (Baltimore: John Hopkins University Press, 1984), 324–25.

CHAPTER 1. Defining the Limits of Alliance:
The Creation of NATO, 1948–1949

1. Winston Churchill, "Mr. Churchill's Address Calling for United Effort for World Peace," *New York Times*, 6 March 1946, 4.
2. "Britain in Crisis," *Life*, 28 April 1947, 105.
3. Churchill, "Mr. Churchill's Address."
4. Editorial, "Our Foreign Policy Crisis," *Life*, 17 March 1947, 38.
5. Editorial, "Mr. Truman Goes to Congress," *New York Times*, 12 March 1947, 24.
6. Editorial, "A Tocsin for World Power," *Washington Post*, cited in "Extracts from American Editorial Comment on President Truman's Message," *New York Times*, 13 March 1947, 4.
7. Sir Nicholas Henderson, *The Birth of NATO* (London: Weidenfeld and Nicolson, 1982), 1. The concept of a "world-wide Article 51 (UN Charter) pact of free nations" was, in fact, discussed in early exploratory meetings between the United States, the United Kingdom, and Canada but rejected on the grounds that "it would be too cumbersome and too long in implementation." See Minutes of the Second Meeting of the U.S.-U.K.-Canada Security Conversations, 23 March 1948, in *Foreign Relations of the United States* (hereafter *FRUS*) *1948*, 3:64.
8. Bevin and his cabinet colleagues did not, however, relinquish their ultimate ambition of creating a worldwide collective security network. As long as the British maintained a substantial presence outside of Europe, they would continue to seek an American commitment to the defense of what they believed were global Western interests.

9. Aide-Mémoire from the British Embassy to the Department of State, 11 March 1948, in *FRUS 1948*, 3:46–47.

10. Letter from Secretary of State Marshall to British Ambassador Lord Inverchapel, 12 March 1948, in *FRUS 1948*, 3:48. See also discussion in Henderson, *Birth of NATO*, 12.

11. For initial exchanges about treaty scope, see the meeting of 9 July 1948, especially pp. 11–13, in U.S. National Archives, Washington, D.C. (hereafter, USNA), doc. no. 840–20/7–748.

12. Ireland ultimately would not be invited to join because its government insisted on linking participation with discussions on the ending of partition. See Telegram from Sir Oliver Franks (British ambassador to Washington) to Foreign Office, 7 February 1949, Foreign Office file (hereafter, F.O.) 371/79224, doc.no. Z1187/1074/72G, Public Records Office, London (hereafter, PRO). Indeed, in a note to the prime minister on the same day, Bevin commented that if Ireland were to join under those conditions, it might "cause a revolution" (F.O. 371/79224, doc.no. Z1188/1074/72G, PRO).

13. Western Germany became the Federal Republic of Germany, or West Germany, when the state was officially divided in 1949. NATO served as the vehicle through which the Federal Republic was slowly integrated into the Atlantic defense system. It officially acceded to the alliance in 1955.

14. Memo from George Butler (deputy director of the Policy Planning Staff) to Messrs. Hickerson (director, Office of European Affairs) and Reber (deputy director, Office of European Affairs), 27 July 1948, in doc. no. 840.20/7–2748, USNA.

15. For subsequent discussion, see Draft Paper on "Territorial Scope" of 2 September 1948, or thereabouts, doc. no. 840.20/9-248, USNA.

16. See revision of "Territorial Scope" paper in doc. no. 840.20/9–248 and 840.20/7–948 TSF, USNA, and the covering note sent to London by the British embassy in Washington, doc. no. 840.20/9–2448, USNA.

17. Henderson, *Birth of NATO*, 64.

18. See George Washington's Farewell Address, 17 September 1796, and Thomas Jefferson's First Inaugural Address, 4 March 1801, cited in Henry Steele Commager, ed., *Documents of American History*, 9th ed., vol. 1 (Englewood Cliffs, N.J.: Prentice-Hall, 1973), 174, 188.

19. James Reston, "We Assume World Role But Cost Bothers Us," *New York Times*, 3 April 1949.

20. Article 2, section 2, clause 2 of the U.S. Constitution states that the president "shall have Power, by and with the Advice and Consent of the Senate, to make Treaties, provided two-thirds of the Senators present concur."

21. Senator Vandenberg, 11 May 1948, in U.S. Senate, *The Vandenberg Resolution and the North Atlantic Treaty*, Hearings Before the Committee on Foreign Relations, 80th Cong., 2d sess. (Washington, D.C.: GPO, 1973), 9.

22. See text of the Vandenberg Resolution in *The Private Papers of Senator Vandenberg*, ed. Arthur H. Vandenberg, Jr. (Boston: Houghton Mifflin, 1952), 407.

23. Article 5 of the treaty states that in the event of an armed attack on

one of the parties, each will assist "by taking forthwith, individually, and in concert with the other Parties, such action as it deems necessary, including the use of armed force." See the Memorandum of Conversation of 3 February 1949, between Secretary of State Acheson and Senators Vandenberg and Connally (Connally became chairman of the Senate Foreign Relations Committee in the 81st Congress, controlled by the Democrats) in which each article of a draft treaty was considered. Particular attention was paid to the wording of article 5. (Doc. no. 840.20/2–349, USNA). See, too, Franks's analysis of congressional reservations in cable from Washington to Foreign Office on "Senate Debate on North Atlantic Pact," 15 February 1949, F.O. 371/79225, and personal letter from Franks to Bevin, 17 February 1949, F.O. 371/79228, PRO.

24. In *Imperialism at Bay: The United States and the Decolonization of the British Empire, 1941–1945* (New York: Oxford University Press, 1978), Wm. Roger Louis discusses the wartime tensions between Roosevelt and Churchill over the fate of Britain's imperial possessions in detail.

25. "An Open Letter from the Editors of LIFE to the People of England," *Life*, 12 October 1942, 34.

26. Walter Lippmann, "Today and Tomorrow," 7 March 1946, cited in Ronald Steel, *Walter Lippmann and the American Century* (Boston: Atlantic Monthly Press/Little, Brown, 1980), 429.

27. Letter from Theodore Achilles to Rear Admiral Arthur C. Davis, 1 December 1948, and Davis's reply, 7 December 1948, doc. nos. 840.20/12–148, 840.20/12-748, USNA.

28. See Minutes of the Eleventh Meeting of the Washington Exploratory Talks on Security, 14 January 1949, in *FRUS 1949*, 4:28, and Telegram no. 301 from Franks to Foreign Office, 14 January 1949, F.O. 371/79221, doc. no. Z422/1074/72G, PRO.

29. See Telegram no. 384 from Franks to Bevin, 19 January 1949, F.O. 371/79222, doc. no. Z5191/1076/72G, PRO, and Minutes of the Eleventh Meeting, *FRUS 1949*, 4:28-29.

30. Foreign Office cable to Franks, 14 January 1949, F.O. 371/79221, doc. no. Z422/1074/72G, PRO.

31. Memo for the Secretary of Defense from the Joint Chiefs of Staff on North Atlantic Pact, 5 January 1949, in response to Department of State 24 December 1948 Report on the Washington Security Talks. This was sent to the secretary of state on 5 January 1949 (doc. no. 840.20/1–649, USNA).

32. See Henderson, *Birth of NATO*, 103, 69; Telegram no. 19 from Franks to Foreign Office, 13 January 1949, F.O. 371/79222, doc. no. Z498/1074/72G, PRO; and Alan K. Henrikson, "The Creation of the North Atlantic Alliance," in *American Defense Policy, Fifth Edition*, ed. Reichart and Sturm, 310. James Reston also referred to the *obligation* to consult "on any threat to the peace in any part of the world," in an article on "West Pact Facing Strong Opposition," *New York Times*, 11 January 1949.

33. Memo from H. M. Gladwyn Jebb (assistant under-secretary of state and U.K. representative on Brussels Treaty Permanent Commission with personal rank as ambassador) to Bevin, 11 January 1949, F.O. 371/79222;

Telegram no. 14 from Franks to Foreign Office, 14 January 1949, F.O. 371/79222, doc. no. Z283/1074/72G; and Telegram no. 19 from Franks to Foreign Office, 19 January 1949, F.O. 371/79222, doc. no. Z365/1074/72G, PRO.

34. See handwritten comments of E. M. Rose, dated 5 May 1949, F.O. 371/76033, doc. no. F6563, PRO. Date on file cover may well be inaccurate, or document may have been improperly filed at PRO.

35. Theodore C. Achilles, "U.S. Role in Negotiations that Led to Atlantic Alliance," part 2, *NATO Review* 27, no. 5 (October 1979): 17. In original text, the author emphasized in italics all words from *casus belli* onward.

36. See Minute on the North Atlantic Pact, from Bevin to the prime minister, late December (no date) 1948, and prime minister's reply, 1 January 1949, F.O. 371/79218, doc. no. Z57/1074/72G, PRO, and Henderson, *Birth of NATO*, 69–72, and appendix A, 115–17.

37. See Minute on the North Atlantic Pact, especially discussion of "Major Points," and Minutes of the Tenth Meeting of the Washington Exploratory Talks, 22 December 1948, doc. no. 840.20/12–2248, USNA.

38. See, for example, the British embassy's report on the observations of Foreign Minister Spaak of Belgium on the question of Italian accession and the inability of the lesser powers in the alliance to change "whatever decision the United States Government requires," in Telegram no. 94 from Brussels to Foreign Office, 2 March 1949, F.O. 371/79229, doc. no. Z807/1074/72G, PRO.

39. See, for example, John Hickerson's comments in U.S.-U.K.-Canada discussions on 22-23 March 1948, doc. no. N.A. 840.20/3–3148, USNA.

40. Hamilton Fish Armstrong, "Regional Pacts: Strong Points or Storm Cellars?" *Foreign Affairs* 27, no. 3 (April 1949): 364–65.

41. For an example of their pointed opposition, see Jebb's memo to Bevin recounting his conversation with the Italian ambassador to the United Kingdom, 28 February 1949, F.O. 371/79229, doc. no. Z1851, PRO. The Italians were painfully aware of British resistance; see, for example, Egidio Ortona, "Diplomacy on the Spot," in *NATO's Anxious Birth*, ed. Nicholas Sherwen (London: C. Hurst, 1985), 103.

42. Telegram no. 77 from Foreign Office (initialed by Bevin) to Rome and Washington, 13 January 1949, F.O. 371/79220, doc. no. Z260/1074/72G, PRO. There is also documentary evidence indicating that Italian officials knew that British opposition to their participation in the envisaged alliance was not based on any focused animosity but rather on what the Italian ambassador to Paris described at the time as the fact "that the English do not take us seriously enough to even carry out a policy against us." See cable from Ambassador Pietro Quaroni to Foreign Minister Carlo Sforza, 3 November 1948, reproduced and translated in Bruno Vigezzi, "Unpublished—How Italy Entered the Atlantic Alliance," *Relazioni internazionali* 1 (June 1988): 136–41.

43. Letter to Jebb from Jo Hollis of the Ministry of Defence, 20 January 1949, F.O. 371/79222, ref. no. c.o.s. 123/20/1/9, PRO.

44. Telegram no. 223 from Foreign Office (initialed by Bevin) to Franks, 7 January 1949, F.O. 371/79219, doc. no. Z78/1074/72G, PRO. See also Jebb

Minute for Bevin, 17 January 1949, F.O. 371/79222, doc. no. Z666/1074/72G, PRO.

45. See Telegram no. 223, F.O. 371/79219, doc. no. Z78/1074/72G, PRO, and Ortona, "Diplomacy on the Spot," 105, 108.

46. Schuman quoted in Telegram no. 893 from U.S. Ambassador to France Jefferson Caffery to Acheson, 3 March 1949, doc. no. 840.20/3–349, USNA. See also Foreign Office Minute from Jebb to Sir Orme Sargent recording his conversation with General Elie (French representative on the Military Committee of the Brussels treaty), 25 January 1949, F.O. 371/79223, doc. no. Z885, PRO; and Henderson, *Birth of NATO*, 68, 95.

47. Memorandum by the Secretary of State (Acheson) of Discussion with the President (Truman), 2 March 1949, *FRUS 1949*, 4:141. See also French Ambassador Bonnet's comments in the Minutes of the Fourteenth Meeting of the Washington Exploratory Talks on Security, 1 March 1949, *FRUS 1949*, 4:129.

48. See Telegram no. 461 from Foreign Office to Washington, 12 January 1949, F.O. 371/79220, doc. no. Z246/1074/72G, and Telegram no. 77 from Foreign Office to Rome, 13 January 1949, F.O. 371/79220, doc. no. Z260/1074/72G, PRO.

49. See Memorandum by the Director of the Policy Planning Staff with attached staff paper on "Considerations Affecting the Conclusion of a North Atlantic Security Pact," 24 November 1948, *FRUS 1948*, 3:283–89.

50. "Arguments Against Inclusion of Italy in the North Atlantic Pact," Annex to Memorandum by the Secretary of State of Discussion with the President, 2 March 1949, *FRUS 1949*, 4:142–43.

51. Letter from Achilles to James C. H. Bonbright (counselor, U.S. Embassy, Paris), 17 January 1949, doc. no. 840.20/1–1749, USNA. Dean Acheson presented this argument almost verbatim to Truman in their 2 March meeting cited in *FRUS 1949*, 4:143.

52. Office Memorandum from Hickerson to Kennan, 26 November 1948, doc. no. 840.20/11–2648, USNA.

53. See analysis of American attitudes prepared by British Joint Services Mission for the Chiefs of Staff at the Ministry of Defence, 31 December 1948, F.O. 371/79219, ref. no. c.o.s. 14/4/1/9, PRO.

54. For discussion of the significance of the debate over NATO membership in the Italian domestic political context, see Primo Vannicelli, *Italy, NATO, and the European Community* (Cambridge, Mass.: Harvard University Center for International Affairs, 1974), esp. 5–9.

55. See, for example, analysis of possible implications in letter from Italian Ambassador to France Pietro Quaroni to Foreign Minister Carlo Sforza dated 3 November 1948, reproduced and translated in Vigezzi, "Unpublished—How Italy Entered the Atlantic Alliance," 138.

56. See account of Jebb's meeting with the Italian ambassador to London, 28 February 1949, F.O. 371/79229, doc. no. Z1851/1074/72G, PRO.

57. NSC 1/2 of 10 February 1948, formally approved by Truman on 15 March, cited in "Arguments for Inclusion of Italy in the North Atlantic

Pact," Annex to Memorandum by the Secretary of State of Discussion with the President, 2 March 1949, *FRUS 1949*, 4:143.

58. For a detailed description of the history of American funding of Italian political parties and their associates, see footnote 448 of the Pike Report, a Memorandum for the Forty Committee, discussing the "Political Action Program for [deleted] to Arrest the Growing Power of the Communists," as reprinted in "The CIA Report the President Doesn't Want You To Read," *Village Voice*, 16 February 1976, 86.

59. See Decision Memorandum from Hickerson to the Secretary of State, 11 February 1949, doc. no. 840.20/2–1149, USNA.

60. Memorandum by the Secretary of State of Discussion with the President, 2 March 1949, *FRUS 1949*, 4:142.

61. Office Memorandum from Satterthwaite (director of the Office of Near Eastern and African Affairs) to Lovett on "Future United States Policy Toward Security of Nations Threatened by the USSR but Not Included in the Proposed North Atlantic Defense Arrangement," 26 October 1948, doc. no. 840.20/10–2648, USNA.

62. Record of London Consultative Council Session of Brussels Treaty Powers, 27–28 January 1949, F.O. 371/79223, doc. no. Z970/1074/72G, PRO. See also Telegram no. 940 from Bevin to Franks, 22 January 1949, F.O. 371/79222, doc. no. Z519/1074/72G, PRO, and Henderson, *Birth of NATO*, 106. Toward the end of the negotiations, there was also discussion of the precise wording of article 6 that revealed the desire of the British to stretch the NATO commitment to cover their "armed forces" in Greece (Telegram no. 624 from Foreign Office to Washington, 15 January 1949, F.O. 371/79221, doc. no. Z365/1074/72G and Telegram no. 2590 from Foreign Office to Washington, 7 March 1949, F.O. 371/79231, doc. no. Z1962/1074/72G, PRO). This terminology was resisted by the Americans as well as by the Dutch and the Canadians. Telegram no. 1282 from Franks to Foreign Office, 4 March 1949, F.O. 371/79231, doc. no. Z1961/1074/72G, PRO. See also text of American draft and British redraft of "Proposed Additional Article (?8)" in Draft of Proposed Atlantic Pact, 20 January 1949, F.O. 371/79223, doc. no. Z892/1074/72G, PRO. As a result the final commitment referred only to the "occupation forces" of any of the parties that were stationed in Europe when the treaty came into effect. The Foreign Office noted ironically, "It is unfortunate that British troops in Greece should be regarded as 'occupation troops'—they are already called that by the Communists" (Comment by John Cormick of 9 March 1949 on cover of Franks cable to Foreign Office of 7 March 1949, F.O. 371/79232, doc. no. Z2025/1074/72G, PRO).

63. See Office Memorandum on "Declaration on Greece, Turkey and Iran," esp. Tab A on "Reasons for Including Iran," Office Memorandum from Satterthwaite to Acheson, 8 March 1949, doc. no. 840–20/3–849, USNA.

64. See Memorandum of Conversation between Franks and Acheson on "Revised British Attitude on Proposed Statement on Greece, Turkey, and Iran," 15 March 1949, doc. no. 840.20/3–1549, USNA, and Henderson, *Birth of NATO*, 106.

65. Telegram no. 76 from Franks to Foreign Office, 22 February 1949, F.O. 371/79224, doc. no. Z1627/1074,72G, PRO.

66. Office Memorandum on "Declaration on Greece, Turkey and Iran" from Satterthwaite to Acheson, 8 March 1949, doc. no. 840.20/3–849, USNA.

67. Jebb to Sir William Strang, 3 March 1949, F.O. 371/79232, doc. no. Z2086/1074/72G, PRO.

68. Memorandum of Conversation on "Revised British Attitude," 15 March 1949, doc. no. 840.20/3–1549, USNA, and Henderson, *Birth of NATO*, 106.

69. Telegram no. 1391 from Franks to Foreign Office, 9 March 1949, F.O. 371/79223, doc. no. Z2115/1074/72G, PRO.

70. In September 1950, Greece and Turkey had been invited to associate themselves with NATO in a limited fashion through participation in military planning for the defense of the Mediterranean, but this did not constitute formal membership entitling them to invoke the NATO mutual defense guarantee in the event of an attack on the territories of either country.

71. See Telegram no. 243 from Franks to Foreign Office, 12 January 1949, F.O. 371/79221, and Memo on the Atlantic Pact from Jebb to Bevin, 4 January 1949, F.O. 371/79220, PRO.

72. See Memo from Hickerson to Lovett, 14 January 1949, doc. no. 840.20/1–1449, and Office Memorandum from Achilles to Acheson on "Points Concerning the Atlantic Pact Which Ambassador Bonnet May Raise," 14 February 1949, doc. no. 840.20/2–1449, USNA. See also Bevin's assessment of the American position in Telegram no. 15 to Paris, 5 January 1949, F.O. 371–79219, PRO.

73. As of 3 July 1962, when Algeria gained its independence from France, the relevant clauses of the treaty became inapplicable.

74. See discussion in Henderson, *Birth of NATO*, 81.

75. See Letter from Rear Admiral Davis of the Joint Chiefs of Staff to Achilles, 9 December 1948, and Department of State Memorandum of Conversation on "Defense of the Belgian Congo," 10 December 1948, doc. no. 840.20/12–948, and Telegram from Lovett (acting secretary of state) to American Embassy in Brussels, 11 December 1948, doc. no. 840.20/12–1148, USNA.

76. Achilles, "U.S. Role in Negotiations that Led to Atlantic Alliance," 16; Henrikson, "The Creation of the North Atlantic Alliance," 306; and Escott Reid, *Time of Fear and Hope* (Toronto: McClelland and Stewart, 1977), 195.

77. See, for example, discussion of British concurrence in the American assessment of the value of including Scandinavia and Portugal in Henderson, *Birth of NATO*, 48.

78. The 10 September 1948 paper on "Territorial Scope of a North Atlantic Security Arrangement" that formed the basis of discussion at the Washington Talks explicitly stated: "To be effective the arrangement must provide for the defense of . . . Portugal (Azores)" (Doc. no. 840.20/9–948, USNA).

79. Text of oral communication from Portuguese government in Tele-

gram no. 6 from Lisbon (Sir N. Ronald) to Foreign Office, 6 January 1949, F.O. 371/79219, doc. no. Z137/1074/72G, PRO.

80. Henderson, *Birth of NATO*, 78, Telegram no. 10 from Washington to Lisbon, 8 January 1949, F.O. 371/79219, doc. no. Z140/1074/72G, and Aide-Mémoire of Meeting of the American Ambassador to Portugal (MacVeagh) with the Portuguese Minister for Foreign Affairs (Caeiro da Matta), 10 January 1949, *FRUS 1949*, 4:20.

81. Translation of memorandum from Portuguese foreign minister contained in Telegram from MacVeagh to Acheson, 9 March 1949, *FRUS 1949*, 4:182.

82. With the introduction of democracy in the late 1970s, Spain was invited to join NATO and formally acceded on 29 May 1982. For material on Portuguese attitudes toward Spanish accession, see text of oral communication of 31 December 1948 to Her Majesty's Ambassador from Portuguese Minister for Foreign Affairs contained in Telegram from Ronald to Foreign Office, 6 January 1949, F.O. 371/79219, doc. no. 2140/1074/72G, PRO, and Henderson, *Birth of NATO*, 78.

83. Letter from Secretary of Defense James Forrestal to Acheson, with Enclosures on "Anticipated Position of Scandinavia in Strategic Considerations" and "Study on the Military Implications to the United States of a Scandinavian Pact" (which was subsequently circulated as NSC 28/2), 10 February 1949, *FRUS 1949*, 4:95–101, esp. 100–101. See also Memorandum from the Policy Planning Staff of meeting on "Scandinavian Countries and the North Atlantic Security Pact," 10 February 1949, doc. no. 840.20/2–1049, USNA. Surprisingly, John Foster Dulles was a leading opponent of Norwegian and Danish membership, arguing that the defensive advantages of their inclusion were outweighed by the prospect that their adhesion would provoke Soviet aggression. See Reston, "We Assume World Role But Cost Bothers Us."

84. See Franks's comments in Twelfth Meeting of the Washington Exploratory Talks on Security, 8 February 1949, *FRUS 1949*, 4:78–79.

85. See paper given by Foreign Minister Schuman to the American Ambassador in Paris, 26 February 1949, doc. no. 840.20/2–2849, USNA.

86. Memorandum of Conversation between Acheson and Norwegian Ambassador (Morgenstierne), 1 March 1949, and Editorial note on unpublished memoranda of conversations of 8 March 1949, in *FRUS 1949*, 4:135–36, 176–77.

87. Henderson, *Birth of NATO*, 66–67, and notes of International Working Group, 13 January 1949, in USNA file no. 840.20 with no document number.

88. "The Atlantic Nations Unite for Defense," *Life*, 28 March 1949, 38.

89. For final texts of North Atlantic Treaty articles relevant to this study, see appendix.

90. Reston, "We Assume World Role But Cost Bothers Us." See also editorial, "The Atlantic Alliance," *Life*, 11 April 1949, 44, and "The Pact Is Signed," *Life*, 18 April 1949, 3.

91. Editorial, "Destiny at the Door," *New York Times*, 3 April 1949, 8E.

See also Bertram D. Hulen, "North Atlantic Pact Erases Last Marks of Isolationism," *New York Times*, 5 April 1949, 8.

92. Truman address, reprinted in *New York Times*, 5 April 1949, 6.

93. W. H. Lawrence, "12 Nations Sign Atlantic Treaty," *New York Times*, 5 April 1949, 1.

CHAPTER 2. Probing the Limits of Alliance, I: Asia, 1949–1956

1. X [George F. Kennan], "The Sources of Soviet Conduct," *Foreign Affairs* 25 (July 1947): 581.

2. Even before the establishment of NATO, the British had endeavored—albeit with little success—to commit the United States to the defense of the region. For London, the harbinger of the Cold War in Southeast Asia had been the Communist insurgency in Malaya in 1948. See Ritchie Ovendale, "Britain, the United States and the Cold War in South-East Asia, 1949–1950," *International Affairs* 58, no. 3 (Summer 1982): 447.

3. Brief prepared for the British foreign secretary on Southeast Asia and the Far East on 23 March 1949, in advance of his visit to Washington, F.O. 371/76023, PRO. See also description of the conversations between Bevin and Acheson, in Alan Bullock, *Ernest Bevin: Foreign Secretary, 1945–1951* (New York: W. W. Norton, 1983), 673.

4. Acheson quoted in Ovendale, "Britain, the United States, and the Cold War in South-East Asia," 460.

5. Acheson knew that London was likely to be uneasy about such a scheme. In preparation for a round of talks to be held in Washington in mid-September, the secretary of state was advised that, with respect to a potential Pacific pact, "the British are reluctant to have a rival to the Empire [in Asia]" and that "they consider the Asiatics will be reluctant to do much unless pressed from behind and they consider the Empire the proper instrument of pressure" (*FRUS 1949*, 7:1207).

6. A Report to the President by the National Security Council on "The Position of the United States with Respect to Asia," *FRUS 1949*, 7, pt. 2:1215–16.

7. *FRUS 1949*, 7, pt. 2:1215–20.

8. Samuel P. Huntington, *The Common Defense: Strategic Programs in National Politics* (New York: Columbia University Press, 1961), 47–48. For more on this subject, see also 49–69.

9. Tracy S. Voorhees, "To Prevent a 'Korea' in Western Europe," *New York Times Magazine*, 23 July 1950, 10–11, 36–37, and Robert Endicott Osgood, *NATO: The Entangling Alliance* (Chicago: University of Chicago Press, 1962), 68.

10. Dean Acheson, *Present at the Creation* (New York: W. W. Norton, 1969), 405.

11. Huntington elaborates on why conventional defense spending remained imperative: "The atomic bomb was of little help in preserving the integrity of Iran, suppressing guerrillas in Greece, or deterring an attack in Korea" (*Common Defense*, 41).

12. Bradley testimony in U.S. House of Representatives, *The Supplemental Appropriation Bill for 1951*, Hearings Before a Subcommittee of the Committee on Appropriations, 81st Cong., 2d sess. (Washington, D.C.: GPO, 1950), 20. See also Samuel F. Wells, Jr., "Sounding the Tocsin: NSC 68 and the Soviet Threat," *International Security* 4, no. 2 (Fall 1979): 139–40.

13. Senator Joseph R. McCarthy maintained that funding for the reconstruction and rearmament of Europe detracted from the struggle against Communism in Asia. Indeed, he accused General Marshall of having been the chief saboteur of congressional efforts on behalf of Korea. See Walter LaFeber, *America, Russia and the Cold War, 1945–1975*, 3d ed. (New York: John Wiley and Sons, 1976), 112–13.

14. Samuel Huntington described the three goals of the newly sanctioned rearmament effort engendered by Korea: "The immediate prosecution of the Korean War; the creation of a mobilization base which could be maintained over a long period of time and which would make possible rapid total mobilization in a general war; and the development of the active forces required to counterbalance the increase in Soviet strength and to deter further Soviet aggression" (*Common Defense*, 54).

15. See Bullock, *Ernest Bevin*, 804.

16. The NAC is NATO's principal political decision-making body.

17. See Acheson, *Present at the Creation*, 443–44.

18. *NATO Final Communiqués, 1949–1974* (Brussels: NATO Information Service), 26 December 1950, 59 (hereafter, NFC).

19. The Western European Union had a military command under Field Marshal Montgomery in Fontainebleau, France, which served as the embryo for NATO's military command center, the Supreme Headquarters Allied Powers Europe (SHAPE).

20. See Roger Hilsman, "On NATO Strategy," in Arnold Wolfers, ed., *Alliance Policy in the Cold War* (Baltimore: The Johns Hopkins University Press, SAIS, 1959), 146.

21. Osgood, *Entangling Alliance*, 74.

22. This proved possible in part because the Soviet Union's U.N. representative, who had been boycotting the Security Council since January in protest against the continued presence of the Nationalist Chinese, was not present at the 25 and 27 June 1950 sessions during which the resolutions were presented that legitimized the United Nations military effort in Korea as a means of upholding the organization's collective security system. For more on these resolutions and on the initial role of the United Nations, see Leland M. Goodrich, *Korea: A Study of U.S. Policy in the United Nations* (New York: Council on Foreign Relations, 1956), 102–25.

23. Acheson testimony, 1 June 1951, in U.S. Senate, *Military Situation in the Far East*, Hearings Before the Committee on Armed Services and the Committee on Foreign Relations, 82d Cong., 1st sess. (Washington, D.C.: GPO, 1951), pt. 3:1715.

24. Lester B. Pearson, *Mike: The Memoirs of the Right Honorable Lester B. Pearson*, ed. John A. Munro and Alex I. Inglis (New York: Quadrangle Books, 1973), 2:151.

25. Pearson, *Mike: The Memoirs*, 153.

26. See David Rees, *Korea: The Limited War* (New York: St. Martin's Press, 1964), 32–33. Specific contributions of the Atlantic allies (including Greece and Turkey) were as follows: Belgium, one infantry battalion; Canada, a reinforced infantry brigade, including tank and artillery forces, part of the Commonwealth Division, some naval forces, and a squadron of transport aircraft; France, one reinforced infantry battalion; Greece, one infantry battalion and transport aircraft; Luxembourg, one infantry company; the Netherlands, one infantry battalion and naval forces; Turkey, one infantry brigade; United Kingdom, two infantry brigades, one armored regiment, one and one-half artillery regiments, one and one-half combat engineer regiments and supporting ground forces, all part of the Commonwealth division, the Far Eastern fleet, and two Sunderland squadrons of the Royal Air Force. This information may be found in Rees, appendix A, 457. See also Matthew B. Ridgway, *The Korean War* (Garden City, N.Y.: Doubleday, 1967), 221, 240.

27. Goodrich, *Korea: A Study of U.S. Policy in the United Nations*, 117.

28. Pearson, *Mike: The Memoirs*, 148.

29. See, for example, State Department draft minutes of discussions at State-Joint Chiefs of Staff Meeting, 30 January 1951, *FRUS 1951*, 5:28. For a study of the relationship between the United States and the United Kingdom at the time of the Korean War, see Jong-yil Ra, "Special Relationship at War: The Anglo-American Relationship During the Korean War," *Journal of Strategic Studies* 7, no. 3 (September 1984): 307–17.

30. "Essential Elements of US-UK Relations," *FRUS 1950*, 3:870.

31. Acheson, *Present at the Creation*, 527.

32. Truman said on 30 November that, with respect to the possible use of the atomic bomb in taking the necessary steps to "meet the military situation," he would consider using "every weapon we have" and that "there has always been active consideration of its use" (Rees, *Korea: The Limited War*, 167). For Truman's account of this event and of his subsequent discussions with Attlee, see Harry S Truman, *Memoirs: Years of Trial and Hope* (Garden City, N.Y.: Doubleday, 1956), 395–413, esp. 395 and 409, respectively.

33. For example, see Lord Bullock's account of these worries in *Ernest Bevin*, 792.

34. "United States Delegation Minutes of the First Meeting of President Truman and Prime Minister Attlee," 4 December 1950, *FRUS 1950*, 3:1366.

35. Cable from Ambassador in France (Bruce) to Secretary of State, 5 December 1950, in *FRUS 1950*, 7:1388.

36. See Special Assistant to the President Averell Harriman's remarks in "United States Delegation Minutes of the Fifth Meeting of President Truman and Prime Minister Attlee," 7 December 1950, in *FRUS 1950*, 7:1458.

37. Truman, *Years of Trial and Hope*, 402.

38. "Communiqué issued at the Conclusion of the Truman-Attlee Discussions," 8 December 1950, *FRUS 1950*, 7:1479.

39. Letter from Attlee to Bevin, 10 December 1950, F.O. 371/81637, quoted in Ra, "The Special Relationship at War," 312. Even the French ac-

knowledged the special position the British occupied in the alliance and, however much it irked them, capitalized on it when it served their interests. Thus they sent Prime Minister René Pleven and Foreign Minister Robert Schuman to London to talk with Attlee before he left for Washington.

40. In March 1951, General MacArthur warned against what he perceived to be a dangerous European complacency: "Here we fight Europe's war with arms, while the diplomats there still fight it with words. . . . if we lose this war to Communism in Asia the fall of Europe is inevitable; win it and Europe most probably would avoid war and yet preserve freedom" (letter from Mac-Arthur to House Minority Leader Joseph W. Martin, quoted in Acheson, *Present at the Creation*, 520).

41. Huntington, *Common Defense*, 63–64, and Lawrence Freedman, *The Evolution of Nuclear Strategy* (New York: St. Martin's Press, 1982), 287–88.

42. Goodrich, *Korea: A Study of U.S. Policy in the United Nations*, 146–48. See also Pearson's observation that the "Korean War underlined the necessity for political consultation and cooperation with the smaller members of the North Atlantic Alliance, including Canada. The Alliance was becoming subject to strains over US policies in the Far East" (*Mike: The Memoirs*, 67).

43. Alastair Buchan, *Crisis Management* (Paris: The Atlantic Institute, 1966), 30.

44. On the tradition of anticolonialism in American foreign policy and on the impact of the Cold War on United States policy toward French efforts in Indochina, see Miles Kahler, *Decolonization in Britain and France* (Princeton: Princeton University Press, 1984), 364; Dwight D. Eisenhower, *The White House Years: Mandate for Change, 1953–1956* (Garden City, N.Y.: Doubleday, 1963), 373–74; and Julius W. Pratt, "Anticolonialism in United States Policy," in Robert Strausz-Hupé and Harry W. Hazard, eds., *The Idea of Colonialism* (New York: Praeger, 1958), 114–51.

45. See discussion of Roosevelt's views in Louis, *Imperialism at Bay*, 25–47; in Walter La Feber, "Roosevelt, Churchill, and Indochina: 1942–45," *American Historical Review* 80 (December 1975): 1277–95; and in chapter on "The Abolition of Imperialism" in Willard Range, *Franklin D. Roosevelt's World Order* (Athens: University of Georgia Press, 1959), 102–19, esp. 106.

46. Memorandum from Roosevelt to Cordell Hull, 24 January 1944, in *F.D.R.: His Personal Letters, 1928–1945* (New York: Duell, Sloan and Pearce, 1950), 1489.

47. See Acheson, *Present at the Creation*, 671; Philippe Devillers and Jean Lacouture, *End of a War: Indochina, 1954* (New York, Praeger, 1959), vii.

48. Roosevelt and Prime Minister Churchill had divergent interpretations of the meaning of the third article of the Atlantic Charter, in which they had declared their respect for "the right of all peoples to choose the form of government under which they will live." Later, Churchill argued that this applied only to European peoples who had been subjected to Nazi domination, while Roosevelt believed that it applied to all peoples seeking indepen-

dence everywhere. See Cordell Hull, *The Memoirs of Cordell Hull* (New York: Macmillan, 1948), 2:1484. See also Louis, *Imperialism at Bay*, 38–39.

49. Roosevelt reply to memorandum from Secretary of State Cordell Hull, 24 January 1944, in *The Pentagon Papers*, Senator Gravel ed. (Boston: Beacon Press, 1971), 1:10.

50. "Memorandum of Conversation [with the president], by the Adviser on Caribbean Affairs (Taussig)," 15 March 1945, *FRUS 1945*, 1:124.

51. Devillers and Lacouture, *End of a War*, vii.

52. Acheson, *Present at the Creation*, 671.

53. Acheson, *Present at the Creation*, 673.

54. Memorandum from Acheson to Truman, mid-February 1950, cited in *The Pentagon Papers* (New York: Bantam Books, 1971), 9.

55. Acheson, *Present at the Creation*, 672–73.

56. Acheson, *Present at the Creation*, 406.

57. See "U.S. Air and Sea Forces Ordered Into Supporting Action," in *Department of State Bulletin* (hereafter, DOSB) 23 (3 July 1950): 5.

58. Record of these talks and extracts of document NSC 105 in *FRUS 1951*, 6, pt. 1:367.

59. For more on French efforts in this regard, see Michael Harrison, *The Reluctant Ally: France and Atlantic Security* (Baltimore: The Johns Hopkins University Press, 1981), 17.

60. See description of these meetings in André Fontaine, *L'Alliance atlantique à l'heure du dégel* (Paris: Calmann-Lévy, 1959), 76–78.

61. See Acheson's instructions to the American ambassador to France in *FRUS 1950*, 3:59.

62. Acheson, *Present at the Creation*, 552.

63. Acheson, *Present at the Creation*, 553.

64. For this and further accounts of these exchanges, see "Memorandum on the Substance of Discussions at a Department of State-Joint Chiefs of Staff Meeting," 5 March 1952, *FRUS 1952–1954*, 12, pt. 1:55–68. This discussion appears on 60.

65. *FRUS 1952–1954*, 12, pt. 1:67.

66. See "Statement of Policy by the National Security Council on United States Objectives and Courses of Action With Respect to Southeast Asia," 25 June 1952, *FRUS 1952–1954*, 12, pt. 1:127–34.

67. Anthony Eden, *The Memoirs of Anthony Eden: Full Circle* (Boston: Houghton Mifflin, 1960), 93.

68. See Eden's discussion of this, *Full Circle*, 92.

69. NFC, 72.

70. See Ruth Lawson, "Concerting Policies in the North Atlantic Community," *International Organization* 12 (Spring 1958): 172.

71. Fontaine, *L'Alliance atlantique*, 73–74.

72. For more on this, see *Pentagon Papers*, Gravel ed., 1:85.

73. Eisenhower, *Mandate for Change*, 338. For Dulles's views on the impact of the Korean armistice, see *Pentagon Papers*, Gravel ed., 1:85–86.

74. Acheson, *Present at the Creation*, 677.

75. *FRUS 1952–1954*, 13:1166.

76. "Un tiers de l'aide U.S. à l'étranger réservé à l'Indochine," in *France-Soir*, 8 April 1954.

77. *Pentagon Papers*, Gravel ed., 1:54.

78. *Pentagon Papers*, Gravel ed., 1:54, 108.

79. See discussion based on message from General Trapnell to Commander in Chief Pacific Command (CINCPAC), January 1954, in Ronald Spector, *Advice and Support: The Early Years of the United States Army in Vietnam, 1941–1960* (New York: The Free Press, 1985), 183.

80. For more on the origins of the plan, see *Pentagon Papers*, Gravel ed., 1:97–98, and Stephen E. Ambrose, *Eisenhower: The President*, 2 vols. (New York: Touchstone, Simon and Schuster, 1984), 2:177–81.

81. Spector, *Advice and Support*, 193.

82. DOSB 30 (12 April 1954): 540.

83. For a detailed account of the meeting, see Chalmers M. Roberts, "The Day We Didn't Go to War," in *The Reporter*, 14 September 1954, 31–35. For discussion of congressional reaction, see Ambrose, *Eisenhower: The President*, 2:178; Bernard Fall, *Hell in a Very Small Place* (Philadelphia: J. B. Lippincott, 1967), 300-301; and Spector, *Advice and Support*, 203. See also analysis of the impact of Korea on Indochina in Alvin J. Cottrell and James E. Dougherty, "The Lessons of Korea: War and the Power of Man," *Orbis* 2, no. 1 (Spring 1958): 60–61.

84. *Pentagon Papers*, Gravel ed., 1:94.

85. Ambrose, *Eisenhower: The President*, 2:177–78.

86. Eisenhower, *Mandate for Change*, 347.

87. At the Berlin Four Power Conference earlier that year, the United States, the United Kingdom, France, and the Soviet Union had agreed to meet on 26 April in Geneva to discuss Korea and Indochina.

88. Eden, quoted in *Pentagon Papers*, Gravel ed., 1:99. On p. 102, there is mention of Downing Street's view that "French cannot lose the war between now [April 1954] and the coming of the rainy season however badly they may conduct it." See also Eden, *Full Circle*, 107.

89. There is some evidence that the British knew of American discussions about the possibility of using atomic weapons to "save" Dien Bien Phu and, as in the Korean case, this may have increased their anxiety even further. For example, in a 29 April cable from the Geneva talks, Dulles reported to Eisenhower that "British seem to feel that we are disposed to accept present risks of a Chinese war and this, coupled also with their fear that we would start using atomic weapons, has badly frightened them." For full text, see *Pentagon Papers*, Gravel ed., 1:481–82. For more on American consideration of nuclear options, see Spector, *Advice and Support*, 200–201.

90. See discussion in *Pentagon Papers*, Gravel ed., 1:102–3, and in Donald Neff, *Warriors at Suez* (New York: The Linden Press, Simon and Schuster, 1981), 146–47.

91. Eisenhower cited in Ambrose, *Eisenhower: The President*, 2:179–80.

92. *Pentagon Papers*, Gravel ed., 1:101–3.

93. *Pentagon Papers*, Gravel ed., 1:103.

94. In an account for Eisenhower of the Franco-American discussions held in Washington during the previous week, Radford observed, "I presented to General Ely our views in regard to expanding the MAAG to assist the French in training the Vietnamese, indicating to him the importance which we attach to this action, first, to obtain better results, secondly to release French officers for combat service. General Ely was most unsympathetic to any encroachment on French responsibilities or significant expansion of the MAAG" (*Pentagon Papers*, Gravel ed., 1:456). See also Spector, *Advice and Support*, 207.

95. Eisenhower quoted in Ambrose, *Eisenhower: The President*, 2:177.

96. These included the Associated States, Australia, France, New Zealand, the Philippines, Thailand, and the United Kingdom.

97. Eden, quoted in Neff, *Warriors at Suez*, 146–47.

98. Nixon, quoted in *Pentagon Papers*, Gravel ed., 1:104.

99. Eden, *Full Circle*, 110.

100. Neff, *Warriors at Suez*, 147.

101. See Eisenhower's account of Dulles's cables from Paris in *Mandate for Change*, 349–50, and report of the same in *Pentagon Papers*, Gravel ed., 1:104.

102. Eden, *Full Circle*, 116.

103. Eisenhower, *Mandate for Change*, 351.

104. See Eden's account of these deliberations in *Full Circle*, 117–19.

105. For more on these views, see Eisenhower, *Mandate for Change*, 348. See also *Pentagon Papers*, Gravel ed., 1:56.

106. Fall, *Hell in a Very Small Place*, 308.

107. Eden, *Full Circle*, 127.

108. *Pentagon Papers*, Gravel ed., 1:142.

109. Eden, *Full Circle*, 113–14. For Dulles's account of this conversation, see *FRUS 1952–1954*, 12:431.

110. The collection of agreements reached at Geneva included provisions for an end to hostilities, the independence and neutrality of Laos and Cambodia, and the supervision of the implementation of the agreements by an International Control Commission whose members were Canada, India, and Poland. This commission was to supervise general elections in July 1956. For texts of the final declaration of the Geneva Conference and of the American unilateral declaration, see Anthony Eden, *Toward Peace in Indochina* (Boston: Houghton Mifflin, 1966), app., 69-77.

111. See discussion in Ambrose, *Eisenhower: The President*, 2:208–10.

112. For the American account of discussions leading up to the signing of the SEATO treaty, see *FRUS 1952–1954*, 12, pt. 1.

113. "Lettre de M. Dulles à Mendès-France (19 août 1954)" and "Réponse du gouvernement français (26 août 1954)," in *Documents diplomatiques français 1954 (annex)* (Paris: Imprimerie nationale, 1987), 165–68. Reflecting French irritation with Dulles's letter, Mendès-France did not reply directly to him but instead instructed the French embassy in Washington to provide the State Department with a response in the form of a series of observations.

114. For the French account of these discussions, see "Conversations franco-américaines relatives à l'Indochine," Washington, 27–29 September 1954, in *Documents diplomatiques français 1954*, 173–201. For exchanges cited here, see 173–75. See also Ambrose, *Eisenhower: The President*, 2:210.

115. *Pentagon Papers*, Gravel ed., 1:182.

116. Alfred Grosser, *The Western Alliance*, trans. Michael Shaw (New York: Vintage Books, Random House, 1982), 137.

117. For more on this subject, see George A. Kelly, "The Political Background of the French A-Bomb," in *Orbis* 4, no. 3 (Fall 1960): 284–306. See also Wolf Mendl, *Deterrence and Persuasion: French Nuclear Armament in the Context of National Policy, 1945–1969* (New York: Praeger, 1970), and Robert L. Rothstein, *Alliances and Small Powers* (New York: Columbia University Press, 1968), 300–301. Rothstein asserts that the decision to acquire nuclear weapons was a purely political decision for France; that it was "unmotivated by strategic considerations."

118. See account of Pineau's speech to the Anglo-American Press Association in Paris in *Pentagon Papers*, Gravel ed., 1:183–84.

119. Eden had tried in 1952 to convince Eisenhower not to choose Dulles as his secretary of state because he felt he could not work with him (Eisenhower, *Mandate for Change*, 142, and Neff, *Warriors at Suez*, 144).

120. Neff, *Warriors at Suez*, 147. See also Dulles's speech of June 10, in which he stated, "We ourselves are the first colony in modern times to have won independence. We have a natural sympathy with those everywhere who would follow our example" (DOSB 30 [21 June 1954]: 936).

CHAPTER 3. Probing the Limits of Alliance, II:
The Middle East, 1950–1957

1. The Anglo-American "Pentagon Talks of 1947" focused on the importance of the Middle East and the Eastern Mediterranean. See *FRUS 1947*, 5:575–76.

2. Elaboration of these ideas appears in "Considerations in Support of Policy in Respect of the Eastern Mediterranean and the Middle East Drawn up After Consultation with the British Group," in *FRUS 1947*, 5:576–80, including discussion of "The Special Role of the British" on 579.

3. See, for example, "Memorandum on Policy in the Middle East and Eastern Mediterranean by the British Group," in *FRUS 1947*, 5:580–81. For a detailed history of the relationship between the British and the Americans in the Middle East before the creation of NATO, see Wm. Roger Louis, *The British Empire in the Middle East, 1945–1951* (Oxford: Clarendon Press, 1984).

4. *FRUS 1949*, 6:61.

5. See "Statement by the United States and United Kingdom Groups," 14 November 1949, in *FRUS 1949*, 6:61–64.

6. *FRUS 1950*, 5:122, n. 6.

7. George McGhee, *Envoy to the Middle World* (New York: Harper and Row, 1983), 53.

8. For text, see *FRUS 1950*, 5:167–68. For further discussion, see

McGhee, *Envoy to the Middle World*, 205–12. Reflecting on the residual competition between the British and French in the region, McGhee recalled that the United States had to persuade the British to include the French, who had less influence than the other two powers but were potentially significant arms suppliers to Israel and would be deeply offended if excluded.

9. Louis, *British Empire in the Middle East*, 588.

10. British-American Chiefs of Staff Meeting in Washington, 26 October 1950, in *FRUS 1950*, 3:1693.

11. Dean Acheson, *Present at the Creation* (New York: W. W. Norton, 1969), 562.

12. *FRUS 1951*, 5:95–97.

13. NATO approved the accession of Greece and Turkey to full membership on 20 September 1951. The two countries were formally admitted on 15 February 1952.

14. Memorandum by the Assistant Secretaries of State for Near Eastern and African Affairs (McGhee) and for European Affairs (Perkins) to the Secretary of State on "Greek-Turkish Security Commitment," 24 April 1951, *FRUS 1951*, 3:511–15.

15. Aide-Mémoire of 15 May 1951, reproduced in *FRUS 1951*, 3:520–22. Although the French did not figure prominently in the discussion of Greek and Turkish accession, their views on the subject may be found in *FRUS 1951*, 3:556–58.

16. United States Minutes of a United States-United Kingdom Meeting on Questions of Atlantic, Mediterranean and Middle Eastern Commands, 19 June 1951, in *FRUS 1951*, 3:535–45 (see especially comments of Air Chief Marshal Sir William Elliot regarding Turkey); Draft Memorandum Prepared by John Ferguson of the Policy Planning Staff on "Command in the Eastern Mediterranean and Middle East," 6 July 1951, *FRUS 1951*, 3:551–54; Draft Anglo-United States agreement prepared by the United Kingdom Representative on the Standing Group (Elliot) on "Command in the Mediterranean and the Middle East," July 1951, *FRUS 1951*, 3:559–61; Draft Anglo-United States Agreement Prepared in the Department of State on "Command in the Mediterranean and the Middle East," 18 July 1951, *FRUS 1951*, 3:563–64.

17. Acheson, *Present at the Creation*, 570.

18. Acheson, *Present at the Creation*, 570.

19. *FRUS 1951*, 3:522–24.

20. *FRUS 1951*, 3:551–54.

21. *FRUS 1951*, 3:559–60.

22. *FRUS 1951*, 3:563–64.

23. See discussion in *FRUS 1951*, 3:563–64, and in a position paper drafted by the United States Defense Department entitled "Three Power Action Regarding an Allied Middle East Command," in *FRUS 1951*, 5:184.

24. Acheson, *Present at the Creation*, 564.

25. See editorial note, *FRUS 1951*, 3:607.

26. Eisenhower quoted in Donald Neff, *Warriors at Suez* (New York: The Linden Press, Simon and Schuster, 1981), 36.

27. Dwight D. Eisenhower, *The White House Years: Waging Peace*,

1956–1961 (Garden City, N.Y.: Doubleday, 1965), 26–27, and Neff, *Warriors at Suez*, 152–53.

28. Selwyn Lloyd, *Suez 1956* (London: Jonathan Cape, 1978), 60–61.

29. For Eden's comments on this episode, see Anthony Eden, *The Memoirs of Anthony Eden: Full Circle* (Boston: Houghton Mifflin, 1960), 374–75, 246–47.

30. Lloyd, *Suez*, 78, 27, 60–61.

31. See Alvin J. Cottrell and James E. Dougherty, "Algeria: A Case Study in the Evolution of a Colonial Problem," in Robert Strausz-Hupé and Harry W. Hazard, eds., *The Idea of Colonialism* (New York: Praeger, 1958), 349–80.

32. See Lloyd's account of French attitudes in *Suez*, 78.

33. For Churchill quotation and further discussion, see Neff, *Warriors at Suez*, 70–71.

34. Lloyd, quoted in Neff, *Warriors at Suez*, 142.

35. Richard E. Neustadt, *Alliance Politics* (New York: Columbia University Press, 1970), 72–73.

36. J. B.-M., "Pour Washington la France n'est plus un 'grand,'" *L'Express*, 8 December 1955; "Le temps des conférences à trois est passé," *Combat*, 8 December 1955; and letter from British Ambassador to France Gladwyn Jebb to Secretary of State Harold Macmillan, 9 December 1955, in F.O. 371/124441, doc. no. F1051/1.

37. See contents of Foreign Office Files 371/121272 and 371/121273, PRO.

38. Pineau, cited in Neff, *Warriors at Suez*, 200–201.

39. Eden's belief that the Egyptians were behind the Hashemite monarch's removal of Glubb Pasha was reinforced by his recollection that Nasser had previously dissuaded Jordan from adhering to the Baghdad Pact (Neff, *Warriors at Suez*, 176–77).

40. There were some American officials, like Treasury Secretary George Humphrey, who believed that the dam project "was a British ploy to gouge money out of the United States," but their views were not widespread. See Leonard Mosley, *Dulles: A Biography of Eleanor, Allen, and John Foster Dulles and Their Family Network* (New York: The Dial Press, James Wade, 1978), 397–98.

41. Eisenhower letter to Eden, 6 April 1956, before Eden and Lloyd met with Soviet Party Secretary Nikita Khrushchev and Chairman of the Soviet Council of Ministers Marshal Bulganin, and Eden's reply, 18 April 1956, F.O. 371/121272, doc. no. V1075 99, PRO.

42. Prime minister's personal telegram and record of 29 July conversation between Lloyd and Pineau in PREM 11/1098, PRO.

43. Neff, *Warriors at Suez*, 289.

44. The original texts of Eden's and Macmillan's communications were not available in the relevant files at the PRO as of March 1988. However, the text of Eisenhower's reply may be found in PREM 11/1098, PRO, and in Eisenhower, *Waging Peace*, app. B, 664.

45. Lloyd, *Suez*, 94–95. In at least one respect, Lloyd's argument was not hyberbolic: British Minister of Fuel and Power Aubrey Jones told a Cabinet meeting on 27 July that the oil passing through the canal represented two-

thirds of Western Europe's fuel supplies and that during the previous year one-third of the ships transiting the canal had been British and three-quarters belonged to NATO members. See description of Jones's presentation in Robert Rhodes James, *Anthony Eden* (London: Weidenfeld and Nicolson, 1986), 460.

46. Eisenhower, *Waging Peace*, app. B, 664–65.

47. See Eden's comments in *Full Circle*, 486–87.

48. The original use of the phrase *Entente Cordiale* refers to the relationship between Britain and France in the first half of the nineteenth century, when a balance of power was maintained in Europe by constantly shifting alliances. See Gordon Craig, "The System of Alliances and the Balance of Power," in J. P. T. Bury, ed., *The New Cambridge Modern History* (Cambridge: Cambridge University Press, 1960), 10: 246–73. British policymakers revived the term to describe the relationship between the United Kingdom and France during the Suez crisis. See, for example, 28 September 1956 Telegram from Ambassador Gladwyn Jebb to Foreign Office in which he observed, "French certainly feel themselves committed as seldom before to the Entente Cordiale" (F.O. 371/12444, PRO).

49. The American chargé attended because Ambassador Aldrich was out of town. For further discussion of this meeting, see Lloyd, *Suez*, 74-75; Mosley, *Dulles*, 404–5; Neff, *Warriors at Suez*, 275; and Rhodes James, *Eden*, 453–54.

50. Eisenhower, *Waging Peace*, 41.

51. Roy Fullick and Geoffrey Powell, *Suez: The Double War* (London: Hamish Hamilton, 1979), 17, 21.

52. Kennett Love, *Suez: The Twice Fought War* (New York: McGraw-Hill, 1969), 392.

53. Mollet and Dulles quoted in Love, *Suez*, 393.

54. See "Final Protocol of the Meeting of the Three Ministers of Foreign Affairs," 2 August 1956, PREM 11/1098, PRO.

55. Eden, *Full Circle*, 497.

56. Spain, which also attended, was not then a NATO member. For a complete list of the invitees and participants in the first London Conference, see *American Foreign Policy: Current Documents, 1956* (Washington, D.C.: GPO, 1959), 608.

57. Lester B. Pearson, *Mike: The Memoirs of the Right Honorable Lester B. Pearson*, ed. John A. Munro and Alex I. Inglis (New York: Quadrangle Books, 1973), 2:229.

58. This included the sixteen major users of the canal plus the original signatories to the Convention of Constantinople, which had first guaranteed use of the waterway. Not suprisingly, Egypt refused to participate.

59. Lloyd, *Suez*, 503. See also Neff, *Warriors at Suez*, 296–97.

60. Neff, *Warriors at Suez*, 296.

61. In a letter to Churchill after the crisis was over, Eisenhower revealed these emotions: "Nothing saddens me more than the thought that I and my old friends of years have met a problem concerning which we do not see eye to eye. I shall never be happy until our old time closeness has been restored." The full text may be found in Eisenhower, *Waging Peace*, app. H, 680–81.

62. Eisenhower, *Waging Peace*, 48.

63. 27 August 1956 letter from Prime Minister Eden to President Eisenhower, F.O. 800/726, PRO.

64. Eisenhower, *Waging Peace*, app. C, 667, or "Letter from the President to the Prime Minister," received at Foreign Office on 3 September, F.O. 800/726, PRO.

65. "Message from the Prime Minister to President Eisenhower," 6 September 1956, F.O. 800/726, PRO, and Eden, *Full Circle*, 518–21.

66. Lloyd, *Suez*, 127–28. See also Eden, *Full Circle*, 511, and Harold Macmillan, *Riding the Storm, 1956-1959* (London: Macmillan, 1971), 113.

67. See Neff's account of the Menzies meetings with Nasser and the stinging response of the Egyptian press toward the proposal in *Warriors at Suez*, 302–3.

68. Eisenhower, *Waging Peace*, app. D, 669–71.

69. See Lloyd, *Suez*, 133, and Eden, *Full Circle*, 536.

70. Christian Pineau, *1956/Suez* (Paris: Editions Robert Laffont, 1976), 101. The British account of Pineau's position is somewhat contradictory: Eden noted that "M. Pineau frankly regarded further talk with the United States Government about the Users' Club as a waste of time" (*Full Circle*, 533–34).

71. For a vivid description of the political crossfire in which Eden was caught, see Rhodes James, *Eden*, 513–16.

72. Dulles quoted in Eden, *Full Circle*, 539. See also account in Macmillan, *Riding the Storm*, 125.

73. Eden, *Full Circle*, 539–40.

74. Rhodes James, *Eden*, 512.

75. Dulles press conference of 2 October 1956 reproduced in *United States Policy in the Middle East, September 1956–June 1957* (Washington, D.C.: Department of State Publications, 1957), 103. Eden also gave an account of Dulles's statement, and although the wording was slightly different, the meaning was essentially the same (*Full Circle*, 556–57).

76. In a draft paper on Anglo-American relations circulated among Foreign Office officials in the aftermath of Suez, the British observed that "one must frankly feel little hope of being able to get things straight so long as Mr. Dulles remains Secretary of State. It would probably be quite practicable to have some basic discussion with him, but one would have the fear that, as so often in the past, what ultimately emerged in public did not correspond with the impression we obtained in private" (Paper with cover memo of 23 November 1956 in F.O. 115/4545, PRO).

77. Eisenhower, *Waging Peace*, 52.

78. See suggestion to that effect in Neff, *Warriors at Suez*, 321, 341, 430.

79. Macmillan, *Riding the Storm*, 139.

80. Lloyd noted, "I gather that he [Dulles] had become very angry that we had taken the matter to the Security Council without his permission" (Memorandum by Selwyn Lloyd on "M. Pineau and Mr. Dulles in New York," 15 October 1956, F.O. 800/725, PRO).

81. Details of the Six Principles may be found in Eisenhower, *Waging Peace*, 54.

82. Pineau was still in New York at the United Nations.

83. Telegram from Ambassador Gladwyn Jebb in Paris to Foreign Office, 28 September 1956, F.O. 371/124444, PRO.

84. Letter from Ambassador Gladwyn Jebb to Assistant Under Secretary of State Harold Beeley, 9 August 1956, and Beeley's reply, 11 August 1956, F.O. 371/118871, PRO.

85. Eisenhower, *Waging Peace*, 56. William P. Bundy described the halt in the exchange of intelligence information in "Crisis and Consensus: Western Experience," April 1984 draft for speech to Naval War College on 9 May 1984.

86. Dulles phone conversation of 18 October with his brother Allen, quoted in Neff, *Warriors at Suez*, 341.

87. Neustadt, *Alliance Politics*, 143.

88. Rhodes James, *Eden*, 539.

89. Stephen E. Ambrose, *Eisenhower: The President*, 2 vols. (New York: Touchstone, Simon and Schuster, 1984), 2:354.

90. For the text of the Treaty of Sèvres, see Rhodes James, *Eden*, 531.

91. Selwyn Lloyd memorandum of 24 October 1956 in F.O. 800/725, PRO.

92. Interview with a French social scientist and political commentator (unnamed), and with a French senator (unnamed), in Herbert Luethy and David Rodnick, *French Motivations in the Suez Crisis* (Princeton: The Institute for International Social Research, 1956), 76–77, 88.

93. Pineau, quoted in Neff, *Warriors at Suez*, 324. See also Mollet's comment to the same effect in Eisenhower, *Waging Peace*, 77.

94. Macmillan and Eden quoted in Mosley, *Dulles*, 407 and 412, respectively.

95. Lloyd, *Suez*, 193.

96. Macmillan, *Riding the Storm*, 157.

97. The willful deception was most blatant at a dinner meeting on 28 October between Lloyd and American Ambassador Winthrop Aldrich. The latter asked Lloyd directly about the signs of Israeli mobilization, and Lloyd put him off the scent by replying that Britain knew no details and only the day before had warned Israel not to attack *Jordan*. Then Aldrich asked if Israel was going to attack Egypt, to which Lloyd disingenuously replied that his government had no information (Neff, *Warriors at Suez*, 360).

98. Eisenhower, *Waging Peace*, 77.

99. Eisenhower, *Waging Peace*, app. G, 678–79.

100. Eisenhower, *Waging Peace*, 76.

101. Eisenhower telegram quoted in Rhodes James, *Eden*, 543. This document is not reproduced in Eisenhower's memoirs, nor is it available in the relevant files at the PRO.

102. "U.S. Strengthens the Sixth Fleet" and "Special Unit Quits Rotterdam," *New York Times*, 31 October 1956, 12.

103. Keightley quoted in Peter Hennessy and Mark Laity, "Suez—What the Papers Say," *Contemporary Record* 1, no. 1 (Spring 1987): 8. Evelyn

Shuckburgh recorded that the Anglo-French force "was delayed twenty-four hours by the American 6th Fleet getting in its way" (*Descent to Suez: Diaries, 1951–56* [New York: W. W. Norton, 1986], 305). Rhodes James also discussed the movement of the Sixth Fleet (*Eden*, 565, 568).

104. Lloyd, *Suez*, 42.

105. William M. Blair, "Nixon Hails Break with Allies' Policies," *New York Times*, 3 November 1956, 1. See also quotations and discussion in Eden, *Full Circle*, 606, and in Lloyd, *Suez*, 201–2.

106. Message from Prime Minister to President Eisenhower, 5 November 1956, F.O. 800/726, PRO.

107. Drew Middleton, "Naval Bombardment Aids Commandos at Port Said," *New York Times*, 6 November 1956, 1.

108. Eisenhower applauded Eden's agreement "to order a ceasefire this evening" in a message to the prime minister sent at 2:45 A.M. on 7 November 1956 (F.O. 800/726, PRO).

109. Eisenhower, *Waging Peace*, 65, 89.

110. Allen Dulles quoted in Mosley, *Dulles*, 420.

111. Texts of Bulganin messages in Eden, *Full Circle*, 619–21; Eisenhower, *Waging Peace*, 89.

112. Chester L. Cooper, *The Lion's Last Roar: Suez, 1956* (New York: Harper and Row, 1978), 200.

113. Their communications resumed apace with a telephone conversation on 6 November and a return to their traditionally warm salutations in an exchange of cables on 7 November (Messages from president to prime minister and from prime minister to president, 7 November 1956, F.O. 800/726, PRO).

114. Eisenhower, *Waging Peace*, 94.

115. At the time, Britain got 75 percent of its oil from the region and France 90 percent (Fullick and Powell, *Suez*, 159, and Cooper, *Lion's Last Roar*, 213).

116. Eisenhower, quoted in Neff, *Warriors at Suez*, 414.

117. See 11 November 1956 message from Eden to Eisenhower, in which the prime minister offers support—at Mollet's request—to the French proposal for consultations among the three (F.O. 800/726, PRO).

118. See comments of Under Secretary of State Herbert Hoover, Jr., in Neff, *Warriors at Suez*, 415. Hoover was acting secretary of state because Dulles had fallen ill.

119. See messages from prime minister to president of 7 November 1956 in F.O. 800/726 or F.O. 371/127274, 8 November 1956 in F.O. 371/127274, and 11 November 1956 in F.O. 800/726, PRO.

120. The Oral History of Ambassador William Macomber in the *Princeton Papers*, cited in Mosley, *Dulles*, 428.

121. See Eisenhower message to Eden of 7 November 1956 in which the president asserts that "it is vital no excuse be given for Soviet participation in United Nations force, therefore all big Five should be excluded from force" (F.O. 800/726, PRO).

122. Pearson, *Mike: The Memoirs*, 257–73.

123. Cable from Caccia to Foreign Office, 28 November 1956, F.O. 115/4550, PRO.

124. Cooper, *Lion's Last Roar*, 231.

125. Editorial, "Greatness," *Observer*, 9 December 1956, 8.

126. Joseph Frankel, *British Foreign Policy, 1945–1973* (London: Oxford University Press, Royal Institute of International Affairs, 1975), 162. See also Lloyd, *Suez*, 225, and Pineau, *1956/Suez*, 188.

127. Draft paper on Anglo-American relations, 23 November 1956, F.O. 115/4545, PRO.

128. Albert Hourani, "A Moment of Change: The Crisis of 1956," in *St. Antony's Papers*, 4 (London: Chatto and Windus, 1958), 134.

129. Letter from Ambassador Harold Caccia to Secretary of State Selwyn Lloyd, 28 December 1956, p. 3, F.O. 115/4545, PRO.

130. For further discussion of the concept of the "permanent" alliance between the United States and the United Kingdom, see Raymond Aron, *Peace and War*, trans. Richard Howard and Annette Baker Fox (Garden City, N.Y.: Doubleday, 1966), 28.

131. See the 1957 White Paper on defense, *Defence Outline of Future Policy*, cmnd. 124 (London: HMSO, 1957).

132. See Philip Darby, *British Defence Policy East of Suez, 1947-1968* (London: Oxford University Press, Royal Institute of International Affairs, 1973), 100–101. See also Alastair Buchan, "Britain and the Nuclear Deterrent", *Political Quarterly* 31, no. 1 (January-March 1960): 39.

133. For text, see DOSB 38 (11 November 1957): 739–41.

134. See Macmillan, *Riding the Storm*, 756–59, 319–27.

135. In summarizing the outcome of the December 1957 NATO discussions, Macmillan highlighted the singularity of the Anglo-American relationship: each needed the other to protect its global role. He credited these meetings—and especially his renewal of close and constant communications with Eisenhower—with "the reconstitution of the Western world and its determination to maintain its liberties and freedom by all the means in its power. . . . Thus in spite of some misunderstandings, the old alliance remained firm" (*Riding the Storm*, 341).

136. Macmillan, *Riding the Storm*, 336–37. See also *The North Atlantic Treaty Organisation: Facts and Figures*, 10th ed. (Brussels: NATO Information Service, 1981), 37.

137. See, for example, French statesman Maurice Couve de Murville's comments on this uncomfortable state of affairs in *Une politique étrangère* (Paris: Plon, 1971), 33.

138. There was strong popular support for the decision to use force. The abortive military mission was blamed on the Americans, the Russians, and the United Nations. See results of public opinion polls in Alfred Grosser, *La IVème république et sa politique extérieure* (Paris: Armand Colin, 1961), 372–73.

139. Luethy and Rodnick, *French Motivations*, 58.

140. Pineau, *1956/Suez*, trans. E. D. Sherwood, 191.

141. See Kelly, "Political Background of the French A-Bomb," 297–98.

142. Pineau, 1956/Suez, 59.

143. Pineau, 1956/Suez, 190–91.

144. Lloyd, Suez, 254.

145. For Eisenhower's initial thinking, see Waging Peace, 96–97; for the message to Congress of 5 January, see U.S. Foreign Policy in the Middle East, 15–23; for the Joint Resolution of Congress of 9 March, see U.S. Foreign Policy in the Middle East, 44–46, or DOSB 36 (25 March 1957): 481.

146. Eisenhower, Waging Peace, 17.

147. U.S. Foreign Policy in the Middle East, 45.

148. An Israeli anecdote illustrated the interdependent relationship between NATO and the actions of its individual members. During the fighting at Suez, Israeli troops were given protection by French fighter jets, and some of those planes still had their NATO colors on them (Michel Bar Zohar, quoted in Peter Calvocoressi, Suez: Ten Years Later, ed. Anthony Moncrieff [New York: Pantheon Books, 1967], 101). Some critics of the Anglo-French action also alleged that the British used weapons at Suez supplied by the United States and intended exclusively for NATO use. Although British military officials acknowledged the employment of American weapons, they argued that it was impossible to distinguish those designated for NATO use from the rest. See letter with marginalia from Admiral Sir Michael Denny, Office of the Representative of the United Kingdom Chiefs of Staff in Washington, to Ambassador Harold Caccia, 16 November 1956, F.O. 115/4545, PRO.

149. Benjamin Welles, "NATO Allies Chide London and Paris," New York Times, 3 November 1956, 4.

150. This discussion draws heavily on an interview with Dr. Lincoln Gordon, Staff Director of the "Report of the Committee of Three on Non-Military Co-operation in NATO," 22 February 1985, Washington, D.C. Significantly, none of the principal allies participated in the project, due to what has been described as a "discreet mutiny" by the smaller countries (Alastair Buchan, NATO in the 1960s, rev. ed. [New York: Praeger, 1963], 45).

151. The North Atlantic Treaty Organisation: Facts and Figures, 275, par. 46; 273, par. 32; 274, par. 40.

CHAPTER 4. Times of Turbulence: De Gaulle Confronts the Anglo-American Special Relationship, 1958–1961

1. Selwyn Lloyd, Suez 1956 (London: Jonathan Cape, 1978), 257. See also Christian Pineau, 1956/Suez (Paris: Editions Robert Laffont, 1976), 195.

2. Harold Macmillan, Riding the Storm, 1956–1959 (New York: Harper and Row, 1971), 506.

3. Robert McClintock, "The American Landing in Lebanon," United States Naval Institute Proceedings 88, no. 10, whole no. 716 (October 1962): 69.

4. Dwight D. Eisenhower, The White House Years: Waging Peace, 1956–1961 (Garden City, N.Y.: Doubleday, 1965), 273.

5. Fahim I. Qubain, *Crisis in Lebanon* (Washington, D.C.: The Middle East Institute, 1961), 115.

6. Eisenhower, *Waging Peace*, 279.

7. Combine II, however, was canceled on 1 July on the grounds that the crisis in the Mediterranean had subsided (Jack Shulimson, *Marines in Lebanon, 1958* [Washington, D.C.: Historical Branch, G-3 Division, Headquarters, U.S. Marine Corps, 1966], 7–9).

8. Macmillan, *Riding the Storm*, 513. See also Eisenhower, *Waging Peace*, 273.

9. De Gaulle quoted in David Schoenbrun, *The Three Lives of Charles de Gaulle* (New York: Atheneum, 1966), 292.

10. Schoenbrun, *Three Lives*, 292.

11. See Robert C. Doty, "France Protests Lags in Lebanon," *New York Times*, 20 July 1958, 13.

12. Maurice Couve de Murville, *Une politique étrangère* (Paris: Plon, 1971), trans. E. D. Sherwood, 33. Indeed, in an interview with the former foreign minister nearly three decades later, on 25 April 1985 in Paris, French pique over the episode was still very much in evidence.

13. Charles de Gaulle, *Memoirs of Hope: Renewal, 1958–62, Endeavour, 1962–*, trans. Terence Kilmartin (London: Weidenfeld and Nicolson, 1971), 204.

14. Khrushchev quoted in André Fontaine, *History of the Cold War: From the Korean War to the Present*, trans. Renaud Bruce (New York: Vintage Books, Random House, 1970), 300.

15. See "U.S. Informs Allies of Lebanon Landing," *New York Times*, 16 July 1958, 3, and "U.S. Mideast Move Endorsed in NATO," *New York Times*, 17 July 1958, 2.

16. See Shulimson, *Marines in Lebanon*, 24–25, and Jack Raymond, "Atomic Unit in Germany Among Forces Dispatched," *New York Times*, 17 July 1958, 1.

17. See M. S. Handler, "Adenauer Raises Mideast Doubts," *New York Times*, 19 July 1958, 3.

18. Robert Murphy, *Diplomat among Warriors* (Garden City, N.Y.: Doubleday, 1964), 398. For further elaboration of the argument that strengthening the credibility of the American deterrent was a determining factor in Eisenhower's decision to invade Lebanon, see Alexander L. George and Richard Smoke, *Deterrence in American Foreign Policy: Theory and Practice* (New York: Columbia University Press, 1974), 309–58.

19. See "Memorandum Re Formosa Strait Situation," in Eisenhower, *Waging Peace*, app. O, 691–93.

20. George and Smoke, *Deterrence*, 364–67.

21. Eisenhower, *Waging Peace*, 301.

22. Couve de Murville, *Une politique étrangère*, trans. E. D. Sherwood, 33.

23. Interview with Couve de Murville, 25 April 1985, Paris.

24. See, for example, comments in Lloyd, *Suez*, 258–59.

25. Couve de Murville, *Une politique étrangère*, trans. E. D. Sherwood, 45.

26. A decade earlier, de Gaulle had called for a Western defense organization directed by a committee of the heads of governments of France, the United Kingdom, and the United States, in which there would be three separate theaters of operation: Europe and North Africa under French responsibility, the Middle East and East Africa under British responsibility, and the Far East under American responsibility (de Gaulle press conference reported in Telegram no. 1664 from Paris to Foreign Office, 18 November 1948, F.O. 371/73082, doc. no. 39877, PRO).

27. George Ball, *The Discipline of Power* (Boston: Little, Brown, 1968), 128–29; John Newhouse, *De Gaulle and the Anglo-Saxons* (London: Andre Deutsch, 1970), 56.

28. Ball, *Discipline of Power*, 129.

29. See, for example, the excerpted article from *Combat* of 4 July 1958 in Newhouse, *De Gaulle and the Anglo-Saxons*, 57–58.

30. Couve de Murville, *Une politique étrangère*, trans. E. D. Sherwood, 33.

31. The ensuing citations from the Directorate proposal may be found in Memorandum and accompanying correspondence from General de Gaulle to President Eisenhower, 17 September 1958, at the Dwight D. Eisenhower Presidential Library, Abilene, Kansas. French text published in *Espoir* 15 (Paris: Plon, 1976) as "Memorandum of 1958 on NATO," 3.

32. See also Couve de Murville's question about whether Dulles's "wisdom" in handling Quemoy could be relied on in all situations, in *Une politique étrangère*, 57.

33. Macmillan, *Riding the Storm*, 453.

34. See discussion in Newhouse, *De Gaulle and the Anglo-Saxons*, 75, and in George Ball, *The Past Has Another Pattern* (New York: W. W. Norton, 1982), 259.

35. Couve de Murville quoted in Schoenbrun, *Three Lives*, 300. In what can only be interpreted as an instance of selective memory, Couve de Murville insisted nearly three decades after the fact that there was never any proposal for increased French control over the use of American nuclear weapons (Interview with Couve de Murville, 25 April 1985, Paris).

36. George Ball used this phrase to describe de Gaulle's tactics in *The Past*, 259.

37. Interview with Couve de Murville, 25 April 1985, Paris.

38. Newhouse, *De Gaulle and the Anglo-Saxons*, 72.

39. "Note de M. Spaak (Très Secret)," 15 October 1958, trans. E. D. Sherwood.

40. See Macmillan's account of his conversations with Chancellor Adenauer in *Riding the Storm*, 452–53.

41. Newhouse, *De Gaulle and the Anglo-Saxons*, 72–73. See also Ball, *Discipline of Power*, 130.

42. De Gaulle, quoted in J.-R. Tournoux, *La tragédie du général* (Paris: Plon, 1967), trans. E. D. Sherwood, 321.

43. Eisenhower interview, 25 August 1964, in Schoenbrun, *Three Lives*, 335–36.

44. Letter from Eisenhower to de Gaulle, 20 October 1958, Eisenhower Library, Abilene, Kansas.

45. Eisenhower interview in Schoenbrun, *Three Lives*, 336.

46. Eisenhower, *Waging Peace*, 427.

47. Schoenbrun, *Three Lives*, 303. Emphasis on the strategic value of Africa to France and by extension to NATO is prevalent in French literature of the late fifties. For example, in an article on "NATO and North Africa" (*Revue de défense nationale* 14 [June 1958]: 911, trans. E. D. Sherwood), General J. Allard, the first French commander in Algeria in 1954, argued that the French troops withdrawn from France proper and from Germany to fight in Algeria were not distracted from the defense of Europe because "without North Africa, the defense of Europe would no longer make sense." See also Colonel Parisot, "Valeur stratégique de l'Afrique pour l'Otan," in *Revue de défense nationale* 14 (March 1958): 430–35, esp. 434.

48. Macmillan, *Riding the Storm*, 453–54.

49. Newhouse, *De Gaulle and the Anglo-Saxons*, 76.

50. See de Gaulle's press conference remarks of 25 March 1959, reprinted in Newhouse, *De Gaulle and the Anglo-Saxons*, 87.

51. Charles de Gaulle, *Mémoires d'espoir: Le renouveau, 1958–62, l'effort, 1962–* (Paris: Plon, 1970), 215; Newhouse, *De Gaulle and the Anglo-Saxons*, 86–87; Couve de Murville, *Une politique étrangère*, 65.

52. Ball, *The Past*, 259–60.

53. De Gaulle speech in Gap, France, on 21 October 1960, cited in *Nouvelles atlantiques/Atlantic News*, no. 1296, 4 March 1981.

54. Information on diplomatic exchanges in 1959 and 1960 drawn from State Department Statement recording the events pertaining to General de Gaulle's Directorate proposal of 1958 and the response of the United States to it, transmitted to Senator Jackson, 11 August 1966, in U.S. Senate, *The Atlantic Alliance*, Hearings Before the Subcommittee on National Security and International Operations of the Committee on Government Operations, 89th Cong., 2d sess. (Washington, D.C.: GPO, 1966), 228–29.

55. Charles de Gaulle, *Discours et messages: Avec le renouveau, mai 1958–juillet 1962* (Paris: Plon, 1970), trans. E. D. Sherwood, 247–49.

56. Schoenbrun, *Three Lives*, 316–17.

CHAPTER 5. Grand Design or Troubled Partnership: Challenges to the Alliance, 1961–1968

1. Stanley Hoffmann, "Europe's Identity Crisis: Between the Past and America," *Daedalus* 93, no. 4 (Spring 1964): 1291.

2. John F. Kennedy, Inaugural Address, 20 January 1961, in *Inaugural Addresses of the Presidents of the United States* (Washington, D.C.: GPO, 1974), 268.

3. Henry A. Kissinger, *The Troubled Partnership* (New York: McGraw-Hill, Council on Foreign Relations, 1965), 8–9.

4. The Fouchet Plan was named after French ambassador to West Germany Christian Fouchet, who headed the commission to develop the concept.

5. See Harold Macmillan, *Pointing the Way, 1959–1961* (New York: Harper and Row, 1972), 323, 349.

6. David Schoenbrun, *The Three Lives of Charles de Gaulle* (New York: Atheneum, 1966), 317.

7. John F. Kennedy, "The Doctrine of National Independence," 4 July 1962, in *The Burden and the Glory* (New York: Harper and Row, 1964), 111. See also second State of the Union message, 11 January 1962, *Burden and Glory*, 16.

8. Kennedy, "Partnership with Germany and a United Europe," speech at the Paulskirche, Frankfurt, Germany, 25 June 1963, *Burden and Glory*, 119.

9. Christian Herter, "Atlantica," *Foreign Affairs* 41, no. 2 (January 1963): 301. See also Kissinger, *Troubled Partnership*, 236–37.

10. Kennedy, "Doctrine of National Independence," *Burden and Glory*, 115–16.

11. Kissinger, *Troubled Partnership*, 234.

12. For further discussion of the historic tensions between Britain's imperial and European vocations, and of the shift to dependence on the United States, see Michael Howard, *The Continental Commitment* (London: Temple Smith, 1972).

13. Harold Macmillan, *At the End of the Day, 1961–1963* (London: Macmillan, 1973), 1.

14. Macmillan, *End of the Day*, 13, 17, 20. The quotation is taken from Macmillan's statement during the Common Market debate in the House of Commons, 2–3 August 1961.

15. *Statement on Defence, 1962: The Next Five Years*, cmnd. 1639 (London: HMSO, 1962). For quoted text, see par. 15.

16. Max Beloff, *The United States and the Unity of Europe* (New York: Vintage Books, 1963), 141. See also Kissinger, *Troubled Partnership*, 76.

17. Lawrence Freedman, *The Evolution of Nuclear Strategy* (New York: St. Martin's Press, 1982), 310–11, and Richard E. Neustadt, *Alliance Politics* (New York: Columbia University Press, 1970), 49–55.

18. Coral Bell, *The Debatable Alliance* (London: Oxford University Press, Royal Institute of International Affairs, 1964), 96.

19. L. W. Martin, *British Defence Policy: The Long Recessional*, Adelphi Paper no. 61 (London: International Institute for Strategic Studies, 1969), 2.

20. Rusk, quoted in Robert Kleiman, *Atlantic Crisis* (New York: W. W. Norton, 1964), 55.

21. Under Secretary of State George Ball speech to NATO parliamentarians on "NATO and the Cuban Crisis," 16 November 1962, DOSB 47 (3 December 1962): 831.

22. "The Cuban Crisis: A Step-By-Step Review," *New York Times*, 3 November 1962, 6. Norstad actually disagreed with and resisted Washington's urging of a NATO alert, as did Macmillan, who argued that "'mobilisation' had sometimes caused war. Here it was absurd, since the additional forces made available by 'Alert' had *no* military significance" (Macmillan, quoting from his diary of 22 October 1962, in *End of the Day*, 190).

23. David A. Welch and James G. Blight, "The Eleventh Hour of the Cuban Missile Crisis: An Introduction to the ExComm Transcripts," *International Security* 12, no. 3 (Winter 1987–88): 7–8.

24. Arthur M. Schlesinger, Jr., *Robert Kennedy and His Times* (Boston: Houghton Mifflin, 1978), 515.

25. Welch and Blight, "Eleventh Hour," 10–11.

26. According to a recent account by Dean Rusk, Kennedy understood that the missiles in Turkey were to be withdrawn once Polaris submarines became available to patrol the Mediterranean in the spring of 1963 (Rusk letter to James G. Blight, 25 February 1987, cited in Welch and Blight, "Eleventh Hour," 17, n. 36).

27. McGeorge Bundy, transcriber, James G. Blight, ed., "October 27, 1962: Transcripts of the Meetings of the ExComm," *International Security* 12, no. 3 (Winter 1987–88): 71–72. See also Kennedy comments, 83.

28. "October 27, 1962: ExComm Transcripts," 39, 49, emphasis in original.

29. Summary Record of NSC Executive Committee Meeting No. 8, 27 October 1962, 4:00 P.M., 5, John F. Kennedy (JFK) Library, Boston. For more on McNamara's logic, see "October 27, 1962: ExComm Transcripts," 74–75. From the outset, the ExComm members had worried about the vulnerability of Turkey and Berlin to a Soviet retaliatory strike. See Theodore Sorensen's account of the 16 October 1962 ExComm meeting in Donald L. Hafner, "Bureaucratic Politics and 'Those Frigging Missiles': JFK, Cuba and U.S. Missiles in Turkey," *Orbis* 21, no. 2 (Summer 1977): 312.

30. "October 27, 1962: ExComm Transcripts," 44, 58.

31. See Welch and Blight, "Eleventh Hour," 11, 19, and "October 27, 1962: ExComm Transcripts," 57–60, 82–83.

32. See "The Cuban Crisis: A Step-By-Step Review," *New York Times*, 7, and White House Statement, 27 October 1962, and Kennedy Letter to Khrushchev, 27 October 1962, in U.S. President, *Public Papers of the Presidents: John F. Kennedy, 1962* (Washington, D.C.: GPO, 1963), 813–14.

33. Robert Kennedy, *Thirteen Days* (New York: W. W. Norton, 1969), 98, and Walter Pincus, "Standing at the Brink of Nuclear War," *Washington Post*, 25 July 1985, 1, 10. For McNamara's arguments regarding defusing the Jupiters, see "October 27, 1962: ExComm Transcripts," 52–53.

34. According to his recent account of the sequence of events, McNamara ordered the missiles "withdrawn, cut up, and photographed" on 29 October ("Proceedings of the Cambridge Conference on the Cuban Missile Crisis," Cambridge, Massachusetts, 11–12 October 1987, 85).

35. Kennedy quoted in Hafner, "Bureaucratic Politics," 309. Documents recently made available by the JFK Library support the existence of such an arrangement, and it was confirmed in a joint statement by former Kennedy administration officials Dean Rusk (secretary of state), Robert McNamara (secretary of defense), George W. Ball (under secretary of state), Roswell L. Gilpatric (deputy secretary of defense), Theodore Sorensen (special counsel to the president), and McGeorge Bundy (national security adviser), on "The

Lessons of the Cuban Missile Crisis," *Time*, 27 September 1982, 85–86, esp. point eight. For more background on the deal, see Robert Kennedy's notes to himself in preparation for his meeting with Dobrynin, 30 October 1962, in Schlesinger, *Robert Kennedy*, 523; Kennedy, *Thirteen Days*, 108–9; Bundy's remarks in Pincus, "Standing at the Brink," 1, 10; and Bernstein, "Cuban Missile Crisis," 122.

36. During a March 1987 conference on the Cuban Missile Crisis at Hawk's Cay, Florida, Dean Rusk made this public for the first time. See James Blight, Joseph S. Nye, Jr., and David A. Welch, "The Cuban Missile Crisis Revisited," *Foreign Affairs* 66, no. 1 (Fall 1987): 178.

37. Rusk letter of 25 February 1987 to James G. Blight, reproduced in part in Blight, Nye, and Welch, "Cuban Missile Crisis Revisited," 179.

38. "October 27, 1962: ExComm Transcripts," 52.

39. Macmillan, *End of the Day*, 216. See also his rebuttal of the opposition party's attacks on Anglo-American cooperation during the crisis, 219–20. For a vivid picture of the intensive consultations between the two leaders and their governments during the crisis, see chapter entitled "On the Brink," 180–220.

40. See Macmillan comments in Schlesinger, *Robert Kennedy*, 519.

41. De Gaulle quoted in André Fontaine, *History of the Cold War: From the Korean War to the Present*, trans. Renaud Bruce (New York: Vintage Books, Random House, 1970), 447. See also George Ball, *The Past Has Another Pattern* (New York: W. W. Norton, 1982), 296.

42. Excerpts of de Gaulle commentary and "Note sur les relations franco-américaines," 21 March 1966, Ministère des affaires étrangères, in J. R. Tournoux, *La tragédie du général* (Paris: Plon, Paris-Match, 1967), 460, 652–53.

43. State Department analysis prepared by Raymond L. Garthoff cited in Welch and Blight, "Eleventh Hour," 14. See also evaluation by American policymakers of potential impact on Turkish government, and attitudes of other allied governments, in Barton J. Bernstein, "The Cuban Missile Crisis: Trading the Jupiters in Turkey?" *Political Science Quarterly* 95 (Spring 1980): 107–8, 112–16, respectively.

44. "October 27, 1962: ExComm Transcripts," 37, 39, 50. See also Ball, *The Past*, 295.

45. The communiqué issued at the 13–15 December NAC meetings stated that the "peril [in Cuba] was averted by the firmness and restraint of the United States, supported by the Alliance and other free nations" (NFC, 147). See also Roger Hilsman, *To Move a Nation* (New York: Delta, 1967), 212.

46. De Gaulle, quoted in Bernstein, "Cuban Missile Crisis," 114.

47. Fontaine, *History of the Cold War*, 496–97.

48. De Gaulle, Press Conference of 14 January 1963, quoted in Bell, *Debatable Alliance*, 104.

49. Interview with Maurice Couve de Murville, 25 April 1985, Paris.

50. See Maurice Couve de Murville, *Une politique étrangère* (Paris: Plon, 1971), 77–78; also John Newhouse, *De Gaulle and the Anglo-Saxons* (London: Andre Deutsch, 1970), 237–39.

51. Philippe Devillers, "La politique française et la seconde guerre du Vietnam," *Politique étrangère* 32, no. 6 (1967): 583.

52. Joint Resolution of Congress, H.J. Res. 1145, 7 August 1964, in *Documents of American History*, 8th ed., ed. Henry Steele Commager (New York: Appleton-Century-Crofts, 1968), 714.

53. Telephone interview with Robert Komer, 30 January 1985, and Komer, "Looking Ahead," *International Security* 4, no. 1 (Summer 1979): 109.

54. See Drew Middleton, "Analysis of a Failure," *New York Times*, 6 July 1985, 13. See also Hanson W. Baldwin, "U.S. Combat Forces Spread Thin," *New York Times*, 21 February 1966, 1.

55. Martin Binkin, an expert on military manpower issues, has written that "President Johnson's decision *not* to mobilize reserves was made partly to demonstrate his intent to limit U.S. involvement." See Binkin's *United States Reserve Forces: The Problem of the Weekend Warrior* (Washington, D.C.: Brookings, 1974), 20–21. See also James T. Currie, "The Army Reserve and Vietnam," *Parameters* 14, no. 3 (Autumn 1984): 76–77.

56. See Baldwin, "Forces Spread Thin," 28, for a service-by-service breakdown of the war's impact as well as an enumeration of shortages of matériel in early 1966.

57. Benjamin Welles, "15,000 U.S. Troops to Leave Europe," *New York Times*, 8 April 1966, 1.

58. Hanson W. Baldwin, "Army Personnel Squeeze: Withdrawal of 15,000 Specialists from Europe Accents Manpower Shortage," *New York Times*, 8 April 1966, 4. See also testimony of John McCloy, 25 May 1966, in U.S. Senate, *The Atlantic Alliance*, Hearings Before the Subcommittee on National Security and International Operations of the Committee on Government Operations, 89th Cong., 2d sess. (Washington, D.C.: GPO, 1966), 147.

59. McNamara testimony, 21 June 1966, in U.S. Senate, *Atlantic Alliance*, Hearings, 193–94. See also his remarks as reported in Welles, "15,000 U.S. Troops," 1.

60. See William Beecher, "U.S. Temporarily Cutting Back Its Troop Commitment to NATO," *New York Times*, 11 October 1967, 1.

61. Official sources in the public domain have not documented this withdrawal. For two estimates, see Henry A. Kissinger, *White House Years* (Boston: Little, Brown, 1979), 394, and Richard J. Barnet, *The Alliance* (New York: Simon and Schuster, 1983), 266.

62. Beecher, "U.S. Temporarily Cutting Back," 2, and interview with Couve de Murville, 25 April 1985, Paris.

63. Javits on 27 April 1966, quoted in U.S. Senate, *Atlantic Alliance*, Hearings, 29. See also discussion between Javits and former Secretary of State Christian Herter, 5 May 1966, 43–45, and between Senator John Stennis and Dean Rusk, 16 June 1966, 167.

64. Jackson on 16 June 1966, quoted in U.S. Senate, *Atlantic Alliance*, Hearings, 179.

65. For text of Mansfield resolution, see U.S. Senate, *Congressional Record*, 31 August 1966, 21442. See also Richard Eder, "13 Senators Urge Europe Troop Cut," *New York Times*, 1 September 1966, 16. For more on the history of the Mansfield Amendments, see Stanley R. Sloan, *Defense Burden Sharing: U.S. Relations with NATO Allies and Japan*, CRS Report no. 85–101F (Washington, D.C.: Congressional Research Service, 1985), 8.

66. Alastair Buchan, "The Changed Setting of the Atlantic Debate," *Foreign Affairs* 43 (July 1965): 580.

67. Dean Rusk, Speech on "Our Atlantic Policy" to the Cleveland Council of World Affairs, 6 March 1965, DOSB 52 (22 March 1965): 431.

68. See, for example, discussion in Robert O'Neill, "The Vietnam War and the Western Alliance," unpublished paper prepared for the Symposium on the Second Indochina War, Airlie, Virginia, 7–9 November 1984, 14.

69. Harold Wilson, *A Personal Record: The Labour Government, 1964–1970* (Boston: Atlantic Monthly Press, Little, Brown, 1971), 39.

70. O'Neill, "Vietnam War," 3.

71. Wilson, *Personal Record*, 96. See also account of meetings at the end of 1965 between Johnson and Macmillan in Richard Crossman, *The Diaries of a Cabinet Minister*, vol. 1: *1964–1966* (New York: Holt, Rinehart and Winston, 1975), 418.

72. Johnson quoted in Wilson, *Personal Record*, 80, 264.

73. Martin, *Long Recessional*, 3.

74. See discussion in Phillip Darby, *British Defence Policy East of Suez, 1947–1968* (London: Oxford University Press, Royal Institute of International Affairs, 1973), 295–96.

75. Wilson, quoted in Crossman, *Diaries*, 456.

76. *Statement on the Defence Estimates, 1966: Part 1, The Defence Review*, cmnd. 2901 (London: HMSO, 1966), esp. 7, para. 19.

77. See discussion of the impact of Vietnam on British thinking in Martin, *Long Recessional*, 6, 20.

78. See text of Wilson's statement to the House of Commons, *New York Times*, 17 January 1968, 14; and Anthony Lewis, "Britain to Close Far East Bases; Won't Buy F-111's," *New York Times*, 17 January 1968, 1; as well as the *Statement on the Defence Estimates, 1968*, cmnd. 3540 (London: HMSO, 1968).

79. *Statement on the Defence Estimates, 1969*, cmnd. 3927 (London: HMSO, 1969), 9, par. 45.

80. See Couve de Murville, *Une politique étrangère*, 113, and Devillers, "La politique française et la seconde guerre du Vietnam," 580.

81. See Pierre Viansson-Ponté, *Histoire de la république gaullienne*, 2 vols. (Paris: Fayard, 1970), 1:75.

82. Since 1954, the Southeast Asian security organization that included the three principal NATO powers (along with Australia, New Zealand, Pakistan until 1973, the Philippines, and Thailand) had created in substance a three-power directorate among them. However, SEATO was disbanded in 1975, due largely to the allies' divergent views on threats to the region and appropriate responses to them, although the treaty obligations remained in

effect. See also Couve de Murville, *Une politique étrangère*, 127, and Viansson-Ponté, *Histoire de la république gaullienne*, 77.

83. See Drew Middleton, "De Gaulle Begins Trip to Nations of South America," *New York Times*, 21 September 1964, 1.

84. Excerpt of de Gaulle press conference, 9 September 1965, French Embassy press files, Washington, D.C.

85. Couve de Murville, *Une politique étrangère*, 134.

86. De Gaulle, quoted in Devillers, "La politique française et la seconde guerre du Vietnam," trans. E. D. Sherwood, 587. Text of de Gaulle's 7 March 1966 letter to Johnson, and Johnson's reply, reproduced in *New York Times*, 25 March 1966, 7.

87. See, for example, Devillers, "La politique française et la seconde guerre du Vietnam," 587.

88. Couve de Murville, *Une politique étrangère*, 136.

89. Couve de Murville, *Une politique étrangère*, 122–23.

90. In his first meetings with Kennedy in June 1961, for example, de Gaulle had warned that "once the Berlin crisis was over, he would pull France out of NATO—in his eyes an outmoded organization—while remaining in the Atlantic Alliance." See Fontaine, *History of the Cold War*, 413.

91. See "Note sur les relations franco-américaines," 21 March 1966, Ministère des affaires étrangères, in Tournoux, *Tragédie du général*, and *New York Times*, 25 March 1966, 7.

92. Testimony of Secretary of State Dean Rusk, 16 June 1966, U.S. Senate, *Atlantic Alliance*, Hearings, 160.

93. Text of de Gaulle's speech in *New York Times*, 2 September 1966, 13.

94. See David Halberstam, "De Gaulle Believed Seeking Role as Future Mediator on Vietnam," *New York Times*, 3 September 1966, 2. See also Max Frankel, "De Gaulle Stand Irks U.S. Officials," *New York Times*, 3 September 1966, 1.

95. Devillers, "La politique française et la seconde guerre du Vietnam," 588.

96. With the exception of Robert O'Neill's unpublished paper, "The Vietnam War and the Western Alliance," there is also a curious lack of literature on the subject of allied attitudes toward the war and its impact on NATO.

97. See chart in "What the U.S. Can Expect from Allies in Vietnam," *U.S. News and World Report*, 14 March 1966, 31–33.

98. Henry Gemmill, "Europe's Opposition to War in Asia Chills Its Relations with U.S.," *Wall Street Journal*, 9 May 1967, 12.

99. Interview with Couve de Murville, 25 April 1985, Paris.

100. Interview with Couve de Murville, 25 April 1985, Paris.

101. "The Future Tasks of the Alliance," Report of the Council, 13–14 December 1967, NFC, 199, 201.

102. Rusk quoted in Eugene Rostow, "A Practical Programme for Peace: The 20th Anniversary of the Harmel Report," *NATO Review* 35, no. 4 (August 1987), 13.

103. Gemmill, "Europe's Opposition to War," 12.

CHAPTER 6. Retrenchment and Renewed Commitment: From the Nixon Doctrine to the Carter Doctrine, 1969–1979

1. Richard N. Haass, "Filling the Vacuum: United States Foreign Policy Towards Southwest Asia, 1969–1976" (D.Phil. thesis, Oxford University, 1982), 1.

2. George Ball, *The Past Has Another Pattern* (New York, W. W. Norton, 1982), 433.

3. Haass, "Filling the Vacuum," 4, 6.

4. The transcript of Nixon's remarks was subsequently released and can be found in U.S. President, *Public Papers of the Presidents of the United States: Richard Nixon, 1969* (Washington, D.C.: GPO, 1971), 543–56. See especially 549 for Nixon's comments that the United States would encourage and expect that problems of internal security and military defense would "be increasingly handled by, and the responsibility for it taken by, the Asian nations themselves."

5. Nixon address to the nation on the war in Vietnam, 3 November 1969, in U.S. President, *Public Papers: Richard Nixon*, 905–6.

6. U.S. President, *U.S. Foreign Policy for the 1970s: A New Strategy for Peace*, A Report to the Congress by Richard Nixon, 18 February 1970 (Washington, D.C.: GPO, 1970), 6.

7. Acheson speech, "Crisis in Asia—An Examination of U.S. Policy," to the National Press Club, Washington, D.C., 12 January 1950, in DOSB 22 (23 January 1950), 111.

8. Statement of James H. Noyes, Assistant Secretary of Defense for Near Eastern, African, and South Asian Affairs, 2 February 1972, in U.S. House of Representatives, *U.S. Interests in and Policy Toward the Persian Gulf*, Hearings before the Subcommittee on the Near East of the Committee on Foreign Affairs, 92d Cong., 2d sess. (Washington, D.C.: GPO, 1972), 14.

9. Robert S. Littwak, *Détente and the Nixon Doctrine* (Cambridge: Cambridge University Press, 1984), 140.

10. Henry Kissinger, *White House Years* (Boston: Little, Brown, 1979), 1264.

11. Gary Sick, *All Fall Down: America's Tragic Encounter with Iran* (New York: Random House, 1985), 14.

12. Testimony by Assistant Secretary of State for European Affairs Martin Hillenbrand, in U.S. House of Representatives, *United States Relations with Europe in the Decade of the 1970's*, Hearings before the Subcommittee on Europe of the Committee on Foreign Affairs, 91st Cong., 2d sess. (Washington, D.C.: GPO, 1970), 34.

13. See the testimony of Ronald J. Spiers, Director of the Bureau of Politico-Military Affairs, Department of State, in U.S. House of Representatives, *The Indian Ocean: Political and Strategic Future*, Hearings before the Subcommittee on National Security Policy, Committee on Foreign Affairs, 1971, 167–68 and 175–76.

14. Marvin Kalb and Bernard Kalb, *Kissinger* (Boston: Little, Brown, 1974), 482.

15. Z, "The Year of Europe," *Foreign Affairs* 52, no. 2 (January 1974): 238.

16. See discussion in William B. Quandt, "The Western Alliance in the Middle East: Problems for U.S. Foreign Policy," in Steven L. Spiegel, ed., *The Middle East and the Western Alliance* (London: George Allen and Unwin, 1982), 10.

17. Statement by State Department Spokesman Robert J. McCloskey, cited in David Binder, "Nixon Says Some Allies Failed U.S. in Middle East: Oil Is Called a Factor," *New York Times*, 27 October 1983, 1, 11.

18. See book by the Insight Team of the London *Sunday Times* on *The Yom Kippur War* (Garden City, N.Y.: Doubleday, 1974), 424–25; Tad Szulc, "Is He Indispensable? Answers to the Kissinger Riddle," *New York Magazine*, 1 July 1974, 33–39; Henry Kissinger, *Years of Upheaval* (Boston: Little, Brown, 1982), 709; and "The Unfriendly Friends," *The Economist*, 9 February 1974, 18.

19. Leslie H. Gelb, "U.S. Jets for Israel Took Route Around Some Allies," *New York Times*, 25 October 1973, 1, 18; Kissinger, *Years of Upheaval*, 709; and Robert J. Lieber, *Oil and the Middle East War: Europe in the Energy Crisis*, Harvard Studies in International Affairs no. 35 (Cambridge: Harvard University Center for International Affairs, 1976).

20. Gelb, "U.S. Jets for Israel," 1, 18. Alfred Grosser also suggested this was the case in *Affaires extérieures: La politique de la France, 1944–1984* (Paris: Flammarion, 1984), 248–49.

21. The German request was made privately on 23 October and issued publicly on 25 October. For text of German statement, see "Bonn Bids U.S. Halt Arms to Israel via Germany," *New York Times*, 26 October 1973, 20. For more on American operations through Germany, see book by the Insight Team of the London *Sunday Times*, *Yom Kippur War*, 425; Gelb, "U.S. Jets for Israel," 18; Binder, "Nixon Says Some Allies Failed U.S.," 1, 11; Kissinger, *Years of Upheaval*, 712, 714; and Lieber, *Oil and the Middle East War*, 12. The *Sunday Times* Insight Team suggested that the United States stripped aircraft from American squadrons based in Germany in order to resupply Israel, but this is not substantiated elsewhere.

22. Kissinger, *Years of Upheaval*, 520.

23. Gelb, "U.S. Jets for Israel," 1, 18.

24. Spain, although not yet a NATO member, had a treaty of friendship and cooperation with the United States but also refused to allow Spanish bases to be used for this purpose.

25. Kissinger, *Years of Upheaval*, 709. According to the *New York Times*, Soviet resupply aircraft heading for Egypt and Syria flew over Turkey, and the Turkish government did not make a public protest (Gelb, "U.S. Jets for Israel," 1, 18).

26. Letter from Brezhnev to Nixon reproduced in Kissinger, *Years of Upheaval*, 583. For further discussion of the superpower dimension of the conflict, see Scott D. Sagan, "Lessons of the Yom Kippur Alert," *Foreign Policy* 36 (Fall 1979): 160–77.

27. DefCon II would indicate that attack is imminent and that troops are ready for combat; DefCon I is war. Under normal peacetime conditions, the

United States remains at DefCon IV. See "The 5 Conditions of 'Defense Readiness,'" *New York Times*, 26 October 1973, 20, and Kalb and Kalb, *Kissinger*, 489–92.

28. See Herbert J. Coleman, "U.S. Forces Stay on Alert as NATO Politicians Fume," *Aviation Week and Space Technology*, 5 November 1973, 14–16.

29. Kissinger added that precisely because they did not want to draw attention to their "preferential status in Washington, British officials did nothing to stem the tide of criticism from other allies" (*Years of Upheaval*, 590, 712). See also Coleman, "U.S. Forces Stay on Alert," 14.

30. Kissinger, *Years of Upheaval*, 713, 590. See also Kalb and Kalb, *Kissinger*, 493.

31. Kissinger, *Years of Upheaval*, 713.

32. Alvin Shuster, "Nixon Says Some Allies Failed U.S. on Middle East: Alert Puzzles Europeans," *New York Times*, 27 October 1973, 1, 11.

33. Statistics on dependence on imported oil as a percentage of consumption cited in Barry M. Blechman and Edward N. Luttwak, eds., *International Security Yearbook, 1983/84* (New York: St. Martin's Press, Center for Strategic and International Studies, 1984), 224. Sources are *Basic Petroleum Data Book*, May 1983; *World Energy Industry*, 2d Quarter, 1980; *BP Statistical Review of World Energy*, 1982; *International Energy Statistical Review*, 25 October 1983.

34. For further discussion of the debate within the alliance about energy policy, see Robert J. Lieber, "Cohesion and Disruption in the Western Alliance," in *Global Insecurity*, ed. Daniel Yergin and Martin Hillenbrand (Boston: Houghton Mifflin, 1982), and Lieber, *The Oil Decade: Conflict and Cooperation in the West* (New York: Praeger, 1983), esp. 80.

35. For Kissinger's account of the conference, see chapter entitled "Energy and the Democracies," in *Years of Upheaval*, 896–934. For a collection of statements delivered by American, British, French, German, and Norwegian participants in the conference, see "The Washington Energy Conference," *Atlantic Community Quarterly* 12, no. 1 (Spring 1974): 22–54.

36. See Lieber's discussion of "Response as a Community" in *Oil and the Middle East War*, 12–29. See also "To Washington, with Europe's Hands Just Loosely Tied," *The Economist*, 9 February 1974, 47, and Flora Lewis, "New Rift Casts Doubts on Outlook for Europe," *New York Times*, 15 February 1974, 14.

37. Communiqué cited in Kissinger, *Years of Upheaval*, 920.

38. Instead, they took part in world spot (free) market bidding. The price on the market tripled the official OPEC price and touched off a chain reaction, forcing more purchasers to the spot market for supplies as producers diverted their resources to take advantage of the situation. Moreover, International Energy Agency mechanisms established after 1973 proved useless in the second crisis because the shortfall was below the 7 percent threshold necessary to trigger the emergency oil sharing plan.

39. Craig R. Whitney, "Europeans Urge Mideast Pull Back," *New York Times*, 7 November 1973, 1, 10.

40. Lieber, *Oil and the Middle East War*, 18, and David Allen, "The Euro-Arab Dialogue," *Journal of Common Market Studies* 16, no. 4 (June 1978): 325.

41. See Dominique Moisi, "Europe and the Middle East," in Spiegel, *Middle East and Western Alliance*, 26, and Allen, "Euro-Arab Dialogue," 328. The European Community Council issued the "Venice Declaration" on 13 June 1980, which endorsed full Palestinian self-determination and called for the association of the Palestine Liberation Organization with peace negotiations (Text of Venice Declaration reproduced in *New York Times*, 14 June 1980, 4).

42. Kissinger, *Years of Upheaval*, 930. For more on Kissinger's response, see "Henry's Thunderbolts," *The Economist*, 16 March 1974, 11–12, and in the same issue, "With Such Friends, Who Needs Enemies?" 43–44; and "Convincing Allies to Cooperate Is Biggest Task, Kissinger Says," *Los Angeles Times*, 12 March 1974, 1.

43. Henry A. Kissinger, "The Year of Europe," address to the Associated Press Annual Luncheon, New York, 23 April 1973, in *American Foreign Policy*, 3d ed. (New York: W. W. Norton, 1977) 104–5.

44. For a critique of Kissinger's approach, see Stanley Hoffmann, *Primacy or World Order?* (New York: McGraw-Hill, 1978), 48–49, and A. W. DePorte, *Europe between the Superpowers: The Enduring Balance* (New Haven: Yale University Press, 1979), 216–17. For another view articulating the potential merits of the "Year of Europe" for Europe itself, see Michael Howard, "NATO and the Year of Europe," *Survival* 16, no. 1 (January–February 1974), 21–27.

45. Kissinger quoted in "Kissinger Compared," *The Economist*, 5 January 1974, 52.

46. See Allen, "Euro-Arab Dialogue," 329, and Kissinger, *Years of Upheaval*, 909, 933–34.

47. "Declaration on Atlantic Relations," 19 June 1974, *NATO Final Communiqués, 1975–1980* (Brussels: NATO Information Service), 320 (hereafter, *NFC 75–80*).

48. Sick, *All Fall Down*, 18.

49. Zbigniew Brzezinski, *Power and Principle* (New York: Farrar, Straus and Giroux, 1983), 177.

50. Brzezinski, *Power and Principle*, 456.

51. Richard Burt, "How U.S. Strategy toward Persian Gulf Region Evolved," *New York Times*, 25 January 1980, 6. See Brzezinski's comments on the Pentagon's heel-dragging in *Power and Principle*, 456.

52. Burt, "How U.S. Strategy Toward Persian Gulf Evolved," 6.

53. This is discussed in "Prodding the Allies," in Sick, *All Fall Down*, 240–242. See also Tom Wicker, "The Allies Hold Back on Iran," *International Herald Tribune*, 7 December 1979.

54. Watt quoted in Joseph Fitchett, "Europeans Warn Against Military Action," *International Herald Tribune*, 28 November 1979.

55. Sick, *All Fall Down*, 242.

56. State of the Union address, 23 January 1980, reproduced in U.S. President, *Public Papers of the Presidents of the United States: Jimmy Carter*,

1980–81, book 1: *1 January–23 May 1980* (Washington, D.C.: GPO), 197. See also Drew Middleton, "The President Draws the Line in the Persian Gulf," *New York Times*, 25 January 1980, 1.

CHAPTER 7. Stretching the Limits of Alliance: NATO in the 1980s

1. Confidential interviews with U.S. Defense Department and NSC officials.

2. Michael Field, "Germany and France Stay Cautious," *Daily Telegraph*, 10 January 1980.

3. The president's diary of 9 February 1980, cited in Jimmy Carter, *Keeping Faith: Memoirs of a President* (New York: Bantam Books, 1982), 486–87.

4. See Leonard Downie, Jr., "U.S. Allies Cool to Boycott of Games," *International Herald Tribune*, 22 January 1980; Joseph Fitchett, "EEC Countries to Seek Common Position on Olympics," *International Herald Tribune*, 26 January 1980; and Will Ellsworth-Jones and Keith Richardson, "Support for Games Boycott Growing," *Sunday Times*, 20 April 1980.

5. U.S. Department of Defense, *Rationalization/Standardization within NATO*, Seventh Report, A Report to the United States Congress by Harold Brown, Secretary of Defense, 19 January 1981, 76.

6. These measures included improvements in the areas of war reserve stocks of ammunition; command, control, and communications; electronic warfare; air defense; nuclear, biological, and chemical defense; readiness and availability of units; training; astern refueling (an initiative to fit merchant ships with refueling equipment in order to give NATO an increased capacity to support warships during military operations); mining and other maritime assets; capabilities for land-based tactical air support for maritime operations; and aid to Portugal and Turkey (Department of Defense, *Rationalization/Standardization within NATO*, 76–77).

7. These measures included improvements in readiness; reserve mobilization; war reserve stocks and matériel; reinforcement airlift; maritime defense; support by nations of reinforcing forces (host nation support); the NATO Infrastructure Program; and additional military aid to Portugal and Turkey (Department of Defense, *Rationalization/Standardization within NATO*, 77–79).

8. See Michael Getler, "U.S. Not Expecting Large-Scale Allied Military Support in Gulf," *International Herald Tribune*, 12 February 1980.

9. DPC Communiqué, 13–14 May 1980, *NFC 75–80*, 131.

10. NAC Communiqué, 25–26 June 1980, *NFC 75–80*, 139.

11. DPC Communiqué, 9–10 December 1980, *NFC 75–80*, 149–50.

12. NAC Communiqué, 11–12 December 1980, *NFC 75–80*, 154.

13. Confidential interviews with U.S. Defense Department and State Department officials.

14. F. J. West, Jr., "NATO II: Common Boundaries for Common Interests," *Naval War College Review* 34 (January–February 1981): 59–67, esp. 64.

15. Frank C. Carlucci speech to the Wehrkunde Conference in Munich, Germany, 21 February 1981, News Release no. 57–81, Office of the Assistant

Secretary of Defense for Public Affairs, Washington, D.C. See also David Fairhall, "Britain Backs 'Global' NATO Force," *The Guardian*, 23 February 1981.

16. Confidential interview with U.S. State Department official.

17. Fred C. Iklé, Speech to North Atlantic Council permanent representatives on "The Security Role of Southwest Asia and the Role of the Alliance," 16 October 1981, cleared as amended for open publication on 5 February 1982; emphasis in original.

18. NAC Communiqué, 10–11 December 1981, *NATO Final Communiqués 1981* (Brussels: NATO Information Service), 27.

19. DPC Communiqué, 1–2 December 1982, *NATO Final Communiqués 1982* (Brussels: NATO Information Service), 26–27.

20. NAC Communiqué, 9–10 December 1982, *NATO Final Communiqués 1982*, 33. In response to American pressure, in 1983 NATO also began a series of biannual meetings on regional issues with experts from the sixteen member countries. The discussions covered the Middle East, Africa, Southeast Asia, Latin America, and Eastern Europe (*Nouvelles atlantiques/ Atlantic News*, 24 February 1984, 4).

21. The initial authorization for the SWAIS was given by the NAC in May 1982. This is noted in par. 8 of the communiqué issued from the 6–7 May 1982 DPC ministerial meeting, which stated, "The Military Committee is studying the implications for the Alliance of the United States strategic concept for South West Asia" (NAC Communiqué, *NATO Final Communiqués 1982*, 16. Weinberger quoted in "U.S. Asks Increased Allied Role in Defense," *International Herald Tribune*, 2 June 1983, 1. See also description of the SWAIS in *Nouvelles atlantiques/Atlantic News*, 3 June 1983, and in Nicolas Mosar, "Interim Report of the Sub-Committee on Out-of-Area Security Challenges to the Alliance," Political Committee of the North Atlantic Assembly, November 1983, 4. Some background information was gathered in confidential interview with U.S. Defense Department official.

22. For documentation on USCENTCOM, see "Fact Sheet: United States Central Command," U.S. Department of Defense, March 1983. For more, see Raphael Iungerich, "U.S. Rapid Deployment Forces—USCENTCOM: What Is It? Can It Do the Job?" *Armed Forces Journal International* 122, no. 3 (October 1984): 88–106.

23. U.S. Congressional Budget Office, *Rapid Deployment Forces: Policy and Budgetary Implications* (Washington, D.C.: CBO, February 1983), 19–27. See also George C. Wilson, "Strike Force Held to Hurt NATO Power," *International Herald Tribune*, 21 February 1983.

24. On factoring the supplementary force goals of the SWAIS into planning guidelines, see Herrero de Minon, "Sub-Committee on Out-of-Area Challenges: Interim Report," Political Committee of the North Atlantic Assembly, October 1985, 8–9.

25. For further discussion of the specifics of the burden-sharing issue, see Phil Williams, "The Nunn Amendment, Burden-sharing, and U.S. Troops in Europe," *Survival* 27, no. 1 (January–February 1985): 2–10; and Graham Allison, Thierry de Montbrial, and Nobuhiko Ushiba, *Sharing International*

Responsibilities, Report of the Trilateral Task Force on Sharing Global Responsibilities to the Trilateral Commission (New York: The Trilateral Commission, 1983).

26. See Senator Glenn's exchange with Under Secretary of State for Political Affairs Lawrence S. Eagleburger, in U.S. Senate, NATO *Troop Withdrawals,* Hearing before the Committee on Foreign Relations, 97th Cong., 2d sess. (Washington, D.C.: GPO, 1982), 74–77. For another example of the congressional effort to get the NATO allies (and Japan) to take an active role in the Persian Gulf program, see U.S. House of Representatives, *Making Appropriations for Military Construction for the Department of Defense for Fiscal Year Ending September 30, 1983,* Appropriations Committee Conference Report no. 97–913, 97th Cong., 2d sess., 6–7, which stated: "The Conferees agree that prior to the obligation of Ras Banas construction funds, the Secretary of Defense is to certify through specific documentation that negotiations have proceeded with our NATO and Japanese allies which would insure either direct funding or indirect offset funding support for the Persian Gulf program. Direct participation would be through funding a portion of U.S. planned facilities. Indirect offsets should include increased funding for U.S. projects by host nations or, in the case of NATO, increased expenditures in the NATO infrastructure program."

27. U.S. Senate, *Europe and the Middle East: Strains on Key Elements of America's Vital Interests,* Report of Senator William S. Cohen to the Committee on Armed Services, 97th Cong., 2d sess. (Washington, D.C.: GPO, 1982), 8.

28. Compare *Statement on the Defence Estimates, 1975,* cmnd. 5976 (London: HMSO, 1975), 7, 14–15, on the government's decisions regarding the withdrawal from non-NATO commitments wherever possible, with *The Falklands Campaign: The Lessons,* cmnd. 8758 (London: HMSO, 1982), 31–36, for the decision to augment defense spending and increase flexibility, mobility, and readiness in support of operations in NATO and non-NATO areas.

29. Confidential interview with British Foreign Office official.

30. Thatcher quoted in William Tuohy, "Thatcher Says NATO Must Enlarge Scope," *International Herald Tribune,* 2 March 1981.

31. "NATO Naval Operations Out-of-Area," *Naval Forces* 8, no. 1 (1987): 32.

32. For more details of the American contribution, see "America's Falklands War," *The Economist,* 3 March 1984, 29–31, and Michael Getler, "U.S. Aid to Britain in Falklands is Detailed," *Washington Post,* 7 March 1984, A9. See also Mosar, "Interim Report," 4.

33. The three levels are described in *The Falklands Campaign: The Lessons,* 31, par. 303.

34. Information derived from *The Falklands Campaign: The Lessons,* 31; *Statement on the Defence Estimates, 1987* (London: HMSO, 1987), 23–24, and *Statement on the Defence Estimates, 1988* (London: HMSO, 1988), 31–33; confidential interviews with British Foreign Office and Defence Ministry officials; and Maj. Gen. T. A. Boam, "Defending Western Interests Outside

NATO: The United Kingdom's Contribution," *Armed Forces Journal International* 122, no. 3 (October 1984): 116. For more on the relationship between Oman, the United Kingdom, and the United States, see Judith Miller, "U.S. Is Said to Develop Oman As Its Major Ally in the Gulf," *New York Times*, 25 March 1985, A1; and David Buchan, "Oman and Friends Keep Gulf Open," *Financial Times*, 28 November 1986.

35. See list of "Forces Abroad" in International Institute for Strategic Studies, *The Military Balance, 1987–1988* (London: IISS, 1987), 82, and *Statement on the Defence Estimates, 1988*, 31.

36. *The Falklands Campaign: The Lessons*, 32, and confidential interviews with British Foreign Office and Defence Ministry officials.

37. For details of upgrading, see Boam, "Defending Western Interests Outside NATO," 118, and James Digby, Robert W. Komer, and John Van Oudenaren, *Security Partner Support of U.S. Maneuver Forces*, Confidential Rand Note N–2299–USDP (Santa Monica, Calif.: Rand Corporation, 1985), 30. See also British Atlantic Committee, *Diminishing the Nuclear Threat: NATO's Defence and New Technology* (London: British Atlantic Committee, 1984), 53–54, and Drew Middleton, "British Panel on Military Seeks to Rouse the Allies," *New York Times*, 11 March 1984, 9.

38. For an American version of this argument, see Joshua M. Epstein, "Soviet Vulnerabilities in Iran and the RDF Deterrent," *International Security* 6, no. 2 (Fall 1981): 127–58.

39. Confidential interviews with British Defence Ministry and Foreign Office officials.

40. In the agreement between the United States and the United Kingdom providing for American use of Diego Garcia, Washington agreed in exchange for real estate and a promise of equal access to spend about £12 million on lengthening the aircraft runway from 8,000 to 12,000 feet (making it accessible to almost any aircraft), improving parking ramps, building more fuel storage tanks, providing maintenance facilities for ships and aircraft, and deepening the anchorage area. See "Indian Ocean: A Little Help Where It Counts," *The Economist*, 9 February 1974, 38–39, and also chapter on "The Bases Problem: Diego Garcia and Elsewhere," in Robert J. Hanks, *The U.S. Military Presence in the Middle East: Problems and Prospects* (Cambridge, Mass.: Institute for Foreign Policy Analysis, 1982), 24–28.

41. Confidential interview with British Foreign Office official.

42. Charles Hernu, "Face à la logique des blocs, une France indépandante et solidaire," *Défense nationale* (December 1982): trans. E. D. Sherwood, 16.

43. Mitterrand cited in Jean-Marie Colombani, "Le pacifisme peut-il prendre en France?" *Le Monde*, 19–20 June 1983, 1.

44. Interview with former French ambassador to the United States François de Laboulaye, 23 March 1983, Paris, and confidential interviews with French Foreign Ministry and Defense Ministry officials.

45. François de Rose, "La sécurité de l'Europe après l'Afghanistan," in *La securité de l'Europe dans les années 80*, ed. Pierre Lellouche (Paris: Institut français des relations internationales, 1980), trans. E. D. Sherwood, 341–42.

46. Confidential interview with French Foreign Ministry official.

47. Prime Minister Pierre Mauroy's Annual Defense Policy Speech, delivered at the Institute for Higher Defense Studies, Paris, 20 September 1983.

48. IISS, *The Military Balance, 1987–1988*, 63–64; James Brooke, "The French in Africa: Old Ecole Ties," *New York Times*, 25 December 1988, 8; and John Chipman, *French Military Policy and African Security*, Adelphi Paper no. 201 (London: IISS, 1985), 20, table 2.

49. See Michael Dobbs, "France: Some Libyans Still in Chad," *Washington Post*, 17 November 1984, A13; "France Criticizes U.S. Policy on Libya," *New York Times*, 21 November 1984, A3; Chipman, *French Military Policy and African Security*, 29; James Brooke, "Desert Cunning Brought Victory to Chadians," *New York Times*, 2 April 1987, A8; James Brooke, "After a Day of Glory, What's Next for Chad?" *New York Times*, 5 April 1987, E3; U.S. Department of State, "Update on Chad," unclassified briefing paper, 21 January 1987.

50. IISS, *The Military Balance, 1987–1988*, 63.

51. Information drawn from confidential interviews with French Foreign Ministry and Defense Ministry officials and U.S. NSC official. Bernard Rogers cited in Ian Davidson, "France Rejoins Its Allies," *Financial Times*, 3 May 1983.

52. See discussion in D. Bruce Marshall, "The Evolving French Strategic Debate," *Strategic Review* 8, no. 2 (Spring 1980): 63–65.

53. For more on the intended structure and capabilities of the FAR, see "Un entretien avec M. Charles Hernu sur le programme militaire," *Le Monde*, 22 April 1983, 1; "La France crée une force antichar pour assister ses alliés en Europe," *Le Monde*, 18 June 1983, 1; Defense Minister Hernu speech "Balance, Deterrence and Will: The Narrow Path to Peace and Liberty," Institute of Higher Defense Studies, Paris, 15 November 1983; General Georges Fricaud-Chagnaud, "Origins, Capabilities and Significance of the Force d'Action Rapide," paper prepared for the 1983–84 International Security Studies Program Core Seminar on "Prospects for Effective Conventional Defense in Europe," The Wilson Center, Washington, D.C., 30 October 1984; Giovanni de Briganti, "*Forces d'Action Rapide*: France's Rapid Deployment Force," *Armed Forces Journal International* 122, no. 3 (October 1984): 122–23; William Durch and Peter Almquist, "East-West Military Balance," in Barry M. Blechman and Edward N. Luttwak, *International Security Yearbook, 1984/85* (New York: St. Martin's Press, Center for Strategic and International Studies, 1984), 156–57.

54. Maurice Delarue, "Le conseil de l'OTAN à Paris," *Le Monde*, 8 June 1983, 1.

55. John Vinocur, "Paris NATO Meeting Signals Affirmation of French Role," *International Herald Tribune*, 8 June 1983, 2. For more on this line of thought, see "La France doit accroître sa rapidité d'intervention aux côtés de ses alliés, estime le général Lacaze," *Le Monde*, 31 May 1983; Hernu speech "Balance, Deterrence and Will," in which he referred to the newly reinforced relationship between France and the Federal Republic as an "alliance within the alliance"; and Davidson, "France Rejoins Its Allies."

56. "M. Hernu admet que l'emploi de la force d'action rapide en Europe serait subordonné à l'accord du commandement allié," *Le Monde*, 25 June 1983, 11.

57. Michael Dobbs, "Paris Boosts Defense Cooperation With Bonn," *Washington Post*, 1 March 1986, A14, and Paul Lewis, "Paris-Bonn Military Accord Is Reached," *New York Times*, 2 March 1986, 3.

58. Paul Lewis, "France Approves Arms Plan Linked to European Allies," *New York Times*, 11 April 1987, 3.

59. Luigi Caligaris, "Italian Defence Policy: Problems and Prospects," *Survival* 25 (March–April 1983): 74.

60. Confidential interview with Italian Foreign Ministry official and discussion in Luigi Caligaris, "Defence Policy and Parliamentary Debate in Italy," in *Relazioni internazionali* 1 (June 1988), 104.

61. The key to this broad-ranging agreement lay in the decision of the Communist party (PCI) to enter into constructive opposition with respect to the new strategic posture. A Communist party spokesman commented, the "PCI tends to agree with what is emerging as a national policy." He added that because of the lack of a foreign policy tradition in postwar Italy, the PCI acknowledged Italy's need to develop "a world strategic outlook" and an expertise in international affairs that had been heretofore unwarranted (Interviews with Mario Zucconi, foreign affairs expert at CESPI [Centro studi di politica internazionale], the Communist international relations institute, 7 April 1983, Rome; with Luigi Caligaris, 6 April 1983, Rome; with journalist Arrigo Levi, 6 April 1983, Rome; and confidential interview with Italian Foreign Ministry official).

62. Interview with Caligaris, 6 April 1983, Rome.

63. See, for example, Renato Ruggiero, "The Atlantic Alliance and Challenges to Security in the Mediterranean: Problems and Policy Choices," in *Prospects for Security in the Mediterranean, Part III*, Adelphi Paper no. 231 (London: IISS, 1988). See also summary of conference on "NATO's Southern Region: Present Issues and Future Challenges," 14–15 April 1988, Istituto per gli studi di politica internazionale (ISPI), Milan. For additional discussion, see *Lo spettatore internazionale* 13, no. 1 (January–March 1978), special issue on the Mediterranean.

64. Ruggiero, "Atlantic Alliance and Challenges to Security in the Mediterranean," 10. Indeed, the Italians specifically resented this aspect of the report issued by four American, British, French, and German foreign relations institutes in 1981. Not only was Italy not invited to participate in the original study, but the report's conclusions suggested that access to "Principal Nations" groups—proposed coordinating bodies for Western policy initiatives— would be determined by geography (Karl Kaiser, Winston Lord, Thierry de Montbrial, and David Watt, *Western Security: What Has Changed? What Should Be Done?* [New York: Council on Foreign Relations, 1981], 45).

65. IISS, *The Military Balance, 1987–1988*, 70, and confidential interview with Italian Foreign Ministry official. Italian troops began their official tour with the MFO on 25 April 1982.

66. Interview with Stefano Silvestri, Deputy Director, Institute for Inter-

national Affairs, 5 April 1983, Rome. See also discussion of how the deployment of the national forces in the MNF mirrored individual national perspectives in Luigi Caligaris, "Western Peacekeeping in Lebanon: Lessons of the MNF," *Survival* 26, no. 6 (November–December 1984): 262–79, esp. 263; Enrico Jacchia, "Beirut Role Has Italians Worrying," *International Herald Tribune*, 6 May 1983; and IISS, *The Military Balance, 1984–1985*, 58, and *The Military Balance, 1987–88*, 70.

67. See Roberto Suro, "Italy to Consider Basing of F-16's," *New York Times*, 5 February 1988, A3; Loren Jenkins, "Italy to Agree to NATO Request to Accept U.S. F16s," *Washington Post*, 26 May 1988, A15; "NATO Aides: US Jets in Spain Should Go to Italy," *Boston Globe*, 27 May 1988, 88; Edward Cody, "Allies Formally Ask Italy to Provide Base for F16s," *Washington Post*, 27 May 1988, A21; Edward Cody, "NATO Agrees on Burden-Sharing, Delays Decision on F16 Move Costs," *Washington Post*, 28 May 1988, A18; Roberto Suro, "Italian Bishops Assail Plan to Accept U.S. Jets," *New York Times*, 12 June 1988, 4.

68. See Philip Windsor's discussion of the Federal Republic's "uncertain role" in his *Germany and the Western Alliance: Lessons from the 1980 Crises*, Adelphi Paper no. 170 (London: IISS, 1981), 7–8.

69. Hans Apel, "A Prepared Statement for an Address Before the 19th Wehrkunde Conference," 13 February 1982, reproduced in U.S. Senate, *Europe and the Middle East: Strains on Key Elements of America's Vital Interests*, app. 1, p. 30, and confidential interviews, German Foreign Ministry and Defense Ministry officials.

70. Basic Law of the Federal Republic of Germany, articles 87 and 24.

71. Confidential interviews with German Foreign Ministry and Defense Ministry officials and U.S. Defense Department official.

72. Confidential interviews with German Foreign Ministry and Defense Ministry officials.

73. Confidential interview with German Foreign Ministry official. For details of Host Nation Support agreement, see 15 April 1982 agreement between the United States and the Federal Republic of Germany, "Defense: Host Nation Support," TIAS 10376 (Washington, D.C.: GPO, 1982), esp. 2, point 1.

74. Confidential interviews with German Foreign Ministry officials and interview with Volker Ruhe, Deputy Leader of the CDU-CSU Parliamentary Group in the Bundeshaus, Bonn, 28 April 1983.

75. Apel, "A Prepared Statement Before Wehrkunde Conference," 29–30.

76. For statistics on German aid, see Europe Information, *Official Development Assistance from the European Community and Its Member States*, May 1988, 4, and Organization for Economic Co-operation and Development (OECD) Report on *Geographical Distribution of Financial Flows to Developing Countries, 1977–1980* (Paris: OECD, 1981).

77. "U.S. to Pay for Upgrading Turkish Military Airfields," *New York Times*, 16 October 1982, 5; Metin Demirsar, "U.S. Upgrades Military Links to Turkey with Eye to Soviet Union and the Mideast," *Wall Street Journal*, 12

January 1983, 32; and Blechman and Luttwak, *International Security Yearbook, 1983/84*, 156–57.

78. See U.S. Assistant Secretary of Defense Richard Perle's 7 March 1984 testimony and exchange with Senator Joseph R. Biden, Jr., in U.S. Senate, *Security and Development Assistance*, Hearings before the Subcommittee on European Affairs of the Senate Foreign Relations Committee, 98th Cong., 2d sess. (Washington, D.C.: GPO, 1984), 362, 396–99.

79. For further discussion of Turkish attitudes, see Duygu Bazoglu Sezer, *Turkey's Security Policies*, Adelphi Paper no. 164 (London: IISS, 1981).

80. See "Technical Agreement in Implementation of the Defense Agreement between the United States of America and Portugal of September 6, 1951," signed at Lisbon, 18 May 1984, U.S. Department of Defense, Washington, D.C.

81. Source: IISS, *The Military Balance, 1987–1988*, section on NATO forces, 56–82; and *The Military Balance, 1984–1985*, 58, and section on NATO forces, 31–49.

82. Caspar W. Weinberger, "A Report to the Congress on Security Arrangements in the Persian Gulf," unclassified, 15 June 1987, p. iii and chronology in table 1.

83. Edward Cody, "U.S. Seeks NATO Support for Bigger Role in Gulf," *Washington Post*, 27 May 1987, A15; "Weinberger Asks for Help in Gulf," *New York Times*, 27 May 1987; Carrington quoted in Peter Maass, "Carrington Opposes NATO Action in Gulf," *International Herald Tribune*, 28 May 1987, 2.

84. For initial allied reactions, see Fay Willey, "Why Europe and Japan Won't Help," *Newsweek*, 8 June 1987, 35; James M. Markham, "France and Britain Uneasy With U.S. Gulf Policy," *New York Times*, 8 July 1987, A3; James M. Markham, "Washington's Course Worries Allies," *New York Times*, 17 July 1987, A8; "Dutch Would Send Ships," *International Herald Tribune*, 28 May 1987, 2.

85. The British had established an "armilla patrol"—a cross between an armada and a flotilla—near the Strait of Hormuz to protect British merchant shipping. See *Statement on Defence Estimates, 1988*, 35. See also Patrick E. Tyler, "U.S. Flags Raised on Two Tankers," *Washington Post*, 22 July 1987, A1; Patrick Tyler, "Letter From the Persian Gulf: Suspicion, Doubt Cloud Emirates' View of Western Interests," *Washington Post*, 4 August 1987, A8; Edward Cody, "Europeans Send Mine Sweepers," *Washington Post*, 12 August 1987, A1.

86. Aspin quoted in George C. Wilson and Helen Dewar, "Aid from Allies Needed in Gulf, Aspin Stresses," *Washington Post*, 10 June 1988, A23.

87. Neil A. Lewis, "U.S. Copter Crashes in Gulf; 1 Is Dead and 3 Are Missing," *New York Times*, 31 July 1987, A3; Karen DeYoung, "Britain Rejects U.S. Plea for Help in Gulf," *Washington Post*, 1 August 1987, A1; David Hoffman, "Britain Still Weighs Mine Sweeper Aid, Fitzwater Says," *Washington Post*, 4 August 1987, A8; James M. Markham, "Europeans Spurn U.S. On Gulf Plan," *New York Times*, 5 August 1987, A1.

88. Giraud quoted in Cody, "Europeans Send Mine Sweepers"; James M. Markham, "European Policy in the Gulf: A Striking Reversal," *New York Times*, 16 September 1987; Thatcher quoted in Edward Cody, "It Took a While, But Our Allies Finally Joined Us in the Gulf," *Washington Post National Weekly Edition*, 5 October 1987, 17.

89. In the eighties, WEU membership included the original signatories of the Brussels Treaty—Belgium, France, Luxembourg, the Netherlands, and the United Kingdom—as well as Italy and West Germany, which had acceded in October 1954. See Jacques F. Poos, "Prospects for the WEU," *NATO Review* 35, no. 4 (August 1987): 16.

90. Joseph Fitchett, "Gulf Armada Seen as a Quiet Plus for West," *International Herald Tribune*, 18 November 1987, 1, and NATO Defense Planning Committee, *Enhancing Alliance Collective Security: Shared Roles, Risks and Responsibilities in the Alliance* (Brussels: NATO, 1988), 44.

91. Van Eekelen quoted in Cody, "It Took a While," 17. For a detailed description of allied forces in the gulf, see "Naval Line-Up in the Persian Gulf," *Jane's Defence Weekly*, 26 September 1987, 671–73.

92. George C. Wilson, "Gulf Pact Set by Britain, Italy, France," *Washington Post*, 24 January 1988, A1; Don Shannon, "U.S., Allies to Join in 'Clean Sweep' of Gulf," *Los Angeles Times*, 25 January 1988, 1; Karen De-Young, "U.S., Allies to Step Up Gulf Coordination," *Washington Post*, 28 April 1988, A33; and confidential interview with State Department official.

93. Captain Edward Mann, quoted in *News Clips*, The Navy Office of Information, 9 May 1988. See also Patrick E. Tyler, "France Expands Role of Its Navy in Gulf," *Washington Post*, 21 January 1988; Richard Pyle, "U.S. Warship Fires Warning at Iranian Boat," *Washington Post*, 3 July 1988.

94. Edward Cody, "U.S., Europeans Consider Joint Gulf Mine-Clearing Operation," *Washington Post*, 9 September 1988.

CONCLUSION

1. George Bush, "Security Strategy in the 1990s," speech at the Coast Guard Academy, 24 May 1989, reprinted as Current Policy No. 1178, U.S. Department of State.

2. "Declaration of the Heads of State and Government Participating in the Meeting of the North Atlantic Council in Brussels" (29–30 May 1989), NATO Press Service, 30 May 1989, Brussels.

Index

Acheson, Dean, 23, 28, 31–32, 34–36, 38, 41–44, 46, 60, 62, 121–22, 136
Achilles, Theodore, 13, 15, 19
Adenauer, Konrad, 91, 105
Afghanistan: Soviet invasion of, 135, 147–54 passim; Soviet withdrawal from, 185
Africa, 103, 107, 108, 114, 127, 132, 167, 168, 169
Algeria: in treaty area, 24–25; rebellion in, 66, 67, 69, 80, 81, 91, 123; relinquished by France, 112, 130
Anglo-American "special relationship," 3; and definition of NATO area, 23; and Korean War, 36–38; strained by colonial issues, 40–41; and Asian security issues, 54–55, 57; and coordination of Middle East policy, 58–68 passim; and Suez crisis, 65, 67, 80, 81–83; post-Suez resuscitation of, 88–90; and nuclear cooperation agreement, 89–90, 102, 115–16; confronted by de Gaulle (1958–61), 95–110; and joint Middle East military action (1958), 95–97, 98–99; and British defense policy, 115–16; and Vietnam War, 127–29, 130; and October 1973 war, 141, 145; in 1980s, 161–65
Angola, 140, 185
Anticolonialism, American, 12–13, 40–41, 51–52, 57, 77
Anticommunism, 30–32, 40, 47, 50, 74
Apel, Hans, 173, 175

Arab-Israeli war (October 1973), 135, 138–42, 144, 145, 146, 175, 176, 186
Arms sales, 64, 66, 67; and Tripartite Declaration, 60; and French pro-Arab policy, 138; by United States to Iran, 146, 179
Asia, 30–32; and postwar Soviet interest in, 6; offshore islands crisis (1958), 100–101; and Nixon Doctrine, 136–37. See also Indochina; and individual Asian countries
Aspin, Les, 180
Aswan Dam project, 68, 69
Atlanticism versus Europeanism, 102, 111–16, 145
Attlee, Clement, 37–38
Australia, 35, 50, 84; and SEATO, 55; and Vietnam War, 132
Austria, 9
Azerbaijan, 6, 22
Azores, 99, 140, 176; and stepping-stone concept, 25, 26

Baghdad Pact, 65, 66
Ball, George, 116, 122, 135
Barjot, P., 71
Beaufre, André, 71, 72
Belgium, 84, 105, 177; and Brussels Treaty, 8, 9; and foundations of NATO, 9, 10; and distribution of power in NATO, 16, 25; as original member of Atlantic alliance, 28; and Korean War, 35; and Olympic boycott (1980), 151;